Hidden New York

A Guide to Places That Matter

Marci Reaven and Steve Zeitlin

Photographs by **Martha Cooper**
and other great photographers of New York City's splendid places

research and interviews by **Elena Martínez**

CONTRIBUTORS
Caitlin Van Dusen
and
Natalie DeYoung
Makalé Faber
David Hochman
Robert Maass
Elena Martínez
Joseph Sciorra
Roberta Singer

RIVERGATE BOOKS
An Imprint of Rutgers University Press
New Brunswick, New Jersey, and London

About the Cover: Only a few lucky New Yorkers have glimpsed an elephant trudging into the Cathedral of Saint John the Divine during the Feast of Saint Francis and the annual procession of pets and their owners for the Blessing of the Animals. Visible throughout the year is the sculptor Simon Verity's carved masterpiece, "the Portal of Paradise," through which the elephant walks. Adorning the lofty archway—which symbolizes the entrance to Christ's tomb—and beckoning pilgrims and visitors into the cathedral are great prophets and other notable figures from the Old and New Testaments, selected by an interfaith group of priests and rabbis. Visitors process beneath carved eight-foot-tall images including Jacob, Moses, Elijah, and John the Baptist and smaller, three-foot-six sculptures of Ruth, Naomi, Jonah, Noah, Solomon, and others. "The procession of prophets leads you through the Portal to be uplifted," says Verity. "We come in as ordinary New Yorkers and leave as a bishop or a martyr or a saint." Photo by Martha Cooper.

Publication of this book was supported, in part, by Furthermore: a Program of the J. M. Kaplan Fund

Library of Congress Cataloging-in-Publication Data
Reaven, Marci, 1954–
     Hidden New York : a guide to places that matter / Marci Reaven and Steve Zeitlin ; photographs by Martha Cooper and other great photographers of New York City's splendid places ; research and interviews by Elena Martínez ; contributors Caitlin Van Dusen . . . [et al.].
         p. cm.
     Includes bibliographical references and index.
     ISBN-13: 978–0–8135–3890–7 (pbk. : alk. paper)
1. New York (N.Y.)—Guidebooks. I. Zeitlin, Steven J. II. Title.
F128.18.R42 2006
917.47′10444—dc22
2005035564

A British Cataloging-in-Publication record for this book is available from the British Library.

Text design and composition by Jenny Dossin
Manufactured in the United States of America

Hidden New York

For our children,

Jean Tanis and Ben and Eliza Zeitlin,

who love New York

and to the memory of

three extraordinary preservationists:

Mike Bornstein, the Magic Table;
Hyman Genee, Kehila Kedosha Janina;

and

Joan Maynard, the Weeksville Society

Contents

Acknowledgments

Hidden New York takes as its subject places that matter in one of the world's largest and greatest cities. The daunting task required a collective effort, and we would like to express our deep appreciation to everyone who took part. At the top of that list are Caitlin Van Dusen, who researched and wrote many superb entries as well as the introduction to the "Urban Palate" section; Laura Hansen, who founded the Place Matters Program with us; Elena Martínez, whose first-rate research and interviews ground this book throughout; and Martha Cooper, whose vivid urban imagery—captured today and over the last couple of decades—brings the book to life.

Other contributors to main entries are Amanda Dargan, Makalé Faber, Ilana Harlow, David Hochman, Rob Maass, Elena Martínez, Joseph Sciorra, Jennifer Scott, Roberta Singer, and Natalie DeYoung. Additional writing was contributed by Tom Klem and Chris Neville. These folklorists and cultural specialists contributed additional fieldwork, research, and writing: Nicole Gilliam, Ilana Harlow, Madaha Kinsey Lamb, Adrienn Mendonca, Jennifer Scott, and Meng Yu. Our thanks to you all. We are also pleased to include the work of inveterate New York City documentary photographers who have worked with City Lore for many years—Audrey Gottlieb, Hazel Hankin, and Elaine Norman—and others we are pleased to work with for the first time.

In addition, a far greater number of New Yorkers allowed us to interview them and contributed their thoughts, ideas, and assistance: Colin Alevras, Mike Amadeo, Aúrea Almeida, Sam Alston, Lon Ballinger, Doug Bellizzi, Peter Benfaremo, Ron Binaghi, Sandra Bloodworth, Mike Bornstein, Laura Braddock, Bill Butler, Ed Callaghan, Anne Palermo Carroccio, Tommy Chan, Mary and George Chinnici, Joe Ciccu, Robert Clayton, Kathleen Condon, Yvette Debow, Carlos Diaz,

Isaac Dostis, Rose Edinger, Dahlia Elsayed, Mark Russ Federman, Michael Feiger, Michael Feller, Terence Fisher, John Fratta, Chester Fried, Hyman Genee, Tom Goodridge, Lorraine Gordon, David Greco, Janet Greene, Nancy Groce, Robert Guilbe, Will Halsey, Laura Hansen, Naomi Haruta, Marcia Haddad Ikonomopoulos, Ali Abdul Karim, Barbara Kirshenblatt-Gimblett, Pat Kirshner, Thomas Klem, Jonathan Kuhn, Gabrielle Langholtz, Annie Lanzillotto, Simon Lemmer, Joe Liberatore, Donald Loggins, Brian Luebcke, Thomas Lunke, Queva Lutz, Anna Magenta, Richie Mojica, Dr. Uma Mysorekar, Larry Nash, Gary Page, Alex Pathenroth, Eric Paulin, Jim Power, Ethel Raim, Mike Rella, Calixto Rivera, Steve Ross, Gary Ryan, Charlie Sahadi, Mohammed Salem, Bobby Sanabria, Jimi Schultz, Khadijah Shaheed, Michael Shaver, Susan Shellogg, Arthur Sheppard, Peter Siegel, the members of the Society of Our Lady of Mount Carmel, Robert Stewart, Marcos Tejeda, Yakov Tsibushnik, Debbie Van Cura, Simon Verity, Mitchell Vlachos, Alex and Stephanie Villani, Imam Siraj Wahhaj, and Dick Zigun, along with the Smithsonian's Folklife Festival.

We also would like to thank all the members of City Lore's wonderful staff and board of directors. Thanks go to staff members Amanda Dargan, Beth Higgins, Elena Martínez, Anika Selhorst, Roberta Singer, and especially to Hiroko Kazama and Lois Wilcken, who did so much work to finalize the manuscript. Our board of directors includes Ray Allen, Josh Brown, Henry Chalfant, Milly Hawk Daniel, Caroline Harris, Dave Isay, Argentina Palacios, Nathan Pearson, Robert Perlstein, Marilyn White, Wendy Wolf, and Sally Yarmolinsky.

Special thanks, as well, to the funders who provided support for the Place Matters initiatives, including this volume: the National Endowment for the Humanities, the National Endowment for the Arts, the New York State Council on the Arts, the New York Council for the Humanities, the Altman Foundation, the E.H.A. Foundation, the J. M. Kaplan Fund, the Lily Auchincloss Foundation, the New York Community Trust, and the Scherman Foundation. We also would like to thank our wonderful editor at Rutgers University Press who believed in us from the beginning, Marlie Wasserman. Thanks as well to our excellent copyeditor, India Cooper.

—Marci Reaven and Steve Zeitlin, City Lore

Hidden New York

Five-foot-three photographer Elaine Norman at the Street of Little Doors, Dennet Place, Brooklyn. Photo: Elaine Norman.

Introduction

"And above all, watch with glittering eyes the whole world around you because the greatest secrets are always hidden in the most unlikely places."

Roald Dahl, *The Minpins*

A wall, a bench, a door, an arch, a corner, and a set of stairs. Commonplace features of the urban environment. But not any wall, the wavy brick wall that winds around Saint Patrick's Cathedral on Prince and Mott, a wall so old and wavy that it surrounds the cathedral like a well-worn coat, comforting passersby. And not any bench, but the bright mosaic benches that surround Grant's Tomb, reminding one visitor that "we the common people compose this world, not just the presidents and generals like Ulysses S. Grant."

And not any door, but the doorways of Dennet Place between Luquer and Nelson in Brooklyn, the Street of Little Doors. "There are no midgets here," one resident explained, "we're all normal size." The height of most entryways hovers around five feet, but it is the occasional four-foot door that truly amazes, proving the ability of the urban environment to surprise, showing that Alice-in-Wonderland rabbit holes exist even in cities.

And not any arch, but the whispering arches of Grand Central. Here in this great American cathedral, where the footsteps of a million strangers echo through vast spaces, just outside the Oyster Bar a visitor can stand facing one tiled arch, whisper sweet nothings to the wall, and have the sound carry across a domed ceiling along the vaulted arches to a little brother, or a bride-to-be, in the archway opposite. "I think I heard you say, 'I love you,' " we overheard one young girl say to her beau recently as they walked away.

And not any corner, but the Lucky Corner. In the early 1930s,

Congressman Fiorello La Guardia began holding election-eve rallies at the intersection of Lexington Avenue and 116th Street. His political protégé Vito Marcantonio continued the tradition during his fourteen years as a congressman, most of them with the American Labor Party. The rallies resembled Italian and Puerto Rican fiestas, and assuaged tensions between these two neighborhood groups.

And not any set of stairs, but a towering street of stairs that separates Broadway and tranquil Park Terrace East at West 215th Street in Inwood. Close to a hundred steps are matched by hundreds of apartment windows staring out at the New Yorkers as they ascend and descend. A place-bound game of curveball specially designed by kids unfolds at the top of the stairs, and community gardeners work to create a "place in the sun," described by one visitor as unique, "reminiscent of Paris."

WHY PLACES MATTER

Human experiences are written onto the environment. We etch our existence into the landscape with our lives. Then we look back to read our lives between the brick and mortar. We look back to interpret, understand, and pass our experiences along. That is why a sense of place is inextricably bound up with our sense of self. We rely on the tenacity of places to root us not only to our own pasts but also to the lives of those who came before us. The tangible properties of the physical landscape are exactly that: tangible and physical. Their sturdiness connects past and present in time periods that transcend individual lifetimes. Place matters because it marks the physical dimension of our lives and is the home for all our traditions and memories. Sense of place is in the details, in the layers of history, lore, and perceptions that constitute what philosopher Edward Casey terms "place memory."

We say places matter because they are our "old haunts," as if our ghosts still inhabit the places they loved. Place matters because places are the opposite of the virtual world: Books, films, memories, and Web sites are all virtual to a greater or lesser degree; the Web has even opened up to us the concept of virtual time, reminding us that, in a sense, only places are real.

TERMS OF ENGAGEMENT

This book is an invitation to engage with New York City, and we offer these terms of engagement: First, visiting—any curious soul can do that; but then, second, revisiting. For places to acquire the status of cherished spaces—with an interior life inside ourselves—we need to visit more than once, on different days, at different times of year. Third, learning about places through research, talking with people, attending events, participating in their communities, and making those places part of our daily lives. Fourth and finally, advocacy for the place, and genuine stewardship.

The venerable wall surrounding Saint Patrick's Cathedral, Prince and Mott streets, Manhattan. Photo: Martha Cooper.

The heart of the book is a series of thirty-two write-ups of places that matter to New Yorkers, setting the scene, offering insights into their history and significance. We also suggest the issues that challenge the ongoingness of some of the sites, issues that must be confronted to keep each place vital and interesting as this new century unfolds. All through, we include first-person remembrances and commentaries from New Yorkers who have made multiple visits and fallen in love with this or that corner of the city. And because we envision the city as an interlocking chain of associated places, we offer sister sites for some of our main entries, expanding outward from our main sites to side trips that will keep the reader busy for years. We even describe a few "ghost sites" whose absence from the landscape is so palpable as to affect a kind of presence. For so

Competing uses define the urban experience. Photo: Martha Cooper.

many New Yorkers, the destruction of the Twin Towers left a gaping hole in the New York skyline, more visible, perhaps, than their presence, so often taken for granted. "You can see New Jersey in a place you shouldn't be able to," said New Yorker Shirley Newman.

THE BEAUTY OF PLACE-MAKING

Concerned with the experience of place, we have included—along with our thirty-two main sites and occasional sister sites—first-person quotes that give a sense of history experienced first-hand. In addition, we've included poetic evocations—we call them "place moments"—that express the way a given locale is experienced at a given moment. There is no way to see a place just as these writers have—recreating the time of day, the time of year—but their insightful glimpses invite you to see the places they see in your own way, to visit and revisit, to make all the places in this book your own, in your own moments. Oftentimes it's not just a place but how it looks at a certain time of day, a certain time of year, descriptions that evoke the essential experiential qualities that transform space into place: not just the steeple of Trinity Church but the way light plays on it at sunset; not just the Cloisters but its medieval garden on a summer day when, for the imaginative, the aroma of its plants can turn the clock back six hundred years.

"Unwittingly," writes the *New York Times* reporter Somini Sengupta, "I have turned into a student of light. The August light that envelops the beaten-down old streets of Red Hook, I have learned, is more melancholy than the morning light during lilac season in the Brooklyn Botanic Garden. The sun sparkling on the crown of the Chrysler Building is whimsical, like a woman dressed for a party at high noon." Stephanie Nilva, a lawyer, says that "on most days my city protects herself from the sun. But for those few days when the sun lines up with the crosstown streets, she rests like an ice cube in a glass to the west."

In the urban environment, a wavy wall, like the one around Saint Patrick's Cathedral, or Inwood's towering staircase creates a wrinkle in the streetscape. These interruptions often merge with a ripple in the flow of time—the time of day, time of year, a turning point in one's life, to create a vivid place moment, lodged in memory.

LOCATING THE CITY'S COMMUNITIES

Yet place-making involves more than visiting and being moved by the interplay of the place and our own imaginations. Place-making is often about shared structures of meaning, community building, creating places that have significance for a public larger than ourselves. By engaging in an effort to develop a greenmarket in Union Square, to organize regular stickball games in a schoolyard on Bathgate Avenue in the Bronx, or to maintain the last American synagogue for the celebration of Romaniote Jewry, we create places that matter.

Places often matter because they serve as gathering points for communities. The community may be a group of jazz musicians, or the cadre of insomniacs and cops that, until it closed in 2000, gathered at Philip's all night candy shop in Coney Island for coffee and conversation, or the early morning over-eighty crowd that met for breakfast at

FIRST PERSON: BARBARA KIRSHENBLATT-GIMBLETT

"My husband, Max, and I walk the city in entirely different ways. He picks out paths that have the least traffic and the least people. I pick paths so crowded that you can barely make your way through the pack. I love the press of the city, and my favorite place is Chinatown. What I most love about the city is improvisation, and the highest density of improvisation in the city I find in Chinatown. It's a very dense environment, a maelstrom of activity. It's a human ocean—although tourists visit Chinatown, they're minnows. Everything is out in the open, the vegetables, whole pigs, the loading and unloading of crates of vegetables from the corners of the earth. The stores are open to the street—inside is outside. It's a huge open market, and I love open markets. No matter how many times I go there or how long I spend there, there are still edges of the menu yet to be explored, kitchen utensils I don't yet know how to use, vegetables I've yet to cook. It's like walking around inside a living encyclopedia—but the entries are not arranged alphabetically and they change from day to day."

the now defunct Dubrow's cafeteria, where seltzer poured from the water fountain. Often, they are important because they do more than provide a single service; they become a gathering point where people get to know one other, discuss issues, share in one another's lives. Places that matter contribute to a community's sense of identity, provide continuity and character to the community, and are seen as an integral part of the community by those who use them.

"The boundaries of my youth," wrote Fred Ferretti, "were defined by one block in the city of New York." People grow up and still live between two urban corners, on their own block, with its own places that matter—their stickball field with the fire hydrant and manhole covers as bases, and the bodegas and candy stores. These urban villages are stamped out with regularity every few blocks throughout the five boroughs. Yet, the distinctive landmarks, buildings, establishments and institutions that take on meaning for city dwellers are also the product of the many other kinds of communities that New Yorkers inhabit—communities shaped by interests, hobbies, occupations, passions, politics, and sexual orientation. Even the chain stores and strips that have ravaged the landscape of other cities represent only one more ripple in this aggressively diverse metropolis. In this book we ponder the communities of chess players at the Chess Forum, Village Chess Shop, Marshall Chess Club, and Washington Square Park; we slide into the world of the Empire Roller Skating Center in Brooklyn; we contemplate the Hua Mei birds with the community of elderly Chinese men in the bird garden on Forsyth Street; we hang out with the homeless youth at the Cube sculpture on Astor Place. In each case, we discover that the community defines the place. The place provides the physical forms for the community to shape itself around.

In this book, we can defy the conventional spiel of the Manhattan tour guide. A true New Yorker knows that every block in all five boroughs is of enormous interest. As the young writer H. R. Cullinan put it in 2004:

Miss Manhattan,
Why do you get all the attention?
Your sisters are just as interesting

They dance cheek to cheek in Queens basements
They sit on stoops with handsome boys in the Bronx
They stroll hand in hand on the beach in Brooklyn
They lean tight jeans on cars in Staten Island
You always were taller.
You get all dolled up on the weekends.
But aren't you tired?
Don't you want to get on the train
And cross the East River
And go home?

For this book, we journeyed the five boroughs to arrive at the intersections of people and place.

HOLDING HISTORY IN PLACE

Places that resonate have temporal depth, their significance understood if we move not only horizontally across the city but vertically through decades and centuries. We feel the weight of time and the texture of experience. A walk through Union Square, for example, is not just an exercise in getting from point A to point B, it's a journey through urban time and space. On September 11, 2001, New York filled with such overwhelming sorrow that personal rituals of grief spilled out of private lives and homes into public spaces. Although Union Square was not an officially designated site for public grieving (it was the farthest south most people could go once the city below Fourteenth Street was closed off), it marked the epicenter of the response. By three in the afternoon on the eleventh, Jordan Schuster had already put out sheets of butcher paper for people to inscribe their feelings on. City officials left memorials up in most of the city but repeatedly cleaned up the square, not only because it was the site of grief but also because it was the site of protest, with signs from groups like Not in Our Name urging a peaceful response to the attacks. During the Republican Convention in 2004, Union Square was again an epicenter for protest. The march of 500,000 people past Madison Square Garden ended at the square, and so did the candlelit vigil during President George W. Bush's acceptance speech.

Even on peaceful days, the southern tip of Union Square is jammed with countercultural young people with speakers propagating conspiracy theories and picketers with signs. It's as if the temperature in the square is always a little higher than in the rest of the city. It's as if these oppositionists were drawn to the square by a history they may never have known. In 1882 nearly twenty-five thousand workers marched—in the first official Labor Day parade—to demand an eight-hour working day and the end of child labor. In 1910, garment workers

One of New York's tallest staircases marks the path of a glacier, now 215th Street. Photo: Martha Cooper.

rallied here for better working conditions, and just one year later—their pleas ignored—marched here in mourning from Washington Square for 146 victims of a fire at the Triangle Shirtwaist Factory. In 1930, after the stock market crash, the square became the site of violent disturbances when thousands of demonstrators gathered for International Unemployment Day. Even earlier, in 1916, a wonderful photograph shows activist Emma Goldman in Union Square delivering a passionate speech about birth control. She was one of the few radicals skeptical of the Bolshevik Revolution in the Soviet Union, purportedly remarking that she never wanted a revolution that didn't allow people to dance—and dance they do at all the protests in Union Square in recent years.

In one postage stamp of urban soil, Union Square illustrates the layering of associations that are mapped in place, and that we have sought to capture citywide on these pages.

THE DRIVE TO DEFEND PLACES

Places can't defend themselves. Only people can do that. People like Hattie Carthan (1901–1984). Carthan was a neighborhood activist who, in the course of planting and caring for trees in the poor, largely African American neighborhood of Bedford-Stuyvesant, discovered a forty-foot magnolia grandiflora tree that was not supposed to grow north of Philadelphia. The sprawling tree spread its long and graceful branches across three brownstones that protected it from the wind and cold. Over the years, Hattie Carthan went up against four mayors to fight for the trees and the needed brownstones. But the neighborhood had been redlined, the people and places left to fend for themselves by banks and politicians. Immovable as the brownstones, sturdy as a tree trunk, she fought a seventeen-year battle in which she achieved a living landmark status for the tree, purchased the brownstones for four hundred dollars apiece, and established an environmental organization called the Magnolia Tree Earth Center. The tree, the largest of its kind outside the southern United States, continues to bud white, fragrant flowers each summer.

No one is too old or too serious to enjoy the whispering arches at Grand Central Station. Photo: Martha Cooper.

Anyone who falls in love with New York City needs to see it with an eye toward, as the poet William Butler Yeats wrote, "what is past and passing and to come." It's been said that every neighborhood in New York entirely transforms itself every ten years. Oftentimes we think that the city is vanishing before our eyes because places are constantly threatened—but the subtler issue is that we may be losing the eccentric class of holdouts who are willing to stake their identity on keeping one-of-a-kind local establishments going. The writer Kathryn Adisman, a New York native, expressed her admiration for entrepreneurs such as Abel Ornelas, co-owner of the last old-fashioned greengrocery in Manhattan's Greenwich Village, and Dick Zigun, who runs Sideshows by the Seashore and Coney Island USA in Brooklyn, in her story about the closing of Ornelas's Vegetable Garden. Comparing Ornelas to Zigun, she writes: "He's out there preserving something authentic, individual, indigenous, and if you don't know what it is—I can't tell you. I can only tell you it's not a Trump tower: You won't find it in Atlantic City or on Times Square anymore." And Adisman recalls that when she first saw the building on the Boardwalk that was home to Zigun's sideshow until 1995, she said, "I love that place." Zigun replied, "I am that place."

**FIRST PERSON:
ROBERT HERSHON**

The Driver Said

boerum hill?
It used to be
gowanus
this ain't no
neighborhood
if ya butcher
comes to ya funeral
that's a
neighborhood

To make informed choices for the future of urban neighborhoods, we must ground our decisions on what has worked in the past to create a sense of neighborhood and community. The dissolution of communities is real and costly, and cultural conservation is a preventive medicine that can keep neighborhoods and communities from falling apart. Assessing the value of community establishments may be difficult, even costly, but trying to re-create the community after their doors have closed is not possible at any price. We need to conceive an alternate currency backed not by gold bullion but by human values, associations, and memories, correlated to the time and emotional investment put into the places we love. However much some of us may profit from what is optimistically called progress, we cannot let what is most distinctive and most human about our cities be destroyed. As the folk-lorist Alan Lomax warns: "If we continue to allow the erosion of our cultural forms, soon there will be nowhere to visit and no place to truly call home."

EIGHT MILLION STORIES, THIRTY-TWO PLACES

They say there are eight million stories in the naked city. But if there are as many stories as people, it should be said, too, that there eight million cities as well. The city is not the same for any two of us. Nor is it the same for any two moments. In this book, we've tried to chronicle some of those cities within cities, as they existed for us at one particular moment of time. By the time this book is read, all the places we describe will be slightly different; any place in this intense city upon which so many economic and social pressures are brought to bear is going to be in a constant state of change. The exhilaration of urban living is the chance to create one's very own metropolis, one's very own New York, in one's own moment of time.

A wall, a bench, a door, an arch, a set of stairs. A wavy wall, bright-colored mosaic benches, whispering archways, a wide stairway through an urban garden. From the bits and pieces of the urban environment that resonate with one's own spirit, we create an architecture for the soul.

Urban Gatherings

Coming together to honor the ancestors, African Burial Ground, lower Manhattan.
Photo: Martha Cooper.

G athering together in some parts of the country may be simple, but in New York City you may need a permit, a certificate of occupancy, modes of egress, and a pricey rental fee. If a neighbor complains, you may receive a steep summons for making too much noise. Yet the need to gather is powerful, and New Yorkers find a way. Decorated clubhouses, cultural evenings, parades, religious festivals, sporting events, music, and dance are among the activities that mark the city's gathering places. Many of the city's immigrant communities focus their energies around cultural performances, occasions in which members of a community define who they are to themselves and others. Gathering places make possible private cultural celebrations in which rituals and festivals are performed by and for a community, as well as events in which the communities exhibit their cultural traditions to all New Yorkers in street parades and outdoor festivals, developing a measure of visibility and respect. Yet, in New York, even the streets are contested. Since 1971, a moratorium on new parades along Fifth Avenue has kept most of the new immigrant parades away from this choice route. Parades, too, have to cope with neighbors' complaints and fees imposed by the city for cleanup and traffic control.

PLACE MOMENT: ROBERT J. FLYNN, KISSENA PARK

"Kissena Park and the old Chinese ladies who do their tai chi ballet at dawn listening to an inner music that cannot be resisted. Set against the ancient Asian flowering dogwoods in April, they bloom and bend to salute an inner spring."

Like-mindedness is a characteristic of gathering places. Even within our complex and outsized urban setting, gathering spots provide people with a sense of welcome and roots, a place where their type of people

Mosh pit, CBGB, 1987. Photo: Michael Lavine.

can be found. (Selectiveness has its dark side, of course, but is a necessary ingredient of community all the same.) At the Russian and Turkish Baths, featured in this chapter, repeat customers enjoy a particular kind of vigorous bathing in a superheated environment. In many gathering places this shared interest also develops into an impressive expertise about some thing or another. Take the Hua Mei Bird Garden, also in this chapter. Garden regulars amass great amounts of knowledge about the birds they carefully study. Nurturing this expertise becomes its own reason for continuing the connection with the group. The magicians who gather at the Edison Hotel socialize and compete in equal measure. The knowledge created in such specialized settings often stays within the group, creating a kind of insider language and strengthening the bonds of community.

Are there other qualities that are common to gathering places? We propose conviviality, for one, some level of cooperation among members, for another, and certainly some degree of commitment to making the gathering happen. Whenever you find a gathering place that works, you are sure to find individuals whose efforts or charisma keep it going. The Czech social club at Bohemian Hall might have closed in the 1990s if not for the dedicated few who reworked the club's policies and finances.

Gathering places contribute to our collective well-being because they are places where people can act purposefully and creatively in pursuit of their goals. Webster Hall and other halls for hire that once dotted New York City's landscape were places where this history- and culture-making happened in abundance. By hosting everything from ordinary bar mitzvahs and weddings to the extraordinary political events of their day, New York's public halls have been places of opportunity and of movements waiting to happen. Communities need gathering places, and gathering places, in turn, sustain communities. A collective effort is needed on the part of the government and society to ensure that spaces can be made available—spaces within which to meet, dance, revel, and mourn.

Hua Mei Bird Garden

Sara Delano Roosevelt Park, just south of Delancey Street between Forsyth Street and Chrystie Street, Lower East Side, Manhattan

Hours: Every day, year-round, rain or shine, from about 7:00 a.m. to noon.

Public Transit: F train to Second Avenue. Second Avenue turns into Chrystie Street on the south side of East Houston Street. Walk three blocks south on Chrystie and turn left onto Delancey Street.

J, M, Z trains to Bowery. Walk east on Delancey Street about a block and a half.

It's 10:00 a.m. on a sunny Monday in Chinatown. On Forsyth Street, the rush-hour breakfast-bun vendors and shoe polishers are beginning to spread out their wares on over-turned milk crates. Fish trucks back up, beeping, to the loading docks of the markets, where grocers are hosing down the morning's array of bok choy, navel oranges, and eggplants. In the distance, the Chrysler Building soars toward the sky, its scaled tower like the plumage of a bird taking flight. Beneath its sparkling shadow, in a tiny crescent in the northern stretch of Sara Delano Roosevelt Park, the songs of the Hua Mei birds have just begun to drown out the cacophony of traffic on Delancey Street. Each bird has its unique song, and the twittering, kissing, whistling, warbling, lilting, chirping, and chuckling transform this destitute corner of downtown Manhattan into a magical—if ephemeral—oasis.

"RESPECT THE BIRDS"

Were it not for the birdsong, it would be easy to pass right by the Hua Mei Bird Garden—and still, many do. But for some passersby, the haunting refrain of the birds, or perhaps just a subtle shift in the dappled light falling on the cobblestones, is enough to make them stop for a closer look. A hand-painted sign announces: "Hua Mei Bird Garden. Respect the birds. Respect the plants." A low gate—locked at all times—is flanked by two gently swaying pine saplings (Hua Mei birds flourish in pine trees). Only members can actually enter the garden, but passersby are welcome to look in. Beyond the gate, nestled under peeling birches and flowers, and lining the wending flagstone path, are up to thirty handmade bamboo birdcages, some covered in white cotton sheaths. Other cages hang from poles cobbled together from old plumbing pipes or swing from loops on a nylon line that stretches above the fence. It is from these birdcages that the songs of the Hua Meis issue forth into the din of the Chinatown morning.

Just outside the fence, leaning against the iron railing that surrounds an abandoned wading pool, is a group of elderly Chinese men. Some are gathered in clusters, talking and gesticulating, tapping each other on the shoulder, pointing under and over the shrubbery toward a particular cage, but most are hunched in silence, gazing into the foliage with rapt attention. These are the members of the Hua Mei Bird Club, an informal convocation of roughly forty Chinese men who gather from dawn to noon, every day of the week, rain or snow or sun, because they share a passion for the exotic Hua Mei bird.

Its varied songs aside, the Hua Mei bird itself is unremarkable to behold. Both male and female are a dun-colored brown, with blue-white rings around the eyes that sweep upward into their signature feature: the eyebrows—a thin white line that runs toward the back of the head. Their position is a barometer of each bird's mood and physical condition. Indeed, in Mandarin hua mei means "beautiful" or "raised eyebrow." The beak is orange, the tail dark, its plumage splayed out like a paper accordion fan.

Inside their handmade cages, the birds hop about on swinging perches, flitting between porcelain dishes painted with flowers. Every so often, one of the men lets himself in through the gate and eases the cover off one of the cages, then crouches by its side for a moment as the bird adjusts to the sudden rush of daylight. After gauging the bird's reaction, he picks up the cage and carries it to a new location, and a new set of neighbors, who might or might not respond to its song.

HEAD HIGH, CHEST OUT, TAIL DOWN

Hua Meis are a breed of fighting thrush from the forests of southern China and are said to have come into fashion through the tastes of a particular Chinese emperor, whose lover's beautiful eyebrows inspired their moniker. Each bird has its own distinct song, which changes—or is refined, some owners argue—when exposed to the songs of other birds. In Hong Kong, public Hua Mei competitions take place, akin to dog and cat shows in the United States.

The subtleties of Hua Mei appearance, song, and temperament are indecipherable to the casual bystander. Most of the birds in the garden are males, competing for the attention of one or two females—primarily with their song, but also with their appearance. The birds' "beautiful eyebrows" provide one indication of attraction: When the eyebrow slants up, it means a connection has been made; when it slants down, it means no sparks. Unhappy males also puff up their feathers like a hat and sulk in the backs of their cages.

The elegant bamboo cages are another point of competition, with their frail wooden bars arching upward to a crown. Bamboo is the chosen material because it is strong, lightweight, and durable; the birds' claws cannot split its fibers, and there is no risk of rust poisoning the birds' delicate constitutions. The bars are carefully spaced to provide the optimum ratio of protection and visibility. The porcelain food dishes are also carefully selected, and, as one of the club members, Tommy Chan, avers, antique dishes can cost up to a quarter million dollars for a set of three.

Tommy drives down twice a week from his home in upstate New York to bring his Hua Meis to the garden. Younger than most of his compatriots and competent in English, he has become a de facto leader for the group. The regulars at the moment are almost exclusively retired Chinese men. Despite this demographic homogeneity, the economic diversity is great: Members currently include a businessman, a restaurant worker, a doctor, a chef, a construction worker, a plumber, an electrician, an engineer, and a former nationally ranked volleyball player. All share a passion for the Hua Mei.

The birds are imported from China and Vietnam and have to undergo four weeks of quarantine—at great expense—before they can be brought into a domestic environment. Hua Meis cost anywhere from a few hundred to few thousand dollars each; the most expensive currently in the United States are valued at tens of thousands of dollars. A bird's value is determined by its physical characteristics—feathering, feet coloration, eye coloration, beak coloration, the bird's shape, even

In the garden, the male Hua Meis sing for the attention of the females while the men just watch. Photo: Martha Cooper

its eyelids—and how it performs in competition. It's considered desirable for a bird to hold its head high, its chest out, its tail down.

Hua Meis live an average of sixteen years and subsist on a carefully monitored diet of fruit, vegetables, and insects. The wild Hua Meis are the most coveted, though many of the birds in the garden are hand raised. The wild birds, unaccustomed to the stimulation of an urban environment, are kept in the covered cages while they acclimate. It's best to catch the wild birds when they're young, Tommy says. "Those are the better ones because they still have some wildness in them, but they can also learn from the domestic songs."

It may be difficult to imagine waking at the crack of dawn each day to lean against an iron railing and watch birds for six hours, but for these men it's sheer pleasure. "If you don't take the birds out, they cannot compete," Tommy explains, "because they don't have the stamina to sing or perform for a long time. We want to learn as much as we can, understand why they sing this way, what they react to." The birds also have to be exercised each day. "You walk with them, it's the best way. You just swing the cage a little bit," Tommy says. The birds also must be bathed at least once a week: they're either sprayed or left to bathe themselves in a special bathing cage, similar to an enclosed bathtub.

Beneath the apparent congeniality of the old men is a deeply rooted system of alliances and competition. "They are mostly bird fanatics here. Everybody makes his own food. It's like a secret," Tommy says. "If someone's a good friend, you serve them secrets, but to others you don't." One of the garden's founders, Anna Magenta, claims that in between periods of silent observation, the men bicker. She recounts their conversations: "You know, 'My bird's better,' or 'No, that's not the right thing to feed it.'

FIRST PERSON:

HUA MEI

BIRD GARDEN MEMBER

"Before I came to the bird garden, I used to be very depressed. But here they showed me how they compare the colors: 'This one's dark brown, this one's light brown.' You're just focusing on the colors and you drop all other reality. It slows you down. I started to relax."

'What do you know? How many years have you had one?' " She insists, however, that the competition is good-natured, and that the men are re-

Quiet wonder at the garden. Photo: Martha Cooper.

lieved not to have to talk about personal problems, feeling free to restrict their conversation to the specifics of bird-raising.

Anna Magenta and Federico Sabini started the Forsyth Street Garden Conservancy in 1994, to protect and improve Sara Delano Roosevelt Park, which lay just outside the window of their converted tenement loft on Forsyth Street. One day in 1995, while Anna was working in the garden, a Chinese banker and two former waiters approached her, encouraged, they said, because she was planting evergreen trees—a Chinese symbol of good fortune. The banker asked Anna if she would consider devoting a section of the park to a small population of older Chinese men who had been bringing their birds to the park to sing each morning. Anna had, in fact, noticed the men and their birds, but she had hesitated to approach them. "We didn't want to intrude," she explains. She learned that the men had first begun to congregate in the park because there was a pet store nearby that sold crickets, a staple of the Hua Mei diet. The park wasn't heavily used at the time; their cohabitants were mostly drug dealers, and the men felt they could "squat" without fear of taking over anyone's territory.

Anna applied to the Trust for Public Land and received a grant designed to encourage children to work with older adults in improving a location in the city. She felt sure that the local Dominican children would be eager to help out because they used the park, and she was right. The drug dealers didn't relinquish their turf easily, though. Anna recalls an early incident when a group accosted her one morning. "They said, 'I'm gonna bust your head open,' and I said, 'Look, who's got the wrench, yo?' If I wasn't as crazy as I am, we would have gotten nowhere."

Word of the burgeoning garden spread through a local controversy over use of nearby park space. A rival organization made up mostly of the neighborhood's more affluent residents had begun bringing dogs to the abandoned wading pool adjacent to the garden, much to the chagrin of the bird club, as well as the local children, who used the pool for their games. In protest, the children—both Chinese and Latino—set up tables in the park and collected signatures to oppose the building of a dog run, ultimately convincing the local Community Board to reject the proposal. The controversy and the children's efforts garnered sufficient coverage in local newspapers to bring attention not only to the park but to the Hua Mei Bird Club, attracting curious visitors and new members. "I think it's something that they're very proud of now," Anna remarks. Despite her delight in the attention the bird garden has attracted in recent years, Anna remains ever protective of the club's privacy and integrity. "I was concerned at first that [the men] would be stared at. But I think people pass by and discover the sound. That's fun, 'cause it's like, 'What's that?' They see it and they just can't believe it."

Affectionately dubbed "the Dragon Lady" (her Chinese Zodiac sign is the dragon), Anna was once offered a Hua Mei bird of her own. But she demurred. "I took care of a parakeet once over Christmas, but these things, you have to bathe them every morning. And you have to be careful that they don't get a draft. Then you have to give them special food. They give them congee, rice porridge. So you have to cook for them—

it's like an infant. I mean, I liked the idea of having one, but I didn't like the commitment."

A MATCH MADE IN HEAVEN

D r. Yu, an acupuncturist and one of the most revered members of the club, reflects on the value of the bird garden to the broader populace, having been a regular for close to thirty years. "It's a place for retired bird fans to commune and be active," he says. "Also, a lot of visitors come by, so in that way it's valuable for the city." For two other members, a father and son, the garden is less about communing with other bird owners and more about the birds themselves. However, when asked about the hope for passing on the Hua Mei tradition to the next generation, both father and son are skeptical. "The interest is dying out," the son explains. "They're more interested in computers now." Tommy Chan claims there are only two or three people in their twenties who visit the garden regularly, and they mostly come to pick up tips for competitions. Also, among the younger generation, Hua Meis are regarded more as pets than as a lifestyle, as they still are in China and among the older club members. Tommy notes that in Hong Kong, special restaurants cater to the Hua Mei clientele; visitors can bring their birds in and hang them up while they eat and chat.

Anna Magenta remarks that the garden has begun to attract an increasing number of visitors from outside the immediate vicinity. Granted, they are still older men, but word of the garden has spread, and that is encouraging. "Now the old men come in cars from Albany, the tri-state area, Queens. Before it was just neighborhood people." The men have the local street-cleaning rules memorized; at noon, it's as if a wind has swept through the small park, carrying away a substantial contingent of men and their birds, dashing off to move their cars.

Both Tommy and Anna have visions of improving the garden. Anna imagines an urban oasis. In place of the police offices currently stationed in the middle of the park, she envisions a teahouse, and a covered area where the men could bring their birds in the rain or snow. "I think it would be beautiful if we had a pavilion where somebody would come with a cart and sell tea and dim sum." Such a teahouse might transform the Hua Mei Bird Garden from an intriguing sight into a recreational destination. Many hurdles still need to be jumped, but all of Anna's troubles are redeemed when she sees parents and babies pass by the bird garden, pause, and look in. Something in the combination of old men and young children, the quiet wonder, and the birdsong distills the garden to its essence and reminds her of what she really wants to preserve in this space. "The babies love the sound; they drink it up. And I think that's a match made in heaven."

—Caitlin Van Dusen

Russian and Turkish Tenth Street Baths

If you come to the Russian and Turkish Baths expecting soothing balms, thick towels, and gentle ministrations of flower-scented infusions, head elsewhere. This is a rough-hewn place —and proud of it. In fact, the tenaciously shopworn character of the Tenth Street Baths, as they are also known, has been one of the reasons for their longevity. The meticulously achieved balance of old and new is evident even in the sign above the door: Gold adhesive letters spelling out "268 E" have been affixed just to the left of the tenement tile sign proclaiming "Tenth Street Baths."

268 East Tenth Street, East Village, Manhattan

(212) 674–9250 or (212) 473–8806

www.russianturkishbaths.com

Hours: Monday, Tuesday, Thursday, Friday 11:00 a.m. to 10:00 p.m., Saturday 7:30 a.m. to 10:00 p.m. (coed); Wednesday 9:00 a.m. to 2:00 p.m. (women only), 2:00 p.m. to 10:00 p.m. (coed); Sunday 7:30 a.m. to 2:00 p.m. (men only), 2:00 p.m. to 10:00 p.m. (coed).

Public Transit: F train to Second Avenue. Use the First Avenue exit. Walk ten blocks north (against traffic) on First Avenue. Turn right onto Tenth Street.

6 train to Astor Place. Walk north (with traffic) on Fourth Avenue. Turn right onto Tenth Street and walk east three and a half blocks.

TWO HUNDRED DEGREES OF GLORY

Stroll down East Tenth Street on a weekday afternoon in midwinter (hint: the best time to visit the baths), and you'll notice a plume of smoke rising from a metal shaft climbing the facade of a bedraggled red-brick building. Bolstered as it is by both a Pilates and a tai chi studio, a holistic pet shop, and a raw foods restaurant, its vapors seem to issue from another era. After ascending the steps and pushing through the

Nudity is never out of style at the Russian and Turkish Baths. Photo © Harvey Wang.

heavy doors, you find yourself in a haphazardly arranged room: At one end, Formica tables are arrayed before two televisions, broadcasting different channels simultaneously (often a football game and the Weather Channel). A dazed audience of men and women with steam-pinkened flesh basks in the din. Russian masseurs on break hunch over bowls of chicken legs; twenty-somethings in mud masks sip wheatgrass juice; burly men shake out the pages of Cyrillic newspapers and gnaw on buttered hunks of rye bread; a gay couple exchange tips on sample-sale shopping. A cramped food counter proffers a menu that reflects the appetites of the baths' motley clientele: blintzes, fresh-squeezed juice blends (including a "liver cleanser" and a "heartbeat"), Russian beer, borscht, candy bars. The air smells like peppermint, chicken, and damp towels, but conspicuously absent is the nostril-searing chlorine usually associated with public pools.

Behind the seating area rises the baths' business epicenter: an intimidatingly high counter, presided over by an invariably surly attendant. You reach up to relinquish your wallet and valuables to an iron strongbox stowed in a rack in the wall, in exchange for a numbered key on a rubber band. Accounts are settled upon departure, lest you be seduced by the subterranean mists into a platza beating or a sea salt scrub. You are instructed in no uncertain terms to keep your key with you at all times, and over the years, clients have devised clever ways to adhere to this dictum: Svelte young women slip the rubber bands ornamentally around their biceps or ankles; burly Russian men, around their wrists.

A board above the front desk spells out the baths' hours (women-only Wednesday mornings, men-only Sunday mornings), regulations, and roster of "special treatments." The ransom-note quality of the adhesive lettering is perhaps fitting for the baths' somewhat ominous-sounding offerings: A "Russian massage" is

FIRST PERSON: A TURKISH BATH ENTHUSIAST

"I would rather take a Turkish bath any day than to eat the daintiest dinner that ever was cooked. There is more refreshment in a thorough bath than in all the wine that was ever bottled or in all the delicacies evolved from the fancy of a French culinary artist. . . . It will add to your beauty, fortify your health and frighten old age [back] at least twenty years."—*Washington Post*, January 6, 1889

administered by a scantily clad Russian strongman or -woman who beats, squeezes, and unravels muscles into a limp pulp—an experience at once exhilarating and debilitating. The "Dead Sea salt scrub" and "Dead Sea mud treatments" deliver a thorough epidermal sloughing. But perhaps the most exotic treatment is the "platza massage," during which a masseur beats your back with a broom made of fresh oak leaves saturated in soapy water. An astringent quality in the leaves is said to open the pores, the leaves exfoliate dead skin, and the olive oil in the soap—thankfully—soothes. The platza massage is the most daring, and reputedly the most authentic, of the treatments offered; it is also the only one that is administered publicly, in the pulsing heart of the Tenth Street Baths: the Russian sauna.

These treatments are offered at an additional cost; the modest regular admission fee guarantees you a pair of outsized white rubber slippers, an unlimited supply of tiny, threadbare towels, and free access to cotton swabs and disposable razors. It also includes the baths' trademark uniform, undoubtedly one of the secrets of its success in building a sense of community among its diverse clientele: a one-size-fits-all sleeveless robe, or a pair of shorts, the elastic waistband of which inevitably crackles out into stretchlessness. Much as patrons have devised ways to wear their keys, they have also risen to the baths' sartorial challenge: The waistbands of the shorts can be rolled into a low-rise hipster look, towels tied into strapless bikini tops or (for the slender) sarongs,

FIRST PERSON: A *NEW YORK TIMES* REPORTER

"If cleanliness is next to godliness, New York must be a very upright city, for certainly no people in the world can do more bathing than we on Manhattan Island. . . . For all this bathing New York offers every facility. . . . [This] *Times* reporter has spent the spare hours of a month or more in learning what there is to be learned in these places where heat and electricity are supposed to be the panacea for all ills. He has gone through the dry heat of the Turkish bath, the steam of the Russian, the twists and jerks of the electric, the oleaginous Roman, and the stinging electric shampoo. That he lives to tell the story is no doubt owing to the fact that he did not undertake the sulphur or any of the medicinal baths."—"The Baths of New York," *New York Times,* November 13, 1881

robes worn with the opening to the back and waistband cinched into a makeshift dress. Others abstain from the communal garments altogether, preferring their own swimwear for reasons of sanitation or fashion. After devising a suitable costume, you descend to the baths down a slippery tile staircase past yet another posted ban—"No spitting No shaving No cleaning of teeth"—and the true experience of the Tenth Street Baths begins.

You might choose to ease your way into the experience in the familiar calm of the cedar sauna—or plunge right into the Russian sauna in all its two-hundred-degree glory. The warning sign on the door misleadingly touts its "radiant heat," the source of which is now a gas furnace but formerly was a stucco box filled with boulders hewn from cemetery stone and heated with coals. Should you choose the Russian option, the heat hits you like a wall upon opening the door; newcomers often duck for refuge in the lower altitudes. So intense is the heat that it sears the nostrils upon impact; within seconds the pores are pulsing. Seat yourself on one of the splintered wooden boards set atop the cement benches and bask until you can't stand it anymore. Then grab one of the plastic buckets that reside under the free-flowing ice water taps, hoist it over your head, take a deep breath, and pour. The moment of impact—when all time, sensation, thought, and consciousness are shocked into absence—is the essence of the Russian sauna experience. The shock of extremes repelling and merging simultaneously is the key to its benefits for body and mind.

After another bout with the radiant heat, you may decide to flee the Russian sauna and plunge instead into the ice water pool, about twelve feet long by eight feet wide, its frigid surface pocked with soggy oak leaves from platza clients. The ice water pool, like a sorbet between rich courses, provides the perfect segue between bathing experiences, cleansing the palate and readying it for the next onslaught of heat.

The peppermint smell in the lobby upstairs issues from the Turkish steam room, a glassed-in closet of slick tiles enveloped in a heady vapor infused with eucalyptus oil. The tiled Turkish steam room offers a less barbarian version of the Russian steam room, with racks of wooden benches and a cold shower on a pull string (apparently woven of old robes) by the door. This is a relatively easy room in which to steep—the thick steam separates occupants from each other, much like being lost in a snowstorm, and the scented air refreshes and soothes. When you've had enough, you can shower in one of the unisex stalls adjacent, shave at the communal sink, or decompress on the edge of the pool alongside fellow bathers belted with rubber-banded keys.

TO SPA OR TO SCHVITZ?

The baths were founded in 1892, when most of the city's immigrants and poor lived without convenient access to clean running water for drinking, let alone bathing. The city built floating baths on the Hudson and East rivers beginning in the 1870s, but the first free public bathhouse didn't open until 1901, on Rivington Street on the Lower East Side. (The last one, the Allen Street Baths, closed in the 1970s.) For those with some change in their pockets, commercial bathhouses presented another option. The Russian and Turkish Baths on East Tenth Street was one of about sixty such private bathhouses in the city in the 1890s; many were used by Eastern European Jews.

The schvitz (meaning "to sweat" in Yiddish) evolved as a mostly male institution, where city dwellers could not only clean up but play cards, drink schnapps, chat, and vent their troubles with friends and strangers alike. At the turn of the twentieth century, New York's schvitz culture was thriving, primarily in the predominantly Jewish quarters of the Lower East Side of Manhattan, and Coney Island in Brooklyn. As living conditions in the tenements improved, and many devotees of the schvitz departed in midcentury for the suburbs, New York City's schvitz culture declined, to be overtaken by upscale spas and gyms, which offered ostensibly the same roster of services but in a less "exotic" environment. Spas were everything the Tenth Street Baths were not: hot stone massages in place of platza beatings; stacks of fresh terrycloth towels and handcrafted soaps in place of raveling brown hand towels and Styrofoam cups of "Black Sea mud"; even minimalist "spa cuisine" in place of hearty borscht, blintzes, and knishes.

In 1974, the Tenth Street Baths were taken over by Al Modlin, who hoped that schvitz culture might catch on with the neighborhood's

Women dancing at the Brighton Beach Baths, which fell prey to development in the 1990s. Photo © Harvey Wang.

changing population. At the time, the lobby floors were covered in mismatched strips of linoleum, the walls papered in 1950s girlie photographs, and the front room filled with the cigar smoke of the then-bastions of schvitz: gray-haired Russian men swathed in white towels, tossing back shots of vodka and yammering in Yiddish.

Modlin managed to escort the baths through a decade, only to be hit with the unexpected fallout of the AIDS crisis in the 1980s. Even today, the baths are not noted for their sparkling conditions, and the rising paranoia about disease sent many regular customers fleeing toward the more modern health clubs, leaving the stained towels and unchlorinated pool in their wake. The long-touted health benefits of communal sweating were overshadowed by fear of the fatal germs that might be seeping into the ancient boards and buckets. Susan Shellogg, a masseuse at the baths, remarks: "There are two types of people: You either really love this place or you hate it. The type of people who love it are not uptight, not quite so concerned about hygiene."

By 1985, the roof was caving in, and mice scurried between the legs of the vacant chairs. A neighbor in the tenement next door filed a lawsuit against the baths, complaining that boiling water was leaking into his apartment. The city threatened to close down the baths—until Boris Tuberman and Dave Shapiro came along. Their faith in the social and gustatory benefits of schvitzing managed to cleanse not only the floors but the baths' squalid reputation.

Tuberman and Shapiro went right to work, adding a new furnace, a renovated kitchen serving fresh-pressed fruit juices in addition to the traditional Russian fare of kasha and borscht, a rooftop sundeck, and an exercise room. Following the heyday of improvements, the pair became estranged (the reasons are one of the many shadowed secrets of the Tenth Street Baths), and to this day they operate the baths on alternate weeks, as is announced by one of the many signs above the front desk. Whatever bad blood might exist between the owners, it hasn't prevented the young and the hip, as well as the old and the nostalgic, from pouring through the doors with as much enthusiasm as they pour buckets of icy water over their heads in the sauna. From LL Cool J and JFK Jr. (whose signed photos adorn the walls) to the housewife or yoga instructor next door, the baths still have the power to mesmerize—and unite.

STEAMING IN COMMUNITY

In recent decades, this monument to the nineteenth-century Russian-Jewish culture of the Lower East Side has enjoyed a renaissance, as the neighborhood's hipsters, artists, and young professionals flock up the tenement staircase, gratefully exchange their DKNY for a worn blue robe and rubber slippers, and open their pores—and sometimes their souls—to their fellow schvitzers.

Simon Lemmer, a regular at the baths and an amateur platza

masseur, attests to the timeless lure of the Tenth Street Baths: "About fifteen years ago there were about fifteen or twenty regulars, most of them between sixty and eighty years old. About five or six years ago things changed drastically where it became the 'in' thing, and now you see younger and younger people. Even all the actors have started coming here. Of late, it's a very hip place. The younger crowd is on the weekends. Saturdays it fills up; after work it can get really busy. The old-timers who remain aren't too keen on it. They used to be the bosses here; they were the ones you would respect. I wish I would have found this place earlier. It would have saved me a lot of bad stuff in my younger life.

"There's two or three new places opening in Manhattan, and another one or two opening in Brooklyn. But as much as anybody tries, they're never going to have the heart and soul that this place has. That's why people keep coming back here; it's over a hundred years old and not much has changed. Maybe the veneer, the woodworking, but the essentials stay: a down-to-earth, old-time bathhouse. There's definitely a million stories in here. If there's any one place in the world that's like a soap opera, this is it. I come here for the heat but also for the social life; without the people here, I have none. I'm in the office supply business. Some of my best accounts, I swear, are from here. You get to know somebody pretty quick—you get to talk about everything. I come here five days a week from Brooklyn. I work to make money, but I come here to play; it's a hobby. I have over two hundred brooms—I'm addicted to it. It's like going back into the womb."

The influx of upscale patrons hasn't managed to oust the more traditional customers, who in fact may be responsible in part for the baths' quaintness quotient—another key factor in their longevity. On any given day, you might find yourself sharing a cedar bench with a Hasidic man with side curls, a bikini-clad fashion model, a Russian bodybuilder, a rock star, a gay couple, a waitress. Somehow, sitting in a two-hundred-degree stone cave beneath the teeming sidewalks of New York City brings people together in unexpected ways. That is the magic of the baths that its patrons and proprietors attest to: It is New York's "unexpected paradise"—and an infernally hot one at that.

—Caitlin Van Dusen

Bohemian Hall and Beer Garden

29–19 Twenty-fourth Avenue, Astoria, Queens

(718) 274–4925

www.bohemianhall.com

Hours: Monday, Wednesday, and Thursday 6:00 to 11:00 p.m.; closed Tuesday (BBQ in summer 6:00 to 11:00 p.m.); Friday 6:00 p.m. to midnight; Saturday noon to midnight; Sunday noon to 11:00 p.m.

Public Transit: N train to Astoria Blvd. (one stop before the last, Ditmars Blvd.). Walk one block to the intersection of Twenty-fourth Avenue and Thirty-first Street. The hall is located between Twenty-ninth Street and Thirty-first Street.

Listed on the National Register of Historic Places, 2001

It's Saturday night at the Bohemian Hall and Beer Garden in Astoria, Queens. Patrons linger outside the front door; dogs bark; cars swish past; in the distance the N train rattles over the elevated tracks. Behind the inconspicuous brick facade strung with white-icicle Christmas lights hides a world inside a world: the last remaining beer garden in New York City.

In the front room, a big-screen TV glows from a high corner perch, and dusty inflatable bottles of Pilsner Urqell, the official beer of Bohemian Hall, dangle from the ceiling. Groups chat peacefully in the tall wooden booths. The air is redolent with the yeasty tang of beer, and glasses thunk across the worn bar top. Were it not for the colorful Czech pennants and coats of arms that festoon the walls, this might seem like any other old-school New York City bar—an appearance belied by what happens when you pass through the back door into the beer garden.

Linden trees and trumpeter elms, strung with yet more pennants and festival lights, rustle their silvery leaves above tidy rows of picnic tables lined with twenty- and thirty-somethings, hunkering over heavy glass mugs or dealing out a game of cards. No rowdy bacchanalia, the courtyard has the ordered disorder of a school cafeteria. At the rear of the garden is an elevated dance floor under a gazebo. Some groups have carried their beer pitchers over and sit cross-legged in small groups on the plywood stage, in the shadow of the spotlights that illuminate the rest of the garden. The courtyard is enclosed by a ten-foot white brick wall, and the picnic tables on the fringes are sheltered by a green corrugated metal roof. Gravel crunches underfoot as patrons walk to and from the outdoor bar, bearing brimming pitchers of golden beer. Surly bartenders bark out orders and yank down on the colorful taps of Pilsner Urquell, Hoegaarden, BrouCzech, Staropramen, and Jever.

Patrons cite the laid-back atmosphere as one reason they keep coming back. "It's a throwback to a different era, a preservation of immigrant culture, which New York is rapidly abandoning," says Duncan, a young journalist who lives in the neighborhood and is a regular at the garden. It has a different ambiance than Manhattan bars, he says; "It's the only place you can come and have unobstructed conversation and hang out for hours."

VÍTÁME VÁS (WE WELCOME YOU)

Today, Bohemian Hall is home to the bar and beer garden, a restaurant, a Sokol gymnastics program, and a Czech school, offering free classes to children interested in learning the Czech language and about Bohemian history, geography, and ethnic lifestyle. The rambling, expansive complex hints at an earlier time when Astoria and other New York neighborhoods were still home to a sizable Czech community and this place was one of its centers. In Bohemian Hall's meeting and assembly rooms, its auditorium and courtyard, its kitchen and dining room, Czechs from young to old studied, played, courted, married, and consumed quantities of food and drink, stealing hours from busy weekdays and relaxing on weekends. Generation after generation created and re-created community life here, and Bohemian Hall evolved into a mainstay of Czech culture in New York City.

Bohemian Hall's walled courtyard continues to provide the perfect setting for ethnic festivals. Photo: Martha Cooper.

But don't imagine its era is over. Bohemian Hall is a place that continues to re-create itself, keeping its function as a Czech ethnic center alive while reaching out widely to partying New Yorkers—be they singles, families, or cultural organizations. From a low point a decade ago, Bohemian Hall has sprung back strong. Its key to success is its best resource: a 200-by-125-foot beer garden that comfortably holds over a thousand people, is secluded from the street, and is the last of its kind in New York City. In addition to informal gatherings, the garden hosts a wide variety of festivals and organized programs. There's the annual Oktoberfest, the Czech and Slovak Festival (think dumplings and Wienerschnitzel, synchronized gymnastics, and the Pilsner Brass

Band), other Czech cultural celebrations, and regular Sokol gymnastic exhibitions. The Sokol is thriving, with both Czech and non-Czech youngsters who practice at the hall regularly and compete internationally. One of the team's memorable experiences took place at a meet in Czechoslovakia. Sokol programs there had stopped under Communist rule. When the Americans got up to perform, the Czechs wildly applauded them for keeping the tradition alive.

Other local ethnic groups also make regular use of the walled garden's old-world charm to bring life to their celebrations. The hall's roster of events typically includes Cuban, Greek, and world folk music events, as well as brass band and bluegrass concerts—and pig roasts. Sokol director Bob Liptek says: "You can tell when you walk down the block what celebration you'll find in the courtyard. If you smell sauerkraut and kielbasa, it's Czech; if it's garlic and tomatoes, it's Italians; if it's lesko—onions, peppers, and bacon—it's Hungarian."

One of the garden's devoted users is El Club Cubano Interamericano, a social and fraternal club started in the 1940s on Longwood Avenue in the South Bronx and sustained today by Jo-Ana Rene Moreno, the daughter of two early members. She holds club meetings in her home and throws an annual dance at Bohemian Hall. Four orchestras played in 2004 at El Baile de Mamoncillo—named for a fruit native to Cuba and a park where such dances were held. Moreno calls Bohemian Hall a wonderful substitute for that early dancing space. "Walk into this enclosed, park space," she writes, "and you find yourself surrounded

PLACE MOMENT: JIM PIGNETTI, BOHEMIAN HALL AND BEER GARDEN

"Beyond the elevated subway line, a hum of human voices rises. Enter the tavern huddled against the building flying the Czech and American flags—pass the bar, the stalls, the restaurant—exit the rear door into the last beer garden in New York, a treed, walled sanctum of Urquell, Staropramen, sanctum of schnitzel and sausage. A thousand or more seats float in a haze of human conversation and intoxication, all filtering through the branches and leaves into the Astoria sky."

by trees and benches. Gravel is thrown on the floor to cover dirt, but that doesn't stop any of us Cubans from wearing white shoes, pants, and guayaberas. And for a little authenticity we hang mamoncillos from the trees." (To join the yearly fun, search the Web for Baile de Mamoncillo.)

The Cypriot men's club has employed the hall for games of kazanti, a primitive version of pinball played for cigarettes and bottles of liquor. Members of the Hungarian Reform Church have danced czárdás in the garden. And residents of Quaglietta, Italy, have processed to the beer garden bearing an icon of their patron saint, Rocco, as have local Hispanics for their own parade, the Desfile de la Raza.

A HOME AWAY FROM HOME

The cornerstone of Bohemian Hall was laid on October 1, 1910, by the Bohemian Citizens Benevolent Society of Astoria, established in 1902 by Czech immigrants and Americans of Czech descent. Like so many other ethnic-origin social clubs, the founders organized themselves for mutual aid and tried to maintain a balance between continuation of the old and incorporation of the new. "The purpose of this Society," intoned the bylaws, "shall be to encourage, support and maintain Bohemian Schools, Dramatics, Lectures and Libraries for Czech children and children of Czech parentage; to maintain a non-profit-making social home for Czechs and people of Czech ancestry in which the Czech culture may be taught and blended with American traditions and culture, thereby tending to make the members better Americans." To do all this, Astoria's Bohemian Hall started a beer garden, a Czech school, and a Sokol club.

The Sokol club (*sokol* translates as "falcon," a bird admired for its courage and endurance) not only fostered a supportive place for Czechs in New York; its very existence was a plug for Czech independence from the Hapsburg monarchy and Austro-Hungarian Empire. The Sokol movement, which was founded in the 1860s in Prague and shortly made its way to the United States via new immigrants, included voluntary gymnastic and cultural organizations that sought to embrace the populace and cultivate a national (anti-imperial) identity. Hundreds of Sokol halls were built across the United States, and they became lively community centers, adding libraries, singing societies, and theatrical

Today, Bohemian Hall still hosts the annual Czech and Slovak Festival. Photo: Martha Cooper.

groups to the original program of gymnastics training, competition, and exhibition. (Bohemian Hall and Sokol New York Hall on East Seventy-first Street are the only two active Sokol buildings remaining in New York City.)

But not all Sokols were the same. The founders of Bohemian Hall's D. A. Sokol (Dělnický americký Sokol and Sokolice) were more vocal about their politics than some others. Self-described workingmen, many of them labored in the city's cigar factories. The club's governing rules charged a one-dollar fine for crossing any picket line, and its uniform was red to announce the club's socialist leanings.

The D. A. Sokol came to Astoria from Yorkville in Manhattan, where

Entrance to the bar and the beer garden at Bohemian Hall. Photo: Martha Cooper.

the Czech enclave stretched from Sixty-first to Seventy-fifth streets and Third to York avenues. Yorkville's first Czech settlers had moved uptown from the Lower East Side, creating what would become the city's principal Czech-speaking enclave from the 1880s through the 1950s. They lived there in the midst of a larger German community and smaller enclaves of Hungarians, Italians, and Greeks. Yorkville's Bohemian National Hall on East Seventy-third Street, a designated New York City landmark, is a survivor from this era. Not until the early years of the twentieth century did the Queens neighborhoods of Astoria and Winfield attract concentrated settlements of Czechs.

In the 1930s, with Astoria's Bohemian Hall going strong, the society erected a wooden fence abutting the simple brick edifice of the building, transforming what was then a patch of Queens farmland into a European-style beer garden. They planted the walled courtyard with linden trees, the national tree of the Czech Republic. New generations of immigrants were incorporated into the society, and the humble brick building quickly grew into a neighborhood center as well as a home away from home for the Czech community. In fact, the letters carved into the arched doorway above the hall's high stoop read *Cesky Domov,* meaning "Czech Home." Choral groups and folk-dance societies practiced in the hall and performed at festivals in the courtyard.

At the time of its construction, German-style picnic parks were a New York City institution. In his book *The Great, Good Place,* Ray Oldenburg discusses the importance of informal public meeting places, which, he says, served as gathering points between home and work, where people found good company, laughter, and lively conversation. In a chapter devoted to the institution of the beer garden, Oldenburg notes that "[Germans] who came to meet and know one another in the happy informality of the beer gardens went on to form drama clubs, turnen [German gymnastics groups], debating societies, singing groups, rifle clubs, home guards, volunteer fire departments, fraternities and associations dedicated to social refinement. It was the basis of community." By the mid-twentieth century, the Czech and German beer gardens in New York had started to close, as the children of immigrants relocated to Long Island and New Jersey. "This is a neighborhood for people on their way up," said John Foray, Bohemian Hall's former manager. But, on the flip side, "once they're up, they're gone."

SAVE THE HALL!

Beginning when he was a six-year-old boy, in 1952, John Foray participated in the Sokol gymnastics club at Bohemian Hall. He was in the "midget boys" class, and the girl he eventually married was in the class of "midget girls." Their wedding took place in the hall; an estimated four hundred guests attended. ("Luckily, we had some extra food in the basement," he quips.) Now, he says, "I'm so close to it all, so familiar with its problems, that I have a hard time remembering the good times." He wondered for a time if the hall wasn't something of an anachronism, a "dinosaur trying to survive."

In the early 1990s, revenue was so low that the hall threatened to close. That's when the SOS went out, and to the surprise of Bohemian Society stalwarts, the scattered community responded. Debbie Van Cura, formerly on the board of directors, remembers her shock when she first heard the news. "I'd been going to festivals for about ten years," she recalls, "but I think this was the first time I had realized the place was in trouble. We all thought it would just be there forever!" Van Cura says about a hundred people showed up for the "Save the Hall" meeting, more than expected—and even more surprising, they weren't all Czech. "What had happened was that Bohemian Hall and Park had become more than a building just for Czech people. It had become a real community building, important to Astoria."

The road back to vigor has been bumpy, but the outcome positive. When Vaclav Havel—hero of the "Velvet Revolution" and former president of Czechoslovakia—stopped by in 2000, he was so moved he stayed for hours and held a press conference in the garden. In 2001, Bohemian Hall was listed on the National Register of Historic Places for its association with the history of Czech and Slavic immigration, its dis-

SISTER SITE: BOHEMIAN NATIONAL HALL

321–325 East Seventy-third Street, Yorkville, Manhattan

Designated a New York City Landmark, 1994

Bohemian National Hall (Národní Budova) is a distinguished building being renovated to house the office of the Czech Consulate General in New York. Like Astoria's Bohemian Hall, it was built by a Czech immigrant organization for use as a social club—a place to host a wide variety of community services and activities. It once housed a restaurant, a bar, club rooms, bowling alleys, a shooting gallery, a ballroom/theater, and classrooms. Unlike Bohemian Hall, this building was constructed in 1895–1897 with an eye to architecture. Designed by William C. Frohne in the Renaissance Revival style, its facade is richly ornamented in buff-colored Roman brick, stone, and terra-cotta and features a projecting entrance porch with columns resting on lion's-head bases.

tinctive meeting-hall and beer-garden design, and its importance in sustaining the activities, customs, and attitudes of the Czech community members who use it.

In other words, Bohemian Hall keeps us linked, visually and materially, to the past. That's not important just for the Czechs; it's important for us all. That's why so many of us are crowding Bohemian Hall's beer garden of a weekend night, voting with our feet for the survival of places that sustain local distinctiveness.

—Caitlin Van Dusen and Marci Reaven

The Magic Table at the Edison Hotel

Café Edison, 228 West Forty-seventh Street, Midtown, Manhattan

Public Transit: N, R, S, 1, 2, 3, 7, 9 trains to Times Square/Forty-second Street. Walk north (against traffic) on Broadway and turn west (left) onto Forty-seventh Street, and walk to about the middle of the block.

Every weekday around noon, for almost thirty years, Mike Bornstein's thoughts turned to scrambled eggs and magic. Fortunately, he could satisfy both cravings at the same time.

He strolled the two short blocks from his ancient apartment in the Broadway theater district to the Hotel Edison coffee shop, where he took his familiar corner seat at the head of the magic table. As waitresses glided past, juggling plates of knockwurst and pancakes, Bornstein and his venerable colleagues in the New York magic community turned nickels into dimes, plucked silk flowers from plastic tubes, and summoned the ghosts of long-gone friends like Cardini, Slydini, the Coney Island Fakir, and even Orson Welles and bandleader Richard Himber. Bornstein presided over the Magic Table four days each week until, tragically, he was killed by a truck on his way home from the café at the age of eighty-three. Currently, Society of American Magicians member Tom Klem presides.

SHARING A TRICK OR TWO

Vegas may have David Copperfield and Lance Burton, but the Edison Hotel, from noon until two on Monday through Friday, is the magic world's undisputed spiritual hub. The café is nicknamed "the Polish Tea Room" and has a section for the many Broadway theater folks who also gather there. Neil Simon wrote a play about the place called *Only 45 Seconds from Broadway*.

For the past sixty-four years, the Magic Table has served as a gathering place for coin snatchers, shadowgraphers, levitation aficionados, and generations of shell-game wizards. "It's a depot, a stopping-off point for magicians from all over the world," said Bornstein, who was known on the vaudeville circuit as Kolma the Magical Mandarin. "We don't really have to be anywhere, so we come, we sit down, break bread with fellow magicians, discuss magic, talk about where you've come from or where you're going, and maybe see a new trick or two."

On a good afternoon, fifteen or more magicians might show up, filling

The late Mike Bornstein, longtime host of the Magic Table. Photo: Martha Cooper.

Regards from the Magic Table. Photo: Martha Cooper.

two or three long tables in the back of the coffee shop. Those who come are an eclectic bunch. On the day we visited, a retired federal judge pulled an oversized deck of cards out of an invisible change purse; a porter, on his half-hour lunch break, responded by making a salt shaker disappear. A few minutes later, Bob Friedman, a world-traveling lawyer who commuted two hours that morning from the suburbs, showed the group how to cheat at poker. Afterward, a former court reporter turned an ordinary deck of cards into a bouquet of wildflowers. "What we have in common is the hobby, like car enthusiasts," said Stanley Hersch, a computer consultant better known for his spoon bending and mind-reading abilities. "The only difference is, we carry our hobby with us."

Over a side order of French fries, Jerry Oppenheimer, the court reporter, recalled the Magic Table's history. "Most of the major magicians—and then some—have been to the table," he says. "Slydini, Copperfield, Chinese magicians, magicians from Texas, magicians from

Germany, kid magicians, women magicians, clown magicians, they've all been here. Magicians are part of a family, and when they're in New York, they know there's always a place for them to come home to."

LET'S DO LUNCH (EVERY WEEKDAY FOR FIFTY YEARS)

S ince a member of the Society of American Magicians swears an oath to hold on tight to the secrets of the craft," Tom Klem told us, "magicians naturally seek and enjoy those who share the same passion of a life in magic and its secrets." Over the years many places have become the focus of these activities and are cherished and loved by this magic community. One of these is the S.A.M. Magic Table that first met in 1942 in Times Square, in a different location from the current one. The founders described their first Table in this way: "S.A.M.'s Parent Assembly Number One reserves a regular table at lunchtime daily for its members and friends at the famous Terrace Dining Room of the Dixie Hotel. Visiting magicians are always assured of a hearty welcome and fine food in friendly company at the Magic Table, Forty-third Street west of Broadway. They will be very glad to see you and swap gags and magic news and views."

Over the years, the group moved from place to place—the Dixie Hotel coffee shop, Rossoff's restaurant, the Gaiety restaurant, and finally the Edison—but the meetings were always in the theater district, close to the major magic shops like Tannen's, Holden's, and Robson's. Bornstein, who sold magic in Times Square, remembers the table in the

FIRST PERSON: TOM KLEM

"In the early 1940s, toward the end of the vaudeville and burlesque eras, Mike Bornstein was the magician at Leon and Eddie's, a nightclub on Fifty-second Street, along with a well-known burlesque stripper, Sherry Britton, who had very long dark hair that went all the way down to the floor. A few years ago, Mike was buying sheet music at a store and ran into this older woman. She said to him, 'Do you know who I am?' He said, 'No.' She said, 'Mike, how you doing? I'm Sherry Britton.' Without skipping a beat, he answered, 'I didn't recognize you with your clothes on.'

Mike told this favorite story of his to the cashier at the Edison Café on the very day he died."

1940s and 1950s as a natural meeting place for busy people in the trade. "We'd go over to Lou Tannen's on Forty-sixth Street and see some new vanishing wands or whatever," he says. "Then Lou would say, 'You going to lunch? Let's all go together.'" And off they'd go.

The years after World War II were literally magic ones in Manhattan. Bornstein estimates that dozens of shops, many featuring demonstration counters open to sidewalk shoppers, dotted Broadway and Eighth Avenue, from Times Square to Fifty-second Street. At Holden's, customers were enthralled by "shadowgraphy" performances—expert

SISTER SITES: MORE MAGIC IN MIDTOWN

The Society of American Magicians Parent Assembly Number One, which sponsors the Magic Table, meets the first Friday of the month at the Soldiers', Sailors', Marines', and Airmen's Club at 283 Lexington Avenue, near Thirty-sixth Street. This 102-year-old national organization has over a hundred thousand members and welcomes new members to the club. On the last Friday of each month at the Musicians' Union Hall, the International Brotherhood of Magicians meets as well. Both groups hold workshops and lectures during the month.

On Saturdays, magicians gather at Café Rustico II at 25 West Thirty-fifth Street from noon on, to swap tricks and talk of the latest news in magic. They call this "the pizza place" and professionals, amateurs and the public mix in a love of the art of magic. After the pizza place, usually around 2:00 or 3:00 p.m., they go to Maui Taco at 328 Fifth Avenue. There they gather in a large downstairs room, hosted by Doug Edwards and others. This is a somewhat younger set, and many very good magicians share their art.

Monday Night Magic at the Saint Clements Theatre at 423 West Forty-sixth Street brings professional magic to the public every Monday. With its stage show of three or more acts, and three close-up magicians at intermission, it is the longest-running professional magic show in New York City.

Louis Tannen's Magic Shop (www.tannens.com) is the last of the great magic shops in Manhattan. It is located at 45 West Thirty-fourth Street and is the place to buy a small trick or large illusion, depending on your interests. Occasionally they schedule a series of lectures from professionals, but any day a demonstrator would be happy to show the latest magic. —*Tom Klem*

shadow puppet shows in which Holden himself would create silhouettes of camels, birds, donkeys, and celebrities like Jimmy Durante. At the Flosso Hornmann Magic Shop, the Coney Island Fakir, a fast-talking coin magician (who happened to be Al Flosso), performed close-up magic routines and sold packs of tricks for ten cents apiece. And at Tannen's, on Forty-second Street, magicians came to buy live canaries and turtles, Svengali decks, vanishing milk pitchers, and both disappearing and reappearing canes.

KEEPING THE MAGIC ALIVE

Today, nearly all the great magic shops are gone, except for Tannen's, which has moved several times since Lou Tannen passed away. The community still endures, however, as magicians from around the world baffle each other and expose their secrets by distributing homemade video cassettes, many of which find their way to members of the Magic Table.

After a few visits to the Edison Hotel coffee shop, you start to see some of the old routines over and over again. A newcomer is traditionally shown the salt trick. Bornstein would open the salt shaker on the table, make a fist, pour some into his hand, and—puff!—it vanishes. The visitor is asked if he knows where it went. Suddenly, fifteen magicians simultaneously empty a handful of salt onto the table. But every once in a while, a fresh gag or inexplicable new trick will surface. Even some of the old-timers seemed genuinely impressed when a twelve-year-old boy showed up at the table a few years ago, mesmerizing the group with close-up card tricks and a few ball-in-cup routines. "There's nothing better," Bornstein says, "than seeing a young magician who's continuing the tradition."

After a little midday magic, the group dissolves, as people head home or back to work. A heap of folded and crinkled dollar bills, used in countless tricks over lunch, is left for the waitress. Even after years of practice, there's one trick no one's been able to master. As Bornstein puts it, "You can't make the check disappear."

—David Hochman

The General Society of Mechanics and Tradesmen

20 West 44th Street, Midtown, Manhattan

(212) 840–1840

www.generalsociety.org

Hours: Weekdays; closed weekends and holidays. Tours are available by appointment.

Public Transit: B, D, F, V trains to Forty-second Street/Bryant Park. Cross Forty-second Street.

4, 5, 6, 7 trains to Grand Central/Forty-second Street. Use the station exit that puts you on Forty-second Street. Turn right on Forty-second Street and walk up to Forty-fourth Street between Fifth and Sixth avenues.

Designated a New York City Landmark, 1988

Stroll down West Forty-fourth Street, past the imposing facades of the New York City Yacht Club and the New York Bar Association. You'll come across what might seem an anomaly on this street of wealth and power: a plaque bearing an immense hammer and hand. In today's society it's an unlikely icon, but as a symbol of skilled labor it has been common since medieval times.

In 1785, master craftsmen in New York City founded the General Society of Mechanics and Tradesmen to secure life's opportunities and protect against its dangers. The founding artisans, including sailmakers, silversmiths, potters, and bell hangers, banded together to support the widows and educate the orphans of fellow craftsmen. They created a philanthropic educational institution dedicated to providing cultural, educational, and social services to members and their families. In time, the members found themselves wealthy enough to extend their philanthropy to the city in the form of a library and school. Not a member yourself? You are still welcome inside to peruse the society's library and special collections or attend an evening lecture.

"BY HAMMER AND HAND ALL ARTS DO STAND"

The modern incarnation of the General Society of Mechanics and Tradesmen consists of several interdependent sections: the Library and Special Collections, the Small Press Center, and the Mechanics Institute—a tuition-free technical school for adults working in industries related to the building trades.

The library occupies the heart of the building, and anyone is free to enter and look around, though to check out books or use the wireless Internet connection you must become a paying subscriber for a modest annual fee. This is the second-oldest subscription library in New York City, founded in 1820, with more than 150,000 volumes of fiction, nonfiction, trade, and technical-related materials.

Inside the door, steps lead down into the vaulted main reading room, flanked with faux marble pillars and topped by a glass skylight two stories high. This is the society's fifth location. As the plaque outside attests, its exterior is a designated New York City Landmark. Steel magnate Andrew Carnegie, himself a member, paid for elegant renovations to the Renaissance Revival–style building after the Society bought it in 1898. The society's insignia—a flexed arm wielding a hammer, and the words "By hammer and hand all arts do stand"—testifies to the importance of tools, skill, and human labor to culture and society.

Inside the library, the clutter and noise of Forty-fourth Street dissipates into the hissing of steam radiators and the rhythmic thumping of the librarian's rubber stamp. Six glass mercury-vapor lamps are suspended from brass chains over the worn oak tables and chairs. Two imposing wooden card catalogs stand to the sides. Until recently, their drawers contained the only complete record of the library's holdings. The drawer labels offer a cursory view of the breadth of the collection: Cartesian; Livery Stable; Ships; Telepathy. Indeed, a printed version of the library's classification system reveals equally quirky subdivisions: "A8: Bees, Silkworms; Dc8: Toilet Articles, Perfumery; Fs5: Conjuring, Ventriloquism; Pe7: Bells, Wiring; Ut8: Hats, Caps, Gloves; V6: Buccaneers, Pirates." The catalogs each have hand-cranked pencil sharpeners mounted atop, with mounds of shavings beneath, as well as boxes of call slips and containers of pencil stubs. The date stamps in the books

In 1904, the General Society commissioned architect Ralph Townsend to design the beautiful, soaring three-story reading room with skylight. Photo courtesy Stephen Amiga.

show when they were borrowed. They go so far back that you can trace the popularity of a volume well into the nineteenth century.

Janet Greene, historian and director of the Library, is eager to tell members and the general public about the breadth of the library's collection and the treasures lurking in the stacks: "This was founded as a general-interest library for apprentices, so we have books on all subjects, from architecture to travel to the 'useful arts,' which are mechanical and technical books. This is a terrific place to do research on urban trades and crafts. The society's early members were craftsmen and manufacturers, some of whom became very well known, such as the furniture-maker Duncan Phyfe; Peter Cooper, who was initiated into the General Society when he was a glue manufacturer; and lithographer Nathaniel Currier of Currier and Ives."

The library divides its collections into circulating and noncirculating books. Fiction and nonfiction published in the twentieth century can be borrowed. Older books must be used in the library. Particularly treasured are the nineteenth-century periodicals, especially those relating to architecture and the building arts and sciences, published by General Society members Harper and Putnam, among others. Also available to researchers, thanks to federal funding, are the records of the General Society itself, which go back to 1785.

Greene maintains that the library has books that even the New York Public Library doesn't have: for example, its significant holdings in engineering. And half of the collection is fiction—first editions of popular books from the past 150 years. However, the library doesn't yet have a catalog on-line, so these titles are part of the "buried treasure" available only by visiting and searching through the not-always-accurate card catalogue. Greene touts the library's small size as an asset, calling it a "boutique research collection"—homey, offering personal service and, to confound any stereotypes, wireless Internet connection.

On a balcony above the reading room, the General Society displays its most tangible evidence of urban manufacturing of the past, the John Mossman Lock Collection, one of the most comprehensive special collections of bank and vault locks in the world. Mossman, an active member in the nineteenth century, donated to the Society his papers and hundreds of locks, keys, and tools dating from 4000 B.C. to the twentieth century. Many of the examples are unique, made-to-order locks that were not produced in commercial quantities, and nearly every lock has protected millions in money and securities. Donations are accepted for tours, which are available by appointment.

Sharing ground-floor space with the library are the collections and book displays of the Small Press Center, established as a program of the General Society in 1984 to support and encourage quality work by independent publishers.

One way the programs of the General Society carry out their shared educational mission is by sponsoring public events. The Small Press Center offers workshops designed to help fledgling publishers and holds a Small Press Book Fair for vendors and book lovers each December. The General Society has offered public lectures since the 1830s, and today the themes are focused on topics related to labor, literature, and landmarks. All draw good audiences and, by bringing top-flight professionals and general audiences together, sustain the New York City tradition—to which the city's working people have long contributed—of broad public intellectual engagement in the issues of our day.

Audience members in these gatherings include students from the Mechanics Institute, working adults who attend evening classes in the upper floors of the society's building. The school was established in 1820 as one of the first providers of free education in New York City. In 1858, after the city founded its own public education system, the General Society opened the Mechanics Institute as an evening school for working adults. This is the oldest technical school in the city, and, true to the General Society tradition, all Mechanics Institute instructors are employed in their trades or professions during daytime hours—for example, air-conditioning, electricity, plumbing, and project management—and teach at night.

MECHANICS, TRADESMEN, AND ARTISANS

The tradition of transmitting knowledge from one generation to the next follows the model of artisan culture prevalent during the years of the society's founding—the tumultuous years that followed the Revolutionary War and the establishment of the United States. In November 1785, twenty-two "mechanics and tradesmen"—men who worked, say, as independent master cabinetmakers, shipbuilders, marble carvers, and shoemakers—gathered at Walter Heyer's Tavern on Pine Street in downtown Manhattan to found a society for mutual help and support. These were tough economic times, and the men hoped to help each other and the widows and orphans of their brethren. They also hoped to improve their situation by advocating for politics and laws favorable to the trades and manufacturing, and by reminding elites that neither the city nor nation would prosper without artisan labor.

The historian Sean Wilentz writes that "a typical gathering at the society's Mechanic Hall brought intense conversations. . . . In a city where merchants and bankers were the most powerful social and political leaders, the activities of the society testified that artisans, too, were a resourceful and purposeful group." In 1810, members of the General Society founded the Mechanics' Bank, hoping to have better access to capital. In 1820, hundreds of artisans contributed their books and money to support the founding of the General Society's Library for Apprentices, reinforcing the claim by master baker Thomas Mercein, president of the General Society in 1827 and a founder of the library, that mechanics were, as Wilentz quotes, "a body of men who do much in sustaining the prosperity of this Metropolis."

FIRST PERSON: CARPENTER EDWIN DOBBS, PRESIDENT OF THE GENERAL SOCIETY OF MECHANICS AND TRADESMEN, 1878

"By Hammer and Hand All Arts Do Stand! Galileo, who discovered that the earth revolved around the sun, was a mechanic, afterwards an astronomer. Columbus was said to have worked at a mechanical business, afterwards a navigator. Gutenberg was a printer [and an] . . . inventor. Fulton, who first applied steam as a motive power on water, was a mechanic. Franklin, who brought lightning from the clouds, was a mechanic. Stephenson, who made the iron horse that moves us in safety fifty miles an hour, on iron and steel rails, was a mechanic; and Morse, who was the first to apply electricity as a printing power, we believe was a mechanic, and in fact all great discoverers of anything useful for men were mechanics."

This symbol of working people was first mounted on the General Society's Mechanics Bank and later moved to its library. Photo courtesy Stephen Amiga.

A man wanting to join the General Society needed to be supported by two members who could attest to his "industry, honesty, and sobriety" and be approved by two-thirds of the membership. The initiation fee originally was five dollars, and monthly dues were twelve and a half cents. At the initiation ceremony, members were charged to "let sobriety, industry, integrity, and uprightness of heart continue to be the ornaments of your name."

In 1820, the society broke new ground by starting the library and the precursor of the trades school that still exist today on the upper floors. No public schools or formal training institutions then existed for the education and improvement of the working classes. The library was aimed at apprentices working in the crafts and trades—ironworkers, barrel-makers, leatherworkers, bricklayers, and so on—while the day school was for the children of society members, both those who could pay and those who were subsidized as charity students. Securing the future for mechanics and tradesmen was critical. The economy was changing rapidly; and where an artisan of good health and habits once could be reasonably sure of improving his lot, the evolving development of capitalism and the new wage economy had thrown everything into flux. Neither men nor women could be so sure where they stood anymore.

The library immediately found an enthusiastic audience. So ardent was the boys' response that on its opening evening three hundred books were checked out. As Greene notes, the first expenses listed in the society's minutes were for candles so the library could continue to maintain its critical evening hours; the children worked at their trades during the day, and hence the evening hours constituted their only free time. "That was the only education these children had," she points out. "Apprenticeship carried with it the obligation of the master to teach the student to read, and as apprenticeship changed and shortened and the work got segmented, the obligation to teach someone to read really got left behind. I think part of the reason for establishing the library was to honor that tradition."

Getting in to use the library was considered a privilege, and boys had to produce a letter of reference attesting to their responsibility. Neither women nor girls were welcomed into the library until 1862, when they became the fastest-growing class of readers. Greene stresses that hierarchy was more pronounced in nineteenth-century U.S. society, and even in the institution's earliest years, when the Apprentices' Library was nothing more than boxes of books in the back of a schoolroom, the children were not allowed to loiter, and the books would be given to them only if their hands were clean. It was not a cozy place, it was a disciplined place. In later locations, there were reading alcoves, and if you paid your subscription money you could sit there and read your magazines. The people who sat there were a little better off than the factory workers, Greene says. But there were straight-backed chairs: the Victorian ethos of "straight spine."

Life did not get appreciably more secure for the city's working people over the course of the nineteenth century. The General Society persisted in its efforts to serve the city through philanthropy and education to benefit the working classes of New York, and it altered the shape of the institution and its offerings to cope with larger changes. A researcher combing the records today for the titles of past classes offered by the society would get a revealing glimpse of the transformation of American society over the course of nearly two centuries: elementary education in the earliest years; a night school for adults after 1858; typewriting for women; classes in lettering, magazine illustration, jewelry design, architectural drawing and mechanical drafting; industrial electricity; training for occupations needed in wartime, such as radio operations during World War II; construction project management; visual literacy; and computer-assisted drafting.

HOW TO SUSTAIN THIS NOBLE ENTERPRISE?

The General Society has sustained its school and library for nearly two centuries. So what can this unique institution begun in the eighteenth century offer to us in the twenty-first? As Greene avows, "The General Society's educational programs in the past were founded on the principle that skill is important, that master craftspeople should teach craftspeople, and that people of all trades deserve the opportunity to achieve a well-rounded education. It takes many skills to support urban life, from writers to printers, from architects to bricklayers, from engineers to electricians, and hundreds of other occupations in between. Urban life and arts are the products of many hands and minds. It's important for people to understand that it takes all those people to make our city; our life is larger than just any one part."

—Caitlin Van Dusen and Marci Reaven

Webster Hall

Since 1886, whatever New Yorkers have been doing in public, they've been doing at Webster Hall. Between its four stories, steep stairs, winding passageways, and rooms and ballrooms of every size and shape, it's hard to imagine a use to which the space could not be put—and indeed has been.

ENTERTAINING NEW YORK AND THE WORLD: AN INEXACT TIMELINE

125 East Eleventh Street, East Village, Manhattan

(212) 353–1600

www.webster-hall.com

Hours: Doors open at 10:00 p.m. nightly. Check Web site for special and theme events.

Public Transit: L, N, Q, R, W, 4, 5, 6 trains to Union Square/Fourteenth Street. Walk east on Fourteenth Street toward Fourth Avenue. Turn south (right) onto Fourth Avenue, then east (left) onto East Eleventh Street.

Today, with its original name reinstated, this big, noisy megaclub offers four floors and forty thousand square feet of party space. *"DJ Sean Sharp keeps the basement thumpin' with the hottest hip-hop and reggae sounds. DJ DAM keeps the XXX Male Revue bumping and grinding."* Webster Hall started in the 1880s as a place for entertainment. In one outrageous form or another, it has maintained that tradition for much of its existence. The four Canadian Ballinger brothers plus one silent partner who now own Webster Hall recognize that their property has a history. "This is where New Yorkers came to gather," says Lon Ballinger, "for union meetings, for weddings, for social gatherings, for political causes, for anniversaries and celebrations. It's always been a gathering of the people of New York."

The historian Kathy Peiss explains why. "For the working-class population packed into small tenement apartments, large halls that could be rented for dances, weddings, mass meetings, and other gatherings were a requirement of social life. The number of public halls in Manhattan rose substantially in a short period; business directories listed 130 halls in 1895 and 195 in 1910, an increase of 50 percent. While some of these, like Carnegie Hall, were cultural spaces of the privileged, most were located in working-class districts. The largest East Side halls . . . were always in great demand."

Webster Hall's many lives present variations on this theme.

Webster Hall: 1990s–2000s

Nicole's Saturday night report: "We try the Grand Ballroom, peek into

Webster Hall's exterior is still intact. Photo: Martha Cooper.

the VIP room, stumble through the food bar (the aroma of fresh pizza almost stops us), carefully traipse down steep stairs, and finally find the party—in the basement. Ah, the power of hip-hop! The ceiling is low, draped with red fabric. A disco ball spins dead center. The place is packed, and everybody is dancing. Across the dance floor and up some more steep stairs, we find the Latin room next, and wouldn't ya know it, more dancing. This room is long and narrow, with high ceilings, a bar, a few tables, and a stage, but mostly all we can see is dancing. Dancing on the stage, dancing between the tables, and lots of happy people. Everywhere we go there is different music playing, mixed in with staring, groping, and messing with cell phones. On our way out, the big bouncer sincerely thanks us for coming."

The Ritz: 1980s

Madonna, Prince, Eric Clapton, Tina Turner, Sting, Kiss, and B. B. King all played here, along with many others. The *New York Times* reported: "When a band lands a job at that enormous, glitzy, impersonal club on Eleventh Street, between Third and Fourth avenues, it's roughly equivalent to landing a job at the Fillmore East in the 1960s. But competition . . . is fierce!"

Casa Galicia: 1970s

The fraternal organization of the Galician Spanish Community of Greater New York made its home here for a while, running a restaurant (fans remember great white bean soup!), holding meetings and social events, and renting to other groups like the Balkan Arts Center—a group beloved by New York's folk and world music connoisseurs, now known as the Center for Traditional Music and Dance (www.ctmd.org). At a Friday night folk dance you might learn a Norwegian waltz. At a Saturday night concert you might hear Scottish or Macedonian bagpipers or Italian friscaletto (cane flute) players. The center's 1978 concert with Dave Tarras helped spark a major revival of the Jewish folk music known as klezmer.

Webster Hall Studios: 1950s and 1960s

The hall's acoustics were so good that RCA Records transformed Webster Hall into the company's major East Coast recording facility. Bill

Evans on piano, Carol Channing and the original Broadway cast of *Hello Dolly!*, the original Broadway casts of *Damn Yankees* and *Fanny,* Sid Caesar, Frank Sinatra, Itzhak Perlman, and mambo kings Tito Puente and Tito Rodriguez all cut records here, along with many, many others.

Hootenannies: 1950s

As a hootenanny hall, Webster Hall was one of the places that gave voice to the folk song revival, that "tremendous surge of singing, strumming, and picking which has swept the U.S.A. in recent years," as Irwin Silber, the editor of *Sing Out! The Folk Song Magazine,* said in 1963. The Almanac Singers staged the first "hoots" in New York in the years before World War II. By the 1950s, new performers had joined the scene and played and recorded at places like Webster Hall. In liner notes to a Folkway Records compilation, Silber named a few things that all the hoots shared: new performers; a variety of forms; youthful audiences (mostly teen- and college-aged) who came expecting to sing as much as possible; and topicality. "Hootenannies," he wrote, "have always served as the basis for musical comments on the events of the world. In general, these comments have reflected a 'left-of-liberal' political outlook characterized by belief in and support for the trade union movement, world peace and coexistence with the Russians, and an antagonism to such representative political symbols as Senators Bilbo, Taft, and McCarthy."

·　　　··　　　·

Readers, our timeline breaks here for a bit. We think Webster Hall went dark for some years, right about at this point . . . a fire in 1938 burned out much of the interior . . . but in the 1910s and 1920s, the place was swinging . . .

The Greenwich Village Ball [c. 1920s]

10 P.M. 'til dawn

Come all ye Revelers!—Dance the night unto
dawn—come when you like, with whom you
like—wear what you like—
Unconventional? Oh, to be

sure—only do be discreet!
Continuous Music
Midnight Divertissements

The Greenwich Village Ball wasn't all. Webster Hall's bohemian years began in the mid-teens, when the *Masses* magazine and the Liberal Club threw fabulous dances there. Seeing the potential, others jumped in—some for the money, others for the fun, and still others to make a place that they could call their own. By the early 1920s, says the historian George Chauncey, "the Village's Webster Hall was the site of an annual gay and lesbian drag ball as well as numerous other masquerades attended by homosexuals." Webster Hall stayed a favorite location, for balls, masquerades and Halloween affairs, or parties with outlandish themes of any sort. "Nudity became something of a trend," writes the author Terry Miller.

The Committee of Fourteen—the vice squad of the era—agreed that the balls fostered sexual permissiveness. "Many of the people are advertising their dances as Greenwich Village dances in order to get the crowd, and it works," droned the committee's report in 1917, as quoted by Chauncey. "The dances are getting quite popular. . . . Most of those present at these dances being liberals and radicals, one is not surprised when he finds a young lady who will talk freely with him on Birth Control or sex psychology."

Webster Hall's troubles with straitlaced New Yorkers began as soon as it was built. In December 1886, Charles Goldstein, the first owner of Webster Hall, appeared before the excise commissioners to answer a protest made by Monsignor Preston, the pastor of Saint Ann's Roman Catholic Church, located directly behind Webster Hall on East Twelfth Street. Church leadership opposed the granting of a liquor license to Goldstein, noting that Saint Ann's parochial school was Webster Hall's direct neighbor. "The building which is objectionable has just been completed at a cost of $75,000," wrote the *New York Times*. "Goldstein said this was the first he had heard about the complaints . . . and that the "hall was intended for balls, receptions, Hebrew weddings, and sociables, and not a bar room. The bar would not be opened until 8:30 or 9 o'clock in the evening, at which hour the school would be closed."

ANOTHER SIDE OF WEBSTER HALL

If fun at Webster Hall was often edgy and subversive, so were the politics. Located in the midst of the working-class, immigrant Lower East Side, the rentable rooms of Webster Hall offered labor unions and many types of political organizations spaces of all sizes in which to gather. The doings of socialists, anarchists, and all manner of unionists were once considered news, reported on by the *New York Times,* the *Jewish Daily Forward,* the *Staats-Zeitung,* and scores of other newspapers—large and small—that kept New Yorkers informed of the world. The news flashes from Webster Hall read like this:

> 1887: Sixth Assembly District Labor League meets to organize a League of the Progressive Labor Party. 1888: Meeting of saloonkeepers interrupted by locked-out journeyman brewers who attempt to make an impression on their bosses but fail. 1890: Demands for an eight-hour day occupy the Central Labor Union meeting. Stonemasons, ale and porter brewers, carpenters and joiners, encaustic tile layers, millers and millwrights, and horseshoers from Brooklyn are all represented. Delegate C. J. Quinn turns in his membership card when fellow ale and porter brewers accuse him of informing on brother workers to the authorities. All demands will be presented on May 1st! 1892: Deaf-mutes gather in the several hundreds to support the Cleveland–Stevenson Democratic ticket. 1914: Amalgamated Clothing Workers of America founded. 1916: Midnight, February 8, 1,500 members of the Jewelry Workers Union gather and vote on a general strike: not wages but an eight-hour day the demand; hope to obstruct the Easter trade to press their cause. 1916: The International Ladies' Garment Workers Union sets up strike headquarters.

Margaret Sanger, already known for her public stand on birth control, made big news in the winter of 1912 when she collected 119 children of striking Massachusetts textile workers at the train station and led them to Webster Hall. Ten thousand men and women in Lawrence, Massachusetts, had walked out of their mills to protest the lowering of wages after a new state law shortened the workweek. Strike leaders

THE GREENWICH VILLAGE BALL

15th Annual Edition

Friday, Jan. 15th
Webster Hall
119 East 11th St.
10 P. M. 'til dawn

Come all ye Revelers!—Dance the night unto dawn—come when you like, with whom you like—wear what you like—

Unconventional? Oh, to be sure—only do be discreet!

Tickets $2.00 in advance or $3.00 at the door
Boxes $15.00

Cynthia White, 11 Fifth Ave.   STuy. 9-4674

CONTINUOUS MUSIC
MIDNIGHT DIVERTISSEMENTS

The walls of Webster Hall have witnessed a changing mix of politics and celebration for over one hundred years. Photo courtesy of Jezebel Productions, www.jezebel.org.

Elizabeth Gurley Flynn and William Haywood of the International Workers of the World (aka the IWW or the Wobblies), had arranged to send the strikers' children to other cities to be cared for by sympathizing families. Flynn believed the tactic would save money and dramatize the workers' plight—which it did, indeed, after Lawrence police were photographed beating several women and children at the train station before departure. At Webster Hall, the children were fed and matched

SISTER SITES: OTTENDORFER BRANCH–NEW YORK PUBLIC LIBRARY AND STUYVESANT POLYCLINIC

135 and 137 Second Avenue. East Village, Manhattan

Public Transit: 6 train to Astor Place; R,W trains to Eighth Street; L train to First Avenue or Third Avenue.

Designated New York City Landmarks, 1977 and 1976

Many structures from the era of Kleindeutschland still exist, but only a few make their heritage visible and can be visited. Walk just a few blocks from Webster Hall to visit the Ottendorfer Library and the Stuyvesant Polyclinic. Both buildings date from 1883–1884 and were built by the German American philanthropists Oswald Ottendorfer, publisher of the *Staats-Zeitung* newspaper, and his wife, Anna, for the benefit of their fellow German immigrants. The library first operated as part of a privately funded system called the New York Free Circulating Library and today is the oldest operating branch of the New York Public Library. The Deutsches (German) Dispensary, next door, quietly changed its name to Stuyvesant Polyclinc during World War I, concerned about anti-German sentiment. Early clients of the dispensary included many garment workers suffering from pneumonia and consumption (tuberculosis)—diseases of the tenements and factories. Both buildings are now official New York City Landmarks. The Landmarks Preservation Commission guide to the city's landmarked buildings describes the library as a "Queen Anne– and Renaissance-inspired building with extensive terra-cotta detail that incorporates such symbols of wisdom and knowledge as globes, owls, books, and torches." The Polyclinic is an "exuberant Italian Renaissance–inspired structure . . . among the first buildings in New York to display extensive ornamental terra-cotta, including busts of important figures in the history of medicine." Both buildings were designed by William Schickel.

up with temporary caretakers. By mid-March, all four demands of the strikers had been met.

A German Establishment

Webster Hall's first proprietor was Charles Goldstein, who not only ran Webster Hall but lived there, too, on the ground floor with his family. His 1898 *New York Times* obituary reported: "He was forty-two years old, and was born in Poland. He came to this country with his parents when he was three years old, and was educated in the east side public schools. He learned the cigar-making trade, and in course of time became a cigar manufacturer. Then he went into the business of constructing meeting and dancing halls. . . . Thirteen years ago he built Webster Hall."

It's likely that Goldstein was of German descent. Hiring the services of architect Charles Rentz, he built Webster Hall at the northern edge and in the waning days of Kleindeutschland, or Little Germany. This enclave of German-born immigrants and their children constituted what the historian Stanley Nadel called the "first of the giant urban foreign language settlements which came to typify American cities by the end of the nineteenth century." Kleindeutschland extended over much of the Lower East Side, though its most heavily German American section (64 percent by 1875) was in its northwest quadrant, the Seventeenth Ward, where Webster Hall was located. According to Nadel, German New York was instrumental in the development of labor unions as well as modern American socialism, so it was fitting that Webster Hall, along with many other public and private spaces, hosted politically inspired gatherings.

HALLS FOR HIRE

In the nineteenth century and throughout much of the twentieth, New York City was filled with halls for hire. These were places where ordinary people could afford to rent space to accommodate their public affairs. The goings-on at Webster Hall may have been more extraordinary than most; in 1938 the *Times* did call it a landmark. Perhaps the opportunity to gather is what counts. The more one looks into the history of the city, the more it becomes clear that people enthusiastically used such spaces to participate in cultural and civic life, to make their mark. Sometimes, as our timeline for Webster Hall shows, they even made national history. Webster Hall no longer fulfills this role, and few remain of the hundreds of halls that once dotted the city's landscape. But Webster Hall still exists with its name intact and structure more or less unchanged. It marks a time in New York City when people of modest means could choose from among a wealth of places to gather. We wonder whether, today, our society isn't poorer for the poverty of places which we can call our own.

—Marci Reaven

The Cube

Remnants of lavish nine-teenth-century wealth linger quietly on the streets of the East Village, unnoticed by daily passersby. A crowd of college students at the 6 train platform obscures mosaics of beavers that line the walls. People surface from underground through an old-fashioned cast-iron kiosk dec-

Large black sculpture at Astor Place, East Village, Manhattan

Public Transit: 6 train to Astor Place. Find the Cube plainly visible from the subway exit and opposite Starbucks.

R train to Eighth Street. Walk one block east (with traffic) on Astor Place to the Cube.

orated with colorful reliefs. The memory of John Jacob Astor, creator of America's first monopoly on the fur trade, filters through the space named after him—Astor Place. Years later, his descendant John Jacob Astor III could be found in his office conducting business above his textile warehouse in the orange brick building with arched windows above Astor Place.

Today, unknowing young consumers drink cappuccinos while talking on cell phones and e-mailing through laptops at Starbucks on the street level of the same building. Despite the recent addition of two Starbucks within eyesight of each other, and a Kmart megastore, Astor Place has become a concoction of novel cultures opposite the refined taste of the uptown elite. Astor (the Place) has little to do with big money and industry anymore.

Welcome to the kernel of youth. An urgency of individuality, trend-setting, and experimentation has flavored Astor Place with raw teen spirit for the last half century. Home to the beat generation of the fifties, the hippies of the sixties, and the punks of the late seventies and eight-ies, Astor Place has developed into a center of unleashed urban self-expression.

AT THE HUB

It is approximately 3:30 in the afternoon. The school day is over; a group of juveniles stakes out its territory on the street. The East Village is open for business. A unique array of ethnic restaurants dots the streets, offering cheap meals and student discounts. Tattoo parlors, underground music clubs, colleges, and theaters sponsor a steady flow of youth lingering late into the morning hours. But the hub of all the action is obvious even to tourists. At the junction of Lafayette Avenue, Fourth Avenue, and Astor Place, a wide strip of sidewalk sits smack in the middle of the traffic interrupting everything. From any neighboring street you can't help but notice this pavement stage that awaits the meeting of a rising generation. In the center of the traffic island stands the Cube, a welcome mat for congregations of teens—a rallying point and a place to call one's own.

For the goths and the ravers, some of them runaways, who have appropriated the island (and sometimes live there), the sculpture defines public space. "It's in the middle of everything," one of the young denizens says. "Everybody sees you. And you can show off that you're a degenerate and you don't do shit and ha ha you're going to work at six in the morning and I'm sittin' here smokin' a cigarette, ya know." A friend adds, "You know, like, you can't lose somebody if you say, 'Meet me at the Cube.' Ya know? You're in between Saint Marks, Kmart, and Starbucks—like, you can't really lose each other.'

The eight-foot-square steel sculpture painted solid black stands as the icon of Astor Place. This is a story of transformation, the story of how a work of art transformed the space, and the space transformed the work of art.

MAXIMUS MINIMUS

The cube in the center of Astor Place was designed by the artist Bernard (Tony) Rosenthal. Born in 1914 in Illinois, Rosenthal graduated from the University of Michigan in 1936. He then studied sculpture under Carl Miles at the Cranbrook Academy of Art. In 1946,

Rosenthal moved to Los Angeles, where he taught at UCLA and completed a number of public art projects. In 1960, just as minimalist ideals took form, Rosenthal moved to New York City. Here he would create his most famous sculpture, *Alamo*—the Cube. All of Rosenthal's sculpture is to be touched, sat on, or walked through, embodying the minimalist's concern for the spatial environment of sculpture. *Alamo* is a unique piece designed to create a kinetic relationship between audience and sculpture. A pole hidden in the center enables the opaque structure to rotate on its corner when pushed by a team of pedestrians. *Alamo* exemplifies the plain structure of minimalism in its cubic form. Decontextualized from tradition, the Cube's meaning exists in its method and presence as an object. Stripped of technical complexities, and impersonal in tone, the plain black cube points the viewer to the medium. Alamo exists solely as a solid black cube made of steel—an object with a clear and straightforward presence. Rosenthal rarely used color in any of his works during the height of minimalism in the 1960s; he left most of his works to rust, bronzed them, or painted them black as he did with *Alamo*. The simple cube refers to nothing but itself, inviting the viewer to connect with the work as an object rather than a means of expression.

One of the first abstract sculptures to be permanently installed in New York City, *Alamo* has no pedestal but the sidewalk beneath. The contemporary sculptor Hans Haacke, also working in New York during the 1960s, says: "When viewers are allowed or even asked to handle an object, its institutional sanctity is no longer intact. It is off the altar." Installed at Astor Place in 1967, *Alamo* was intended to stay in New York City only temporarily. However, students at the Cooper Union for the Advancement of Science and Art across the street petitioned to keep the Cube in its original home community permanently.

HAPPENING

Winter 2002. The Cube is in a period of transition. Stix, sixteen years old, Denise, nineteen, and a man who preferred to be known only as D, also nineteen, are of the old school, the ravers, denizens of the Cube for two years or more. They call themselves "Cube Rats." Gaia, fifteen, barely younger, represents the Goths, or vamps, the new school. "I came here when it was all ravers," D says. "Well, not ravers, I hate that word—party-kids—party-kids."

"The whole goth scene is taking over," Stix says. "The worst—the worst—the worst thing about—about—about the kids who shouldn't be here is basically you have a lot of kids comin' in here seeing that there's—there's goth kids and yadda yadda yadda and then they start makin' up shit like 'I have two personalities and yadda yadda yadda and I met Goth Venus and Goddess This and I was chased by a spirit in the forest and blah blah blah'—not that I don't believe—I'm very spiritual in—in all beliefs. . . . And that was the whole thing that we didn't want—is you come here to try and be cool. You come here to have fun."

When they first appeared on the scene, the goths were shunned from the Cube. They constructed their own variant of it across the street. As Gaia puts it, "I was hanging out with my friends and we found a box and we made a cube and we went over there [she points to an area of sidewalk across the street from *Alamo*]. Yeah, it was like a cardboard box. It was like to be thrown away. Yeah. Like, 'This is our cube—it's black.' But really it was brown. But we wrote 'black' all over it. . . . After that they took it and they smashed it into a van. So it was pretty funny, but then we actually went and got a bigger one the next day and did it again. And—some people sat on it—and then we threw it into the street. . . . People didn't like it. They went over to try and figure out what was going on."

One thing led to another, and eventually the goths intermingled with the ravers. "Oh, well, it's not even 'acceptance,' " Gaia says, " 'cause they don't own it, ya know? But, um, I really didn't care. They thought I was nice so I was like, 'Okay, all right.' "

The runaways and other teens on the island "hate it when tourists and or yuppie alike spin the Cube. Don't spin it!" D says. "Yes it spins! Yes it's cool that it spins, but please don't spin it. Or at least tell us to get up. 'Cause you'll just be sitting down and—see how it's like aligned with his head? Somebody will get on that side and start spinning and he won't be paying attention—*wap!* Could have told me something! That's really annoying. And then you get like the 'Oooo! Ahhh!' Yes, yes, the almighty Cube spins—now go away. . . . No—no don't spin it—no please! Stay away or we'll eat you!"

"And then it pisses rainwater on you," Denise adds.

D explains, "It's got these holes in the top. See those holes up there? There's like another hole on the other side. These holes over here. When it rains, these fill with water. So when you spin it, the water drips out. The water's been there for quite some time and it's not that pleasant. Especially when it hits your jacket, and then it covers the bottom here, and nobody can sit down once again. Ya know, that gets real annoying."

D walks around it to read the inscription. "It was brought here in [he reads] '1966–67. Bernard Rosenthal. An anonymous gift to the city of

"You know, like, you can't lose somebody if you say, 'Meet me at the Cube.' " Photo: Johannes DeYoung.

New York, November 1967.' I'm not sure—but that kind of scares me because, like, nobody knows why it's here. Nobody knows who it came from—ya know. . . . And it's like, wow, what an anonymous gift—ruin the lives of many of New York City's youths by having them hang out here and waste their time. Ya know, what kind of gift is that to give to New York? Ya know like, nobody knows quite what to make of the Cube. It's kinda like the whole Stonehenge mystery. Ya know, we don't know who put it here—we don't know why it's here—they come here anyway. Ya know, they don't know whether they're happier being here, or being away from here. Ya know?"

FIRST PERSON:

GAIA, A K A JOVITA

"Yesterday there was this twelve-year-old kid, and I was like, 'Wow, you do not need to be here! You're twelve—I'm fifteen, okay? Still, I know I shouldn't be here, but still you—you're twelve! Go home!' I mean, I'm really young. I shouldn't be here. I'm not even gonna lie. But he's twelve. He doesn't need this kind of influence on him this early."

D goes on. "Yeah, it can symbolize a waste of your youth, ya know. It can definitely symbolize a waste of your youth. And it can also symbolize, like, a strong deal of friendship and, like, uh, unity amongst different diverse groups. The stupidest thing to be at the Cube is racist. Ya know? 'Cause like—forget having like different races and skin colors. You have many different, like, different genres of people, ya know? There are many different genres of people. And like, within those genres of people you have many different races, ya know? Like you have black, white, and Hispanic."

A new person, Carlos, approaches the scene. "It might be a big bomb. 'Anonymous gift.' It might be a bomb. Just like one day, *boom!*"

"Yeah," D says, "like since September 11 some people had this weird theory on this might be a bomb. 'Cause think about it. It's an anonymous gift from an unidentified country. No one knows quite how it got here, or why it's here. And if you think about it, it's almost in the center of New York. Ya know? It's, like, not so far from midtown. And, like, if you wanted to take New York out, that'd be the perfect way. . . . That's just paranoid cube theory. That's just, like, a running joke. Like—this isn't a bomb or anything like that. It—it—it might be, like, a weapon in a different sense. Like I said—it ruins a lot of New York's youth and, um—America's youth 'cause, like, so many kids from different cities and countries come here to waste their lives. Ya know, but then again, for, like, the most part—for those who do waste their lives, some of them, like, better themselves. Ya know. Like, some of them hit the bottom of the barrel only to climb to the top. Ya know, like—it makes some people stronger, when it puts them at their weakest."

UMBILICUS

A*lamo* is more than a sculpture. Rosenthal's Minimalist concerns unpredictably open the space at Astor Place to welcome public gatherings. Unlike a traditional public sculpture, Rosenthal's simple cube decorates the space without proclaiming a purpose. It serves as a destination point, a marker, an icon of place, a void that onlookers fill with their own meanings. Astor's vision of a thriving cultural center has evolved over a century after his death: Astor Place collects the hippies, the punks, the ravers, the gothic families of youth on its sidewalks. A chunk of steel, no bigger than eight feet square, draws homeless teenagers from across the country together on a single strip of sidewalk. Amid the streaming traffic on Eighth Street, Astor, Lafayette, and Fourth Avenue, *Alamo* sits upon an island of refuge.

For fifteen-year-old Gaia, her haven of only three months presents the possibility of shedding a troubled history and escaping into a new identity. The Cube's plain black surface is a clean slate, and Gaia finds renascence. She confronts a separation from her disapproving family and the challenges of life on the street; so far, she remains optimistic. Stix and Denise, slightly older, continue to linger at *Alamo* after several years of the habit, nostalgic for the comfort it has brought them. D, the oldest, is most polarized by feelings of the bittersweet. Regret for a wasted youth, and guarded sentiment for desperate friendships—both are attributed to the Cube.

Since 1967, Rosenthal's sculpture has spun at Astor Place. It will continue to rotate, unchanged for years to come. As D pointed out, the teenagers don't like it when the Cube is pushed. Even though the sculpture is unchanged when turned, perhaps this slight alteration from an outsider threatens change to the denizens themselves. This stage, nourishing much needed attention, will forever draw new characters into its limelight. "It's actually called the *Alamo*," D says. "And—most of us know that except for like some of the new heads. But, we're always gonna call it the Cube. It will always be the Cube to us."

—Natalie DeYoung

City Play

"The Cage," Sixth Avenue and West Third Street, a legendary spot for street basketball in New York City. Photo: Martha Cooper.

T he rules of stickball dictate how to throw a ball, hit it with a broomstick, and run the bases. But as a game that evolved in the alleyways and streets of New York City, this urban sport cannot be understood without a grasp of the built environment. For instance, you need to understand what "sewers" are (manhole covers) and how far apart they are set to understand what it meant for Willie Mays to be, according to legend, a "four-sewer hitter." In the end, we can't understand stickball without understanding the city— just as we can't understand the city without understanding stickball. Similarly, you can't understand stoopball, for instance, without understanding the configuration of the city's stoops, originally brought here by the Dutch.

The forms of play practiced in the city are hardly limited to children. "The business of old age?" asked Bronx baker Moishe Sacks. "To be young." As adults, we engage in play and sports partly to preserve the vigor of youth, and many adults take up physical activities they loved as children. They are often as fanatical about getting their exercise as children are about playing the game. In this chapter, the Old-Timers striking a ball on Stickball Boulevard in Harlem, the skaters at the Empire in Brooklyn, or the chess players

**FIRST PERSON:
JOHN STEVENS, BRONX OLD-
TIMERS STICKBALL LEAGUE**

"I can remember playing stickball with an ear of corn that was cut in half. That was a ball, and you would be amazed at how many curves you could get on that ear of corn. First floor was a single, second a double. When we graduated to a spaldeen, I can remember once Mrs. Kelly had a pie on the second-floor ledge, and I hit the ball, and the ball hit the pie! It came tumbling down and Jimmy Nolan caught it, and we ran away with it! But Mrs. Kelly spotted us—and told my parents because she wanted her pie pan back. My mother had a discussion with me with her right hand."

Early 1980s breakdancers in a Washington Heights subway station. Photo: Martha Cooper.

happily or not so happily being hustled in Washington Square Park or huddled over the legendary Capablanca table at Marshall Chess Club have, indeed, rediscovered the intensity they had as children at play.

In his essay "Fun in Games," Erving Goffman speaks of play as "focused interaction," in which the rules of playful transformation tell players how the real world will be modified inside the encounter. With the outside world held at bay, players create a new world within. A kind of membrane forms around them that bursts when the game is interrupted. They often experience a sense of intimacy, the closeness of sharing a world apart.

Focused play in New York City seems intent on throwing off the shackles of urban life, the constrictions of traffic, congestion, and work. Yet in escaping the workaday world for play, it's as if the city is rediscovered. After all, the Cyclone and Wonder Wheel on Coney Island lift you above all urban care—at the same time providing a great view of Brooklyn and Manhattan. As children, New Yorkers once played stickball with first base a fire hydrant, third a manhole cover. As one person put it, "a dead pigeon, a car, or your little brother could be second base."

Now, for the Old-Timers stickball players on Bathgate Avenue in the Bronx, a chain-link fence defines a home run, and records are set according to which floor of the adjacent apartments the rubber ball may strike.

Some of our places of play highlight the freedom of skating and bicycle riding. In a traffic-jammed, gridlocked town—where it is said that the shortest unit of measurable time is between the traffic lights turning green and the cars behind honking—unfettered locomotion on skateboards, bicycles, kayaks, or roller skates becomes a precious pleasure. In New York, the intensity of work necessary to make a living in one of the world's most competitive environments is matched only by the intensity with which New Yorkers play—the drive to get somewhere in balance with the playful need to reach nowhere at all.

**PLACE MOMENT:
CAITLIN VAN DUSEN,
BIG APPLE ARCHERY,
FLUSHING, QUEENS**

"Find this inconspicuous garage on a suburban street, surrounded by row houses with chain-link fences and gardens, and rent a bow, arrows, and a quiver. Take your place among the bowhunters in camouflage, shooting at a slide-show projection of game: deer, bear, moose, rabbits. Don't be intimidated; raise your bow and aim it at the paper bull's-eye pinned to the wall, focus on your breath, and let your worries dissolve for an hour as you lose yourself in the rhythms and focus of repetitive precision."

Stickball Boulevard
and the Stadiums of the Street

Stickball Boulevard, between Seward Avenue and Randall Avenue (where games are held), Soundview, the Bronx

Hours: Every Sunday morning and early afternoon from April through September; also Memorial Day Tournament and Columbus Day Tournament.

Public Transit: BX39 bus to White Plains Road and Lafayette Avenue. Walk south on White Plains Road. Turn left on Seward Avenue and walk one block to Stickball Boulevard.

"We called it the poor man's baseball," said Louis Mercado, seated on a beach chair set up on Stickball Boulevard at the annual Memorial Day tournament in May 2001. "Half the kids couldn't afford gloves and equipment, so they invented stickball with a rubber ball, and you'd steal you mother's broomstick, take the straw out—and you had a bat." As he speaks, fully grown men ranging in age from their forties into their eighties swing an upgraded broomstick, whack a rubber ball, and hurl themselves down the city street toward first base, summoning motions ingrained in their bones since their boyhoods.

THE STADIUMS OF THE STREET

In 1987, after two years of persistence by the city's stickball players and, in particular, the local New York Emperors Stickball League, two blocks of Newman Avenue in the East Bronx were officially rechristened Stickball Boulevard. Just a few blocks away from a major shopping center, the boulevard is surrounded by playgrounds and schools (P.S. 152 and Adlai Stevenson High School). On the weekends, the local police precinct keeps these two city blocks clear of cars so stickball teams from the Bronx, Brooklyn, and El Barrio (East Harlem) can play the game that some have been playing for over sixty years.

From spring through autumn, the New York Emperors Stickball League (NYESL) meets here every Sunday, with special events like the Weekend Classic Tournament, held on Memorial Day weekend, and the Columbus Day Weekend Finale Tournament bringing stickball players not only from the Old-Timers League in Manhattan but all the way from Florida, California, and Puerto Rico. The New York Emperors put together the NYESL Official Rules and Regulations of Stickball, which is used by many other stickball leagues and organizations. Currently the league is comprised of eight teams, including the Bronx Knights (sponsored by Willie's Steakhouse), the Brooklyn Knights, the Royals, the Gold, the Bandits, and the Angels/Bad Boys; each of the teams is a rather loose federation of players.

Stickball Boulevard marks the main drag for this New York City sport, but side streets abound. Whereas Stickball Boulevard swings weekly, the 111th Street reunion in East Harlem bats just one day a year—always the second Sunday in July—but it has come to be what is probably the largest reunion/block party in the city, with stickball games in the morning and live music throughout the rest of the day for neighborhood residents, returning residents, and stickball aficionados. El Barrio's tradition of stickball goes back to the 1930s, and, according to www.streetplay.com, the neighborhood is known as "Stickball Territory" because it is the home of some of New York City's best teams and players.

The founder of the Guardian Angels and radio personality Curtis Sliwa serves as the self-proclaimed commissioner of stickball. In addition to occasional appearances on Stickball Boulevard, he runs the annual *Daily News* Stickball Classic, which brings together teams from four or five boroughs in various locations, holds borough championships, and then plays a final citywide contest. Sometimes the hilarious Brooklyn Sym-PHONY Band, made up of old-timers who played in the cacophonous group during the old Brooklyn Dodgers games at Ebbets Field, serenades the players. A long-ball contest determines who can hit a spaldeen farthest for major bragging rights.

The Museum of the City of New York houses the Stickball Hall of Fame, and each year, on 104th Street alongside the museum, the Old-Timers play a game and induct new members. In the Bronx, particularly in the winter, at 189th Street and Bathgate Avenue, players often shovel the snow to play in a schoolyard across the street from Roosevelt High School. Inveterate Bronx Old-Timer John Stevens told us: "We get together every Sunday morning through the fall, winter, and spring, as long as it's not raining or snowing. We've been doing it for about forty years, so I guess you could say it's the longest running pick-up stickball game in history."

According to www.streetplay.com, there are three forms of stickball: (1) fast pitching against a wall, or wallball; (2) bounce pitching, which is also called slow-pitch or pitching-in; and (3) hitting by yourself (a k a fungo, the baseball term for throwing the ball into the air and whacking it). Wallball is usually played with one to three players on each team in a playground or parking lot; any wall can be used as a backstop. The pitching zone is often marked with a large *X*. Fungo and bounce pitching are played in the streets with teams of up to 8 members each. In slow-pitch the ball is pitched in and the hitter has to hit it after it has bounced once. This used to be the most commonly played style, though today more leagues use the fungo style of pitch. The rules are similar to baseball's except that there are one or two strikes and anything that lands on a roof is considered out.

THE DURABLE CHARACTER OF CHILDHOOD

The Old-Timers tournaments and scheduled games that take place on Stickball Boulevard attest to the "durable character of childhood," which, as the French philosopher Gaston Bachelard has written, "returns to animate broad sections of adult life." Stickball became one of the favorite pastimes for the children of immigrant groups that settled in New York City around the turn of the twentieth century, including Jews, Irish, and Italians, and, later, African Americans as well as Puerto Ricans. For kids in lower- and working-class families with little access to money, stickball was the perfect game:

Old-Timers Stickball League, 189th Street and Bathgate Avenue, the Bronx. Photo: Martha Cooper

modeled after baseball, yet with practically no equipment to buy. Every kitchen had a broom, and the field was built right into the city's landscape. Manhole covers became bases, while fire escapes and sidewalks served as bleachers.

Some baseball greats started their careers hitting rubber balls down streets. Joe Torre, the current manager of the Yankees, and players Joe Pepitone, Willie Randolph, and Willie Mays were stickball legends. It is rumored Mays was a four-sewer man: He could supposedly hit the ball a distance of four manhole covers, and the covers are a hundred feet apart! He once claimed that stickball taught him how to hit "the breaking ball. Guys would bounce the ball to you, and you'd have to hit it, and

Seneca Stickball Team lineup at the Old-Timers Stickball Reunion, 111th Street, Manhattan. Photo: Martha Cooper.

sometimes it would bounce this way, sometimes that way." Richie Mojica, currently a member of the board of the New York Emperors Stickball League, remembers who would play baseball and who would play stickball: "It depended on their financial status. How many people can afford a glove and bat? And how many baseball fields are there? We didn't have money for shirts for a team; and my father said, 'If I have to get this kid a glove, I have to get it for all the kids.' You know how much a glove costs? We had ten kids in my family. I had seven brothers and three sisters. 'Buy you a glove, then I gotta buy a glove for everybody.' "

For stickball, not only was the broomstick free, but even the spaldeen could be foraged from gutters and rooftops if a child could not afford the five-and-dime. This quintessential New York City ball was made from the inside of a tennis ball and was called a spaldeen, a mispronunciation of the name of its maker, the Spalding Company. These balls bounced high but were soft enough that they did not easily break windows. As stickball player Mike Kanarek remembers: "A golf ball would have been too springy, and a tennis ball was not lively enough, and there were solid foam balls, which were a bit too heavy, but the pink spaldeen was just right. It gave just the right degree of difficulty for the game."

From the age of seven to the time he graduated from high school, Stephen Swid, now chairman and CEO of SCS Communications, played stickball in the shadow of Yankee Stadium in the Bronx. He remembers how he and his friends would walk around with a rubber ball, constantly bouncing or throwing it against the house, stoop, curb, or wall. "You couldn't stop even though your mother would be screaming at you," he said. Worried spaldeen owners often made their fellow players guarantee "chips on the ball," meaning that everyone would chip in to buy a new one if the ball was lost. "We had one guy, Robert Zellman," Swid recalls, "whose swing sent the balls way up, often landing on the roof. He was a good player, but after a while we wouldn't let him play anymore because he kept losing the balls. He became immortalized throughout the neighborhood as "Over the Roof Zellman.' "

"Where could all the lost real Spaldeens be?" bemoans Bronx-born poet Annie Lanzillotto. "On rooftops, in gutters, in sewerpipes, attics, basements, the East River, floating out into the ocean, washed up along shore on beaches in far off countries, in the bellies of whales."

At a time when many New York City apartment buildings held sufficient numbers of immigrant children for two opposing stickball teams, the game helped define neighborhood culture. Often it was connected to the territoriality of local gangs. Richie Mojica recalls that "the police officers used to resent the gangs partly because we carried sticks. So we used to throw them down the sewers when the police came. The cops used to come and put us against the sidewalk and break our bats."

FIRST PERSON:
ANNIE LANZILLOTTO

How to Catch a Flyball
in Oncoming Traffic

With a car coming at you, you face
   the open sky.
You never miss a pop fly because a
   car is coming at you. . . .
The car came all this way,
down this particular street, around
   several corners,
jumped the exit ramp,
to back up round the corner to see
   you make this play.
The car in the middle of the play is
   part of the play.
It's all in the timing.

"After talking to so many players," said Mick Greene, the founder of Streetplay.com, "I do think that stickball was, as the players see it, a vehicle for peace in the neighborhoods." "In fact," adds Mojica, "the only time you had a Puerto Rican go into an Italian neighborhood was to play stickball."

"We liked going to different neighborhoods and playing on their home field," says Charlie Ballard, a grand old man of stickball. "This would make the pot of money bigger. We regularly played for hundreds of dollars a game, sometimes even as much as between five hundred and a thousand dollars, particularly when we went to Pleasant Avenue, where some of the bookies played and would bet on their team. Those guys really hated losing to us. One year I bought furniture for my kitchen, dining room, and living room with the money I made from stickball." Stickball often broke down racial as well as territorial boundaries. Opened in 1940, Minton's Playhouse, the famous Harlem jazz club, known as a birthplace of bebop, is only slightly less famous to stickball aficionados for its great stickball teams of the forties and fifties. Diehard John Stevens, the late spokesperson for the Bronx Old-Timers, was the first white player to join the team and always referred to himself as "the reverse Jackie Robinson."

HOLDING ON TO THE BALL

On Memorial Day 2001, before the year meant anything, the Memorial Day tournament on Stickball Boulevard was threatened with rain, and Steve Mercado had a problem on his hands. He had promised the young crop of stickball players—the children and grandchildren of the old timers—that their game would take place. The oldsters pressured him to cancel that game so the championship match could take place before the downpour. He refused, steadfast in his commitment to perpetuate the sport.

Later that year, in the summer, just a few months before the city and the country were to change forever, Steve Mercado was part of a contingent of players who brought the game to the Smithsonian's Folklife Festival in Washington, D.C., on the National Mall, a sure measure that the game was now emblematic of the city's folk culture. Led by Mick Greene, the contingent demonstrated stoopball against a specially built brownstone facade. Annie Lanzillotto showed bewildered audiences a bent clothes hanger and said that the "Smithsonian scientists" were seeking to determine the origins of this artifact. Asked to surmise its use, slews of Washingtonians suggested everything from a fishing pole to a homemade golf club, before Annie educated them to its true origins in the Bronx—fishing spaldeens out of the gutters.

On September 11, 2001, Steve Mercado, a firefighter, was killed in the World Trade Center catastrophe. With his death, the game lost one of its great advocates. In his honor, in 2002 Stickball Boulevard was officially designated with signage as Steve Mercado Stickball Boulevard.

Players refuse to loosen their grip on the ball and broomstick of their childhoods. Vito Giannone, nicknamed the "iron man of stickball," recalls playing a game against the Minotaurs when a ball came down off the fire escape. "I caught it," he remembers, "but fell backwards onto the curb and got knocked out cold. They had an ambulance bring me over to Saint Vincent's Hospital, where they brought me around. The funny thing was that the whole time, I wouldn't let go of the ball."

The players on Stickball Boulevard never have.

—Steve Zeitlin

Thomas Jefferson Park Pool

2180 First Avenue at 112th Street, East
Harlem, Manhattan

(212) 860–1383

Hours: Open every day 11:00 a.m. to
3:00 p.m. and 4:00 p.m. to 7:00
p.m., last Saturday in June through
Labor Day.

Public Transit: 6 train to 110th Street.
Walk east on 110th Street to First
Avenue, turn left, and walk north to
112th Street.

Escaping the summer heat has probably been a New York City pastime for as long as humans have lived here. The more we flattened the topography, barricaded ourselves from cooling river breezes, and generated heat and smells from crowding and industry, the greater the search for relief. For generations the well-to-do and well connected have run off in the summertime to wherever the city *wasn't*. Working stiffs and their children mostly have stayed put and made do, inhabiting the worlds of the rooftop, the fire escape, the public park, and the swimming pool. When eleven giant, gorgeous pools opened in city neighborhoods in the Depression 1930s, a product of the Works Progress Administration (WPA), the summer landscape changed forever.

EAST HARLEM'S SUMMER SECRET

Take the Lexington local to 110th Street and walk the long blocks to First Avenue, muttering to yourself that there's no Second Avenue subway. The sounds of salsa and hip-hop, the beep of trucks backing up in small factory driveways, stacked rows of fried foods in Mexican, Dominican, and Puerto Rican shop windows, the busy comings and goings of tenement life—these surround but don't impinge. Turn left on First and look for an Art Moderne–style, curved brick-fronted building, with embedded glass bricks, bordered on both sides by green park. It's the entrance to the pool, with "Thomas Jefferson Play Center" inscribed in cast concrete above the door. The first room is rather dark and nothing special—standard Parks Department rec center stuff—but the guard is nice, the game tables well used, and the atmosphere welcoming. Some mishmashing of architectural styles reveals the piecing together of older and new, but look up to the left and glimpse an original. Large, graceful block letters announcing "Women's Bath House" are cut deeply into an overhang that leads to a northern wing. The structure has been remodeled, linking the formerly separate men's and women's bathhouses, but it's lovely that the architect kept intact some of what was here.

A big patch of sunlight intrudes on the rec room through the open door. Beyond lies a long rectangle of light blue water. The pool deck is simply immense, at least by New York City standards. Nearest the entrance is a big squarish pool for babies and small children. Water just grazes the surface, and a wide cement border makes a fine place to sit and watch over them. A longer-than-Olympic-sized pool lies directly beyond, crystal clear, and—amazingly, on this afternoon in late August— almost empty. That's the secret of Jefferson Park Pool. It's one of the great places in the city that isn't overused, though high season is July, and on hot days the people pack in. Spreading around the pool are ample stretches of spotless cement, made pretty by tall pots of flowering plants, the stepped surfaces of the poolside deck, and benches surrounding it all. Barefoot is no problem here. Feel free to lay down your towel on the cement surface and soak up the warmth after a swim. The water is unheated, though by summer's end it retains accumulated heat from the sun. The oddest thing about the water is its depth, or lack thereof—a shallow four feet, more or less, all around—but the pool was designed that way from the beginning.

As in other municipal pools, swimming lessons are offered here for free. Jefferson Park Pool sits in the middle of Jefferson Park. To the south are basketball courts, softball fields, picnic tables and barbecues, benches, trees, and a polished steel sculpture of abstracted shapes that reflect the light and colors of the environment, installed by the city's

Percent for Art Program (which requires that 1 percent of the budget for eligible city-funded construction projects be spent on public artwork for city facilities). To the north is an even more gracious area. A well-kept running track surrounds a soccer field; handball courts, basketball courts, and picnic areas weave in and around each other. A long allée of trees shades benches running the length of the pool. Kids on bicycles circle its circumference along a paved path. At the eastern end, beyond where some Parks Department personnel are throwing themselves an end-of-the-day, end-of-summer barbecue, lies a patch of grass, then the FDR Drive, then the East River—just a stone's throw away.

The staff of the New York City Parks Department who run the park and pool seem truly to like this place. One stopped to ask us what we thought of it all, watching us stroll slowly around the pool. He shared our delight and said that he was attracted as well to its ethnically diverse New York City public. Two park workers, concerned about the pool's lingering bad reputation, mentioned how good security was, contrasting present times to the decades beginning in the 1960s when years of deferred maintenance and unaddressed urban problems made many public spaces into places of danger. Today Jefferson Park doesn't even have a nighttime curfew. Another staff member described how intensively neighborhood people use the park's picnic spaces. Birthday parties, weddings, anniversaries, quinceañeras, soccer games, religious services—it's a space where local residents can gather and keep their family and neighborhood traditions alive. Increasingly these are traditions born in the pueblas of Mexico and transplanted to East Harlem. Demand is so great that some party-givers camp out the night before to make sure they'll have a barbecue grill come daybreak.

PARKS AND POOLS FOR THE PUBLIC

Until the social movement for small neighborhood parks and playgrounds began to show results around the turn of the twentieth century, few neighborhoods—especially in working-class districts—contained green spaces intended for public health and enjoyment. Thomas Jefferson Park opened in its current location in 1902, at first offering

A single summer moment at a pool that tells the history of a neighborhood. Photo: Spencer T. Tucker, New York City Department of Parks and Recreation.

nothing much more than a baseball diamond. Efforts by local residents to adopt and adapt the cleared land for band concerts and other home-grown activities helped push officials to reopen an improved park in 1905.

East Harlem is one of New York's great ethnic neighborhoods, so the prospects for its people and its places have always been affected by ethnic change, contest, and also collaboration. Through the 1920s, East Harlem harbored assorted ethnic and immigrant groups within an area whose current boundaries are 96th to 125th streets, and the East River to Fifth Avenue. Italians were an important presence from early on. Around the corner from Thomas Jefferson Park on 110th Street, in

1918, were a marble yard, two macaroni manufacturers, three bread manufacturers, three Italian grocers, five fruit and vegetable dealers, two tailors, a milliner, three shoemakers, four saloons, and three barbershops. By 1930, East Harlem hosted the largest Italian American community in the United States.

FIRST PERSON: NEW YORK CITY PARKS DEPARTMENT

"It is one of the tragedies of New York life, and a monument to past indifference, waste, selfishness and stupid planning, that the magnificent natural boundary waters of the City have been in large measure destroyed for recreational purposes by haphazard industrial and commercial developments. . . . It is not exaggeration to say that the health, happiness, efficiency and orderliness of a large number of the City's residents, especially in the summer months, are tremendously affected by the presence or absence of adequate swimming and bathing facilities."—Planning Report, March 2, 1936

As East Harlem's large Jewish and smaller Irish populations moved up to the Bronx, and restrictive immigration laws in 1924 largely barred Europeans from coming to the United States, jobs and apartments began to go wanting. Into the aging real estate moved immigrants from Puerto Rico—whose country had been annexed by the United States in 1898 and who had been declared a less-than-equal type of citizen in 1917, though with the right to emigrate.

As is typical in New York City, East Harlem's various ethnic groups clumped together geographically, and the group closest to Thomas Jefferson Park was Italian. The 1939 *WPA Guide* calls it the "Italian Park," observing with irony that it was hardly a "vast landscaped stretch of green." Still, its six square blocks served as a "retreat for the teeming section [of the city]." The swimming pool was duly noted, as was the park's boccie court.

The WPA writer made little of Jefferson Park's new pool, but its construction was a big to-do at the time. Parks Commissioner Robert Moses built eleven huge public swimming pools in New York City that opened with great fanfare during ten consecutive weeks in the summer of 1936: four in Manhattan; one each in the Bronx, Queens, and Staten Island; and four in Brooklyn. A devoted swimmer himself, Moses apparently gave his all to these pools, funding them at $1 million apiece from WPA monies provided by the federal government to create desperately-needed jobs and stimulate the economy in the midst of the Great Depression. As Robert Caro writes in his biography of Moses, *The Power Broker:*

> [H]is architects produced dozens of innovations that would set a new standard for swimming pool construction, public and private, from pool bottoms of wood-float rough enough to prevent slipping and smooth enough to permit games during the off-season when the pool was drained, to a totally new type of scum gutter wide enough to let in sunlight that could kill the bacteria whose formation had been a problem in older public pools. . . . Despite the WP[A] requirements that only the cheapest materials be used, each pool turned out to be a municipal marvel of the first magnitude.

The second of the new pools to open, Jefferson Park's pool—270 feet long by 125 feet wide—accommodated 2,600 people at a time. Two large fountains emerged from either end of the swimming area, and the separate diving pool featured seven diving boards—one of them a high board. (No longer willing or able to supervise the diving pool, the Parks Department turned it into a wading pool in the 1990s.) Mayor Fiorello La Guardia, an enthusiastic builder and East Harlemite himself, eagerly watched the construction.

Like all the new Moses pools, Jefferson Park's sported innovative underwater lighting that looked particularly spectacular at night when the celebratory ribbon cuttings were held. According to Caro, neighborhood parades preceded the speeches; local priests blessed the clear, chlorinated waters; diving and racing competitions fired the crowd up; and La Guardia took the stage. "It was he," Caro writes, "who pulled the switch that turned on the underwater lighting, an event that never failed to bring a murmur of 'oooohs' from the crowd, it was he who gave the word to raise the flag, and it was he who got to cut the ribbon and shout to the waiting children, 'Okay, kids, it's all yours!' "

POOLS AS TREASURES; POOLS AS TURF

Panache aside, Moses had more on his mind than just the beauty of his pools. He was also concerned that they be used in peace, and consequently, given his prejudices, he set out to prevent racial mixing. Jefferson Park's pool, in ethnically mixed East Harlem, not far from largely African American Central Harlem, was the place Moses most worried about. He solved his dilemma, Caro claims, by employing only white lifeguards and attendants and leaving the water unheated—believing that nonwhites didn't like cold water. Caro concludes:

> Whether it was the temperature or the flagging—or the glowering looks flung at Negroes by the Parks Department attendants and lifeguards—one could go to the pool on the hottest summer days, when the slums of Negro and Spanish Harlem a few blocks away sweltered in the heat, and not see a single non-Caucasian face. Negroes who lived only half a mile away, Puerto Ricans who lived *three blocks away,* would travel instead to Colonial Park, three miles away—even though many of them could not afford the bus fare for their families and had to walk all the way.

Bizarre as it seems, swimming pools defined the front lines of racial segregation—and integration—in both the South and the North. Treasured by all, pools demarked turf. Thomas Jefferson Pool didn't remain as lily-white as Caro suggests, but as Italians and Puerto Ricans bartered and battered for control over neighborhood territory, the pool glowed hot. Tensions mounted further after World War II, when migration from Puerto Rico increased tremendously. As Puerto Ricans evolved into the area's new majority (thus the new neighborhood monikers, Spanish Harlem and El Barrio), their ability to claim territory also increased. Novelist Edwin Torres's character Carlito Brigante recalls the turf wars and the pools in *Carlito's Way:*

> Lemme tell you about them rumbles. The wops said no spics could go east of Park Avenue. But there was only one swimming pool and that was the Jefferson on 112th Street and the East River. Like, man, you had to wade through Park, Lexington, Third, Second, First, Pleasant.

Wall-to-wall guineas. The older guys be standing around in front of the stoops and stores, evil-eyeing us, everybody in his undershirt; the kids would be on the roof with the garbage cans and in the basements with bats and bicycle chains. . . . We took a beating—their turf, too many guys. . . . We was tryin' to melt into the pot but they wouldn't even let us in the swimming pool. Hijos de puta.

Bobby Rodríguez and Frankie Yulfo, still of El Barrio today, remember having to make their way through the Italian gang called the Red-wings to get to the pool. One attempt was particularly unsuccessful, and Bobby got stabbed in the back. Girls' experiences of these things are sometimes different, and Aúrea Almeida remembers that sympa-

Opening Day at the pool that Moses built, June 27, 1936. Photo: Max Ulrich, New York City Parks Photo Archive.

thetic Italians would sometimes watch out for her as she passed through their territory, while others might have made comments but still let her by. Other times, she explained, when the ground was particularly fought over, "you had to cross the Italian section with a lot of Puerto Ricans. And if you were by yourself, honey, you would not walk, you would run."

If it was so hard to get to the pool, why did the Puerto Ricans keep trying? Partly because they wanted to use the pool and have fun like everybody else. Carlos Diaz remembers jumping over the fence at night with his friends after the pool had closed. They would find crowds of kids still swimming, trying to keep away from the patrol cop's flashlight. That's when some of Moses's design innovations came in handy. "When the cops would come, we used to go around what looked like a little house. His flashlight beam wouldn't reach that far out, so it stayed dark and then we'd swim around the other side, and he'd say, 'You guys gotta get out.' But we used to keep switching places, and there are long distances in the pool, and by the time the cop got to one point, we'd be gone and he was following some other kids."

FIRST PERSON: CARLOS DIAZ

"I played a lot of softball in Jefferson Park, and after that we used to go swimming 'cause it was so hot in the summer. . . . After you finished swimming, right across the street on 112th Street, there was a little luncheonette, where you bought your French fries for a quarter and they put it in a basket and you'd eat fries all the way till you got back to your house. If you had enough money, you would buy a soda."

Swimming at the pool was also a way to pick up girls: "If you were a good swimmer," Carlos asserts, "you were able to get the pretty girls. . . . You'd go over to the girls, 'Let me teach you how to swim . . .' "

If play was one reason to persist in using the Thomas Jefferson pool, equal rights was another. Felipe Colón, who owns the popular restaurant El Fogón, puts it this way: "They fought until they were finally left alone. They fought for access. The pool was a nice place built by the city—so it was meant for everyone. The pool is a symbol of determination. Puerto Ricans are very determined. They wouldn't let anyone browbeat them and not let them use a facility that belonged to everyone. Puerto Ricans paved the way for future Latino groups. They suffered and they fought to get a better way of life and the benefits that they have now. Everything had to be fought for."

LANDMARKS OF A KIND

A remarkable fact is that ten of the eleven pools built by the city in 1936 are still in working order; many, like Thomas Jefferson, are in brilliant condition. McCarren Pool, in Brooklyn, is the only one missing. The New York City Landmarks Preservation Commission declined to permanently protect the pools by designating them as landmarks when some citizens suggested that action in the 1990s, but landmarks of a kind they are: marking an era of city leaders willing and able to take responsibility for the population's health and well-being, the painful struggles of the city's diverse populations to claim space for themselves, and the sweetness of triumph over the meanness of racism.

—Elena Martínez and Marci Reaven

Empire Roller Skating Center

200 Empire Boulevard, Crown Heights, Brooklyn

(718) 462–1400

www.us-skating.com (click on Brooklyn)

Public transit: 2, 5 trains to Sterling Street. Walk one block north (against traffic) to Empire Boulevard and turn left.

B, Q trains to Prospect Park. Walk east (away from the park) on Empire Boulevard.

"My name's Terence Fisher. I was born here in Brooklyn, and I'm an old skater from Empire Rollerdrome. I started going to Empire at the age of seven, and that's going back to 1953."

"My name is Khadijah Shaheed. My background is basically city, and I've been going to the Empire Roller Disco as long as I can remember."

"I'm Bill Butler, originally from Detroit. I knew if they were skating in New York it had to be serious. The Empire was the first place I came to when I hit the city. I've been on my skates for sixty years without any breaks in between."

"Oh, the Empire. If the Empire shut down, a lot of skaters would stop skating. I'm telling you there is a spirit attached to this building. There is no way to describe it. There's a feeling that you get once you walk in— if it is supposed to be for you." —DJ Q, DJ at the Empire

Khadijah Shaheed first told us about the Empire. She knew we were scouring the city for places that meant something serious to people, places where people had made their own traditions and culture. To recall what the Empire meant to her, she took a long bus ride back to Crown Heights, soaking in the sights and sounds along the way and materializing the past in forms she could see and describe. Khadijah's memories are Khadijah's, but plenty of other people told us similar stories, shaped by their own era, their own background, their commitment to skating. Generations of Brooklynites, of New Yorkers, have skated here. What's amazing about the Empire is that you can still go.

A FULL HOUSE

One of the rink's best features is its wood floor, installed by the Swanson family in 1941 when they turned a parking garage for Ebbets Field into a roller rink—220 feet long by 60 feet wide. The Swansons owned a flooring business, so they put in high-quality maple. Maple is the best wood for skating, and the Empire's was exceptional. The family marketed its rink with the moniker "Home of the Miracle Maple." They also installed speakers used at the 1939 World's Fair. In the early 1980s a whopping new sound system replaced the old one, keeping up the excellent audio tradition. The Empire is decidedly not one of those places that signals its greatness by its appearance from outside: several tacked-together buildings that resemble a low-lying airplane hangar and, until recently, overlapping generations of signs. Khadijah Shaheed well recalls the signs. "All the colors and fancy writing? It just makes you want to come inside, and for me, the sign's a landmark. I would see it, and instant memory!"

There's not a day in the week you can't skate at the Empire, or a night. Public skating, Gospel Night, Ladies' Night, Teen Night; birthday party packages at prices to make Manhattan parents weep. Skate rentals, refreshments—and DJs who know how to "kind of work people up." DJ Q starts out with the slow jams, works his way to R&B, then disco, and slows back down again before bringing it back up to hip-hop. "Sixty-six beats per minute at the start, but you work your way up to 120 beats, then in the middle you break it back down again. You've got to feel out your crowd. On Sunday afternoon when the whole family comes, you gotta be careful what kind of music you play. No cursing, no thugged-out stuff. And the music always has to be skatable. You have to be able to move side to side."

At thirty thousand square feet, room enough for well over a thousand skaters at a time, the Empire is the last giant rink left in Brooklyn. Purist "quad" (four-wheel) skaters say it's about the only place left to dance on skates. Ruminating on the meaning of the Empire, Bill Butler, one of the rink's—and the country's—star skaters, refers to the rink as a "full house": a place where anything could happen, and did.

NICOLE AND FITZ'S NIGHT OUT

I've heard plenty of stories of the old Empire rink," our friend Nicole Gilliam told us. "The place local kids would go to see their friends and show off the new skates they got for Christmas (you know, the speed skates with the fat laces). But from what I'd heard, it was an empty building and nobody ever bothered to change the sign that reads 'Empire Skate.' " When we told Nicole the rink was still open she asked to help us out. Here's her report:

"When I asked my friend Fitz to come check it out with me, he responded with: 'Really? Empire's still open? Girl, that place is ghetto, but yeah, let's go.' So that next Tuesday night, late, we did. The rink's was the only open door on Empire Boulevard. We wander up to the entrance to be greeted by two security guards. The large man pulls Fitz aside to be frisked while the woman goes through my bag. The next stop is the entry booth, where Fitz has to get over the embarrassment of letting the girl pay—especially on Ladies' Night! After the personal hurdle, we finally get into the rink, where the music hits us. Only then do I realize just how quiet it had been outside. We've walked into another dimension. An oasis of bright neon, music, people smiling, dancing, gliding over the floor; skating together, all in one groove. The rink is kept dark for that club-type atmosphere, so the neon gives the whole place a particular kind of glow.

"Okay, next step—the skates. We walk over to the wall of skates, where we are greeted by a guy who has a huge smile on his face. All that's going through my head is *Why is everyone in here so happy?* It's kind of sad to be surprised by happy, smiling people, but this is New York, and it is Crown Heights. So we throw our stuff into a locker, lace up our skates, and we're ready—for the small ring in the back. Apparently roller-skating is not like riding a bike. Even Fitz, who as it turns out used to be a skate guard—at Empire!—could barely keep himself up and held on to me with the excuse that he was helping to keep me steady. 'Well, then stop pulling on me!' We must have been a sight, but we managed to take ourselves around a few times without toppling over or running anyone else down. Finally, we decided to just sit down and enjoy the view.

"The DJ sits on a perch between the main ring and the small ring spinning today's top hip-hop and R&B hits. Skaters are black Americans, ages nineteen to fifty, all dressed in 'going out' clothes: the younger generation in club clothes—short skirts, tight jeans, small T-shirts—and the older generation in slacks and dress shirts. This is not

Generations of signs. Photo: Martha Cooper.

a sport, it's a night out. It's for couples, for cruisers, and for hangin' out with friends. The majority of skaters had their own wheels (roller skates—I saw only one in-line skater), the best pair being a simple black with wheels that lit up as the guy danced. Smooth.

"The main ring also has an 'island' decorated with palm trees and benches where people can relax and chat or show off their gymnastic abilities. One guy spent quite a long time in a handstand, doing all sorts of configurations with his legs. With balance like that, he must be a great skater. The back ring is a little less crowded, providing enough room to practice tricks, goof off, or flail your arms about in an attempt to keep yourself upright. I only saw two people fall. One minute they're following the flow, the next they're nothing but a heap on the floor. But in the spirit of the evening, they just popped back up laughing.

"When the clock chimes 1:00 a.m., it's closing time. With a few stragglers left in the ring, we walk out through the front doors onto Empire Boulevard. And again, there is nothing but a large empty street. Where did all those people go? Maybe it really is an oasis! There is quite a spirit to be felt in this place. It's obvious that people have spent a lot of time here, shared a lot of memories."

A LITTLE ROLLER RINK HISTORY

By 1956, the brothers Henry and Hector Abrami had bought the rink. A few years later Henry Abrami made a practice rink in the back by shaving off about thirty feet from the main rink and added a bowling alley on one side. When skating experienced a temporary drop in popularity, he put platforms on the rink and transformed it into a miniature golf area. Sometimes he set up a stage in the middle of the rink for boxing and wrestling matches. In 1980, when her father passed away, Gloria Abrami took over management of the building, becoming the first woman in the nation to own a roller rink.

Henry lived in Bensonhurst, and he bought the rink because all his children were skaters. Gloria, his eldest, was a dance skater, and his two sons, Henry and Ronald, competed and won championships. The Empire Rollerdrome, as it was first called, was part of a circuit of rinks in

Love on wheels at the Empire. Photo: Martha Cooper.

the city that skaters went to for competition, lessons, and recreation. In the 1950s, there were at least thirty rinks in the New York City area, including Fordham Skating Palace in the Bronx (where Monroe College is today), Queens Roller Rink in Rego Park, Gay Blades in Manhattan (which is today's Roseland dance hall), and Coney Island Roller Skating Rink on Surf Avenue.

The first generation: "I was ten years old and World War II was easing. My mom and dad told me about this place where I could skate indoors away from the traffic. I boarded the Tompkins Avenue Trolley with fifty cents in my pocket and traveled forty-five minutes to Empire Boulevard and Bedford Avenue. As I passed the Empire Skating Rink on the trolley, I could see a long line of kids waiting to get inside. I could feel my heart racing with anticipation and excitement. I waited patiently until I arrived at the ticket window, paid my twenty-five cents, got my admission ticket that I handed to the floor guard stationed at the door to the rink. Wow! I never imagined anything like this! A huge floor made of wood planks, smooth as a sheet of glass, and live organ music that drew me in like a pied piper."—Barry Brown, *Roller Skaters' Gazette*

The second generation: "I was twelve years old in the sixties, growing up in the Marcy Projects, and every Saturday I saw my friends were heading out someplace without me. I started asking, 'Where is everybody going in groups?' And I found out they were going skating. My friend's older sister Moochie took me under her wing, told my mother that she would be responsible for me. We took the Nostrand Avenue bus to the Tompkins bus, a group of us—ten or more—and when we got to the skating rink we'd stand in line and anxiously wait for the door to open. As soon as we got inside we'd run to check our coats, get our skates. It's all a matter of timing. The faster you get your stuff, the more time to skate!"—Khadijah Shaheed

---

Best wishes from the Empire. Photo courtesy of City Lore.

Trolleys supplanted by buses; tenements felled for housing projects; Irish, Italian, and Jewish neighbors exchanged for African Americans and folks from the Caribbean. Brooklyn changed a lot in the postwar years, but the Empire continued to be a place for coming of age.

"I had the old-fashioned indoor roller skates with the felt wheels that you are not supposed to use on cement," recalls Khadijah. "I got them for Christmas, pure white and no pom-poms. And a skate outfit, something that flowed. The bathroom at the Empire had a ceiling-to-floor mirror, and all the girls would come in there to see how they looked in their skates. When the announcer called for couples, someone you might not even know would reach out his hand for you, and then it's on. After that you exchange numbers and hope that person comes again. And you wear the same thing, so maybe they'll remember you. My friend's sister Moochie helped me a lot, because at first no one would ask me to skate. I asked Moochie why and she said, 'Because you skate ugly.' 'What do you mean?' I said. 'I never fall.' I thought it was all about falling. And she said, 'No, you have to have some movement, you have to sway.' I had learned to skate by going *rmm, rmm* on cement with my old metal pair that you put over shoes—what did I know? So she took me aside and showed me a few steps and how to cross the leg over. I was so thankful because after she taught me I started getting asked to skate. I still can't dance, but when I cross the leg, make a little turn, it looks a lot more graceful."

What also made the Empire sparkle was the star skaters who adopted the rink, like Bill Butler. Butler helped make the Empire's reputation, with his skate-dancing techniques that took old steps like the Brooklyn Bounce and gave them clarity and style. "You can always tell an Empire skater by the way they bounce," says DJ Terence

FIRST PERSON:
KHADIJAH SHAHEED

"I went roller-skating with my former husband, who had never learned to skate. I could see that the guy at the mike playing music was watching us. He watches my husband fall, get up, fall, get up, fall, through the whole session. And when it's over he says, 'Give that man a round of applause.' It was so funny. That's what I like about roller-skating rinks. In a big place you can notice an individual. It makes you part of a group, and that's what ties it all together."

Fisher. By the mid-1960s skaters were already thronging the Empire to watch Butler and his followers "jamming" to jazz, R&B, and, in the 1970s, disco. The rink was renamed Empire Roller Disco in the era of *Saturday Night Fever,* and roller disco caught on big. Club lighting, a faux California décor with plastic palm trees, the best music, and a canopy over the entrance for that Studio 54 look gave the rink a disco atmosphere. With hipness came the stars—like Olivia Newton-John, who took lessons from Bill Butler. Artists like Butler changed the language of skating. Skating had become self-expression through dance, on quads and accompanied by the popular music of the time. Robert Clayton, the former DJ Big Bob, says: "Empire dominated the sixties and seventies. There was no rink hotter than us, nowhere."

SISTER SITE: THE KEY SKATING CENTER

220 East 138th Street (near Grand Concourse and Third Avenue), Mott Haven, the Bronx

Public Transit: 4, 5 trains to 138th Street.

Known as the Key, this is another one of the few rinks left in the city that is truly devoted to skating. Some say the skating is faster here than in Brooklyn. The Key's youngish crowd skates and parties surrounded by huge murals of city trains. The Key is also known for hosting hip-hop jams, in the early days of the music and today.

A RINK REBORN

In the eighties and nineties, the rink became more identified with teenagers and trouble. A lot of people started to stay away. But still there were stellar moments, like the reggae concert for a crowd of eight thousand, and hip-hop performances with new stars like Grandmaster Flash and the Furious 5. (In the slow summer months, the rink adapts itself to whatever brings in revenue.)

When owner Gloria Abrami passed away, the rink closed down. Robert Clayton remembers the date, December 26, 1998: "There wasn't a dry eye in the building." Clayton tried to reopen it with four partners but eventually had to turn to the nationwide chain United Skates of America for assistance. The chain purchased the rink and, to the great relief of longtime fans, reopened the place in the spring of 2000.

Today there's even air-conditioning. The Empire continues to hold sway for socializing and recreation. Old-timers hold reunions. Hasidic congregations rent the rink for gender-segregated afternoons of play. Local kids run over after school and on the weekend. And ladies still come hoping for someone to hold out his hand and say, "Like to dance?"

—Elena Martínez and Marci Reaven

Chess Havens

Greenwich Village, Manhattan

Washington Square Park

Southeast corner, near MacDougal
Street and West Fourth Street

Chess Forum
219 Thompson Street
(212) 475–2369
www.chessforum.com
Hours: Every day, 10:00 a.m. to 1:30 a.m.

Village Chess Shop
230 Thompson Street
(212) 475–9580
www.chess-shop.com
Hours: Every day, 11:00 a.m. to midnight

Marshall Chess Club
23 West Tenth Street
(212) 477–3716
www.marshallchessclub.org
Hours: Monday through Friday, 6:00
p.m. to midnight; Saturday and Sunday, noon to midnight

Public Transit: A, B, C, D, E, F, V trains to
West Fourth Street/Washington
Square. Walk east to find all four
places.

Flush with victory after the world championships in 1972—a championship that presaged nothing less than the American victory in the cold war—Grand Master Bobby Fischer, whom many consider the greatest chess player of all time, declared that he would use his fame and celebrity to promote the art of chess. In an extravagant moment, he promised to build a house in the shape of a chess piece, a castle or rook with a spiral staircase. It would serve as a climactic symbol for the significance of chess in America.

Then, for reasons upon which every chess player speculates freely but only he himself knows, Bobby Fischer disappeared from view, and never kept any of those promises. Still, his image of a magnificent castle in the shape of a chess piece is an apt metaphor for chess in New York, where he began as a child playing in the parks, and where his victories made New York City an epicenter for chess in the Americas. The current epicenter of chess in the city spans a small area of the West Village. It beckons passersby in Washington Square Park, where hustlers continually invite anyone who knows the game to play at one of fifteen concrete tables. From there, it's a short walk south to two warring chess clubs— the Chess Forum and the Village Chess Shop on Thompson Street—or north to the lofty haven of the most serious players, the Marshall Chess Club on Tenth Street.

Chess seems to lend itself to grandiose metaphors, perhaps because it marks one of civilization's most enduring, elaborated-upon creations. Here are some from the players at the Marshall Chess Club: "Chess is a mathematical problem that hasn't been solved yet." "Chess is an absurdity." "Chess is a ball of yarn." "Chess is a language in which you have to develop your own vocabulary." And chess, says Doug Bellizzi, the club's president, is "the search for the truth." It's a search that takes us up the winding staircase of Bobby Fischer's castle but begins at the twelve concrete chess tables in Washington Square Park.

PAWNS IN THE PARK

Jean Paul has been playing in Washington Square for more than twenty years. On a recent afternoon, in an act of unusual generosity, he offered to give us twenty thousand dollars' worth of information for a mere twenty bucks. How could we refuse? For a chess player to hustle in the park, he should be at the 2,200 official rating (or level), he tells us, the cutoff for an official chess master. Then the trash talk begins. "You have to perform in bed, you have to perform here. Any woman will tell you if you're performing. Getting them in bed is checkmate—it's mate in one." The games in the park are fast, played with a punch-clock timer. "It may take five minutes for the whole game," he tells us. "Some women don't like that. They get disappointed." In the middle of his game, he looks up to flirt with a young woman who pauses to watch for a moment. "Do you want next? What's your name?" Then he looks disparagingly down at the board, where his opponent has just protected his king by castling. "Real men don't castle," he says disapprovingly.

As we leave the park, heading for Thompson Street, an older player, a forty-year denizen of the park who's known as "Sweet Pea," decides that we owe him a game. He explains his plight: As a result of "Reaganomics and the Bush War, people just don't have money to spend. Rich middle-class whities—without them we can't exist."

KNIGHTS AND BISHOPS FACE OFF

There is a well-known joke about a Jewish Robinson Crusoe who, when discovered by Jacques Cousteau on a desert island, shows him first one, then another gorgeous synagogue he constructed out of twigs and straw. Approaching the second house of worship, Cousteau asks, "Why do you need two synagogues?" "Well," he answers, "that's the one I don't go to." For at least some of the chess players at the Chess Forum on Thompson Street in the Village, the Village Chess Shop across the street is the club they don't go to. In the sixties, a half dozen chess dens were tucked into Village crannies, among them a shop on Sullivan Street, opened by a half-Russian, half-French Grand Master, Nicholas Rossolino. At night he drove a cab to support the business, which he ran with his wife. Late in the 1960s, Rossolino left his store in the care of his manager, a German immigrant named George Frohlinde, and moved to Europe to play tournaments and take care of some real estate holdings in Spain.

In his absence, an earthquake shook the chess world: Bobby Fischer beat the Russians. Frohlinde's nephew and the current manager of the Village Chess shop, Larry Nash, remembers: "At the time, America was a checkers culture. . . . Bobby Fischer enlightened Americans that chess could be an American game." The influx of interest and money into the game resulted in Rossolino and his former manager running competing shops across the street from one another, like a set of white and black pieces facing off across Thompson Street. The conflict continued through to the next generation, although the various moves have become a bit murky over time. Recently, one manager compared the other to King Lear, the man who divided his kingdom. At the time of this writing, the Thirty Years' War still keeps some patrons of one from crossing the street into the other's parlor.

Today, the shop windows of both stores display miniature sculpture gardens of chess sets: Napoleon chess sets, *The Simpsons* sets, Endangered Animals chess sets, Dinosaur Tea Party sets, *American Gothic* sets, a New York set in which the queen is the Statue of Liberty and pawns are yellow cabs. But the players at the club tables eschew these silly sets designed for dabblers and tourists and instead play with the ancient wooden pieces. And, in the clubs, sexual innuendos are only a tad more sophisticated than they are in the park. At the Village Chess Shop, a Mexican man urges his opponent to give up. "He thinks he's a master, a chess master." Then adds, "A master-bator." Meanwhile, a chalk sign on a blackboard at the Chess Shop playfully cites the prices: $1.00 per hour, $1.50 if they lend you a clock, and "$3.00 for profanities uttered."

Village Chess Shop. Photo: Martha Cooper.

QUEENS AND KINGS: NOBILITY ON THE CHESSBOARD

A few blocks north, a sign on a quiet brownstone marks the pinnacle of the New York chess world, the Marshall Chess Club (at least since the closing of its even more famous rival, the Manhattan Chess Club, in 2000). The mythical winding staircase up to this rarefied spot in the chess world takes us up the uncarpeted steps to the second floor into the well-worn, timeless atmosphere of what might once have been called a gentleman's club, though women are welcome. The largest room is lined with chairs and tables set with chess pieces, and framed photographs of chess champions hang on the walls. Bobby Fischer and, in fact, many of the world's chess greats probably sat and played at every one of those tables, says club denizen and international master Asa Hoffman.

"We're standing here on hallowed ground," says Marshall's president, Doug Bellizzi. Steeped in tradition, the club was founded in 1915 by Frank Marshall, one of the original five grand masters of chess, given that title by Czar Nicholas II. When he won the award, a group photo was taken, and Marshall sent home a photograph of the five first venerable masters, adding the inscription "the five wood pushers." When the stock market crashed, it seemed as if the club would lose its space, but "angels came along out of the sky, and helped us buy this home for chess." The great Cuban player José Raúl Capablanca, world champion between 1921 and 1927, joined Frank Marshall to celebrate the reopening of the club in 1931.

Marshall's pièce de résistance is the famous Capablanca table, with an inlaid wooden chessboard. Capablanca is said to have won the world championship on this table. In 1965, when Bobby Fischer was banned from attending a tournament in Cuba, he played in it anyway—on the Capablanca table at the Marshall Chess Club, with the moves of his opponent telexed in from the island.

But to get to know a place is often to know it at certain times of the day or the week or the year. The best time to experience the Marshall is when the best players play. Until recently that was the New York Masters Tournament on Tuesday nights; call (212) 477–3716 or visit www.marshallchessclub.org for an up-to-date tournament schedule.

Unlike in the park and the clubs, games are played here in total silence. Players don't even say "check" when attacking the king, as most of us amateurs were taught to do. All that is audible is the ticking of the clocks beside each game board, timing the moves, though the players say games go by in a split second when they're "in the flow." At a recent tournament, Asa Hoffman, who played speed or blitz chess against Bobby Fischer at the all-night clubs in Times Square in the late 1960s ("I beat him perhaps one game out of fifty"), won against Irina Krush. In the hallway outside the tournament room, he quipped, "I gave her the poison pawn on the eighth move, and she took it."

At Marshall Chess Club, FIDE Master Asa Hoffman and International Master Renato Naranja confront one another across the famed Capablanca table on which Bobby Fischer won a world tournament. Photo: Martha Cooper.

A KINGDOM OF THE MIND

As we ascend the winding staircase of the chess world, we come to an imaginary turret where the players are locked in eternal combat. At this "Capablanca table of the mind" players are, as Gary Ryan describes, "locked into timeless space—there's only this. There's only this kind of laserlike focus on the board. You make a move—I make a move, and I make a move that is totally riding the edge against your move. It's like a surfer catching a big, big wave."

In this kingdom of the mind, chess mirrors the world. "Every chess piece has its own personality," Asa Hoffman says. "Each is different and moves differently—it's quite different from checkers or Go. People of

Facing off in Washington Square Park. Photo: Martha Cooper.

low self-worth think of themselves as a pawn. We devious ones think of ourselves as knights jumping around and foiling and tricking people. Rigid people are bishops that only move diagonally."

Chess Forum player Gary Ryan suggests, "I'm not sure chess is a game. Chess may be something else—like a dream. I think that dreams are probably our attempts to figure out problems. On the chessboard that's exactly what's going on—it's us trying to figure out problems. I think maybe when I play chess I'm trying to figure out problems that have nothing to do with you."

Beyond a dream, each chess game is a story that unfolds. "You get to make beautiful things happen on the chess board," says twenty-three-year-old Jennifer Shahade, the U.S. champion and the author of the forthcoming *Chess Bitch: Women in the Ultimate Intellectual Sport*. "At certain moments, you think of a move that is so paradoxical or one that makes everything fall into place. Then you get to save it forever on the computer." We asked her if she aspires to the rank of grand master. "I don't relish the idea of studying chess for eight hours a day, which is what it would take. In New York City, there's just too much else to do."

FIRST PERSON: GARY RYAN

"In chess, the pawn is the only piece that can only move forward, never back. Pawns remind me of the legend about the Gurkha soldiers from the days of the British Empire. They wore Gurkha shorts and were famous for their bravery. In a battle they were known to tie up one of their legs so they could not run from a last stand. They could only move forward. The pawn is like the poor soldier named as the point man in Vietnam or Iraq. Someone has to go first."

Meanwhile, Bobby Fischer, who started it all, is living in Iceland, unable to return to the States without facing charges for playing a 1992 rematch with his Russian archrival, Boris Spassky, in what was then Yugoslavia; the United States somehow cannot forgive his violation of sanctions against the Soviet Union, despite all that his victory did for the game. In a clipping on the wall of the Village Chess Shop, Spassky makes an offer to the U.S. government, asking to be punished along with Fischer. He suggests that the government put them both in jail—in the same cell, in fact. Their only request: a chess set.

—Steve Zeitlin

The "mayor of Coney Island," Dick Zigun, Coney Island USA. Photo: Martha Cooper.

Coney Island

W hat is honky-tonk?" we ask Dick Zigun, the founder of Coney Island USA and Sideshows by the Seashore. The Yale theater graduate answers simply, "it's the opposite of hoity-toity." Defined in the dictionary as "tawdry, cheap entertainment," the word was first used in an Oklahoma paper in 1894 to describe a honk-a-tonk, meaning a dance hall. Dick refines the definition: "It's a type of culture—whether it's an architecture or an activity that's totally disreputable and absolutely wonderful. It's inventive and outrageous." Honky-tonk is cheap. Honky-tonk is not corporate. It has a homemade feel to it, with few corporate logos and advertising, putting it at the other end of the spectrum from today's Times Square. "When we paint signs for Coney Island USA," Dick continues, "I sometimes purposely ask for spelling mistakes to be put in just to keep that homemade sense."

> Coney Island, Brooklyn
>
> Hours: Open weekends from Easter; daily Memorial Day to Labor Day.
>
> Public Transit: D train to Coney Island/ Stillwell Avenue.
>
> B, Q trains to Brighton Beach, then B68 bus to Stillwell Avenue.
>
> F train to Avenue X, then shuttle bus to Stillwell Avenue.

Laid out between Surf Avenue and the Boardwalk, with Brooklyn and Manhattan on one side, sand and ocean on the other, the honky-tonk amusement district once called "the World's Playground" still mounts a frontal attack on all the senses. Not one place but a configuration of raucous places, Coney is defined by the way rides, arcades, and sideshow attractions bounce off one another pinball style.

The preservationist Melissa Baldock suggests that a parallel can be drawn between the distinctive walkway pattern of Coney and the landmarked street pattern of lower Manhattan. That pattern of historic walks, and the historic Riegelman Boardwalk, built in the early 1920s, are defining elements of Coney. It's a unique pattern of streets framed by neighborhood on one side and Boardwalk and beach on the other, with walkways connecting the two.

Memories are layered in Coney Island, so let us take a walk from the subway down Surf Avenue to the most intact walkway—Jones Walk—across the Bowery Walk and then along the Boardwalk, following the contours of Coney Island honky-tonk. Let us take that walk in two different eras, first in today's Coney, then around 1940; first in the sensual present, then in memories of sensuous moments more than sixty years ago—traversing the fabled walkways of Coney to find the heart of honky-tonk in New York City.

DESTINATION: CONEY ISLAND

Labor Day 2004. The subway—the world's slowest roller coaster—snakes around the curve from West Eighth Street to its final destination, Coney Island. You bound to the platform at Stillwell Avenue in search of honky-tonk. Seeking to be transported from the urban usualities, you walk down and around the newly renovated station onto the Times Square of Coney Island, the intersection of Stillwell and Surf, where Nathan's announces itself with bright and gaudy homespun signs and a whiff of grease mingles with the fresh sea breeze.

If you can resist a dose of Nathan's French fries with cheese, turn left on Surf, walking along the dividing line separating the currently bedraggled block of urban renewal houses and the rest of Brooklyn from a honky-tonk kingdom. On your left, Coney Island Furniture, then Luna Park Furniture, and vacant lots; on the right side of the street, an invitation to "bump your ass off" on the Eldorado bumper cars, the old Shore Hotel, bells and recorded voices from an arcade, and a chance to win a stuffed dog if you can throw a softball through a suspended toilet seat. The rides are in storefronts, "only louder and more colorful," Charles Denson writes in his fabulous book, *Coney Island Lost and Found*. Crossing Twelfth Street, you catch the splendiferous banner line for Sideshows by the Seashore, with Marie Roberts's color-

Plunge of the Cyclone. Photo © Hazel Hankin Photography.

The House under the Roller Coaster, made famous by Woody Allen in *Annie Hall,* tragically demolished in 2000. Photo © Hazel Hankin Photography.

ful banners ballyhooing Eak the Geek, the snake-charming Ananka, the pierced and tattooed Insectivora, Ravi the Bendable Boy from Bombay, Koko the Killer Clown, and even a parody of Dick Zigun, the Sideshows entrepreneur and unofficial mayor of Coney Island, decked out in a checkered suit. "You can go to the movies and see ten million dollars' worth of special effects," Dick says, "but it is something genuinely astonishing and awe-inspiring to visit Sideshows by the Seashore, and see the somebody ten feet in front of you, live, twist his limbs around without any film editing or any props to hide it. That is undeniably happening for real right in front of you. I think to see that is as astonishing in the twenty-first century as it probably was in the twelfth century."

Turn right on Jones Walk, the last of the bustling narrow walkways that run from Surf to the Boardwalk. Suddenly the come-ons, the amusements and rides, are on both sides, the alleyway creating a convergence of people. "Race for first place in the camel race," a Jamaican girl's voice cries out. Down a little further, Phil Frleta, "the grand old man of Jones Walk," who started working on Coney in 1939, uses a hypnotic three-fingered wave to call you over and talk you into throwing a softball into a bushel basket (he tries to explain how to win, but you keep losing). You pass by the Wonder Wheel and the funky Spookarama dark ride, where the metal car bangs through swinging wooden doors and the darkness is aghast with monsters and screams. Then, crossing the Bowery walkway, you stroll through Deno's tunnel and ramp, with the words *Coney Island* inscribed in bright cartoon lettering on the wall of the pathway, to Astroland's Kiddie Park, where you hear children ring the large bells on the front of each of their brightly colored trucks. "Don't be shy, give it a try," cries a woman inviting you to shoot water into a clown's mouth, as the sound of the winning balloon popping above the clown mixes with the wails of children being dragged out of the park by weary parents (no child ever goes quietly).

Step on the Boardwalk, clamshells at your feet. Walk the wooden slats of another dividing line, at once separating and fusing a natural and a man-made landscape—not Brooklyn from Coney, but Coney's amusements from the expansive and magnificent beach, with its fine white sand, the soothing sounds of waves, and the squeaky squawk of seagulls, almost as numerous as the people, sent into a feeding frenzy with every stray morsel of discarded junk food from the amusements. Above, the upward flight of hands as the Cyclone roller coaster plunges downward, clattering along wooden

FIRST PERSON: ELIZA ZEITLIN

"I asked a friend of mine why he smoked pot all the time, and he told me that it was a 're-creatable good feeling.' You can't always be sure that Peggy Sue will go to the dance with you and that great things will happen, but you can always re-create the good feeling by smoking a joint. He was wrong, of course, but I happen to feel that way about Coney Island. Every time I feel the Cyclone ascending, I get this incredibly good feeling. It's an especially simple, uncomplicated feeling—just the joy of that first climb before the plunge. And it can always be re-created just by taking another ride."

slats not nearly as sturdy as the Boardwalk's, sounding as if it will shake itself apart at any moment. ("The new metal coasters just toy with you," one visitor said, "but on the Cyclone you take your life in your hands.") Turning right, back toward Stillwell, resist—but only if you can—the temptation to "Dunk the Creep" with a powerful throw and "Shoot the Freak" with paintball. "Whereas on the surface," says Dick Zigun, "I don't appreciate the new rage in Coney Island, which is called "Shoot the Freak'—my official party line is people should love the freaks, not shoot the freaks—yet it represents all the best of Coney Island. It's rude, it's obnoxious, it's loud, it's politically incorrect, and it's a lot of fun."

Just a day later, the day after Labor Day, the rides shut down, and the park goes into hibernation.

CONEY ISLAND TIME MACHINE

Some sixty years ago—say, in the era from the 1940s to the early 1950s, when Coney's crowds reached their zenith, numbering more than a million on a sunny day—take that same walk. It's the era when Coney was dubbed "the Nickel Empire" and four subway lines first converged there, an era that followed the years when Luna Park, Steeplechase, and Dreamland dazzled Americans with dreams and amusements they'd never seen before.

As you exit the station, Philips Candy tempts you with saltwater taffy, and a young John Dorman hands giant lollipops to the kids (Philips closed in 2000). Nathan's stands, as it does today, but at the site of Luna Park Furniture on your left you can see the real Luna Park, with its Shoot-the-Chutes lagoon and Carver's Diving Horses that plunged from 150 feet into a pool of water. (Luna burned in 1946.) Again, turn onto Jones Walk, this time at the old Feltman's Restaurant and Beer Garden, where the hot dog was invented (Feltman's closed in the 1950s). You pass the Spookarama, but this time with its one-eyed blinking Cyclops towering above the Bowery. Then you're into the tunnel and on the ramp leading to the Boardwalk below Ward's Baths, one of dozens of now extinct Coney Island bathhouses where people changed before bathing.

Jones Walk in the 1980s. Photo © Hazel Hankin Photography.

Turn right again on the Boardwalk, shuffling your way through the crowds. In 1940, Weegee takes his famous photo that shows people on top of people, the beach standing room only, the sand barely visible

FIRST PERSON:

TOM GOODRIDGE

"On the fall equinox, I finally got to Coney Island to celebrate my annual memorial meal 'with' my late father, George. I took the D train to the last stop and found the station totally renovated. George would have hated the upgrading—he loved sleaze. I was relieved to find Nathan's still across the street, although it seemed cleaned up, too, and the prices reflected it. My father was deep cheap, which makes it hard to spend money to remember him. The young woman must have wondered why I cried as I placed the order for a hot dog, small fries, and a beer. 'Can I make that a medium fries for free?' she responded. My first thought was that she was trying to cheer me up, but then she explained that free fries were the Friday special. I knew better; it was George at work."

through the crowds. A few steps farther on, you stumble across Stauch's Baths and Dance Hall, which burned so many times it was nicknamed Coney's finest "outdoor bar-b-que," then the roaring Thunderbolt roller coaster that nestled in its twists and turns the old Kensington Hotel—the "House under the Roller Coaster" later made famous as the home of Alvie Singer in *Annie Hall.* May Timpano and Fred Moran were soon to call the place home and would live there for more than forty years with the coaster rattling their living room and slanting all the pictures with each ride.

A few steps farther down the Boardwalk is the Parachute Jump, moved here from the 1939–1940 World's Fair and originally developed as a training simulator for the military in the 1930s. Close your eyes as you're strapped into a harness, lifted up by six steel cables, and allowed to free-fall for a few seconds high above Coney until a parachute opens, then is slowed by shock absorbers. You step back out onto the Boardwalk, dazed and awed.

Stroll into founder George Tilyou's Steeplechase Park (1897–1964), where the Funny Face stares at you both from high above and from the Steeplechase ride ticket in your hand, a round cardboard currency good for ten rides. (You can find discarded chads and try to insert them seamlessly back into the card for an illegal free ride.) At the park's outrageous and politically incorrect Blow Hole Theater (later dubbed the Insanitarium), beware! Jets of air blow through grates and send women's dresses billowing up around their ears, and Little Angelo the midget may prod you with an electric rod . . .

Perhaps it's the shock that jolts you back to the present! On the Boardwalk you see on the right an empty lot where the House under the Roller Coaster once stood. The Thunderbolt roller coaster stopped running in 1983 and before long took on the look of an overgrown castle in moonlight, with clouds and bats visible through broken windows and missing crossties. Landmarked and restored as a hotel, perhaps with a boardwalk restaurant, it might have been the gaudy centerpiece of a revived Coney Island, but it was illegally razed by the Giuliani administration on November 17, 2000.

In front of the now landmarked but inoperable structure for the Parachute Jump stands the grand new Cyclones minor-league baseball stadium with its stunning ocean view. It opened in 2001, built by the Giuliani administration, and it may hold the key to a new future for Coney. Ironically, one of its luxury boxes is called the Thunderbolt, after the one-of-a-kind coaster it destroyed.

PRESERVING HONKY-TONK

There is more of Caesar's Rome left than Tilyou's Coney," writes Richard Snow. So little remains of Coney Island's pre–World War II past that priorities for preservation are easy to set. Dick Zigun has a list of five places to research and submit to the landmarks commission: Nathan's, the Shore Theater, Henderson's, the B & B Carousel, and the second Child's Restaurant, the current site of Sideshows by the Seashore. (The original Child's Restaurant with its terra-cotta facade recently became a city landmark.) The key to preserving Coney, though, is not only in saving the buildings but in maintaining their "use," a category eschewed by the landmarks law. In her fine master's thesis, "Preserving the Honky-tonk: Coney Island's Future in Its Amusement Past" (which has informed this essay in a number of ways), Melissa Baldock suggests that preserving the building where Nathan's is housed would be equivalent to putting up a "Nathan slept here" sign, unless the establishment continues as a hot-dog-and-French-fries franchise. But official landmarking, she argues, would still bring prestige.

Currently, Coney is in the throes of a new renaissance. At the close of the documentary *Coney Island,* the historian Elliot Willensky suggests that "where land and water meet, wonderful things always happen. That means to me that Coney Island will forever be an opportunity—because that intersection of sand and waves, the kind of light that you have, the kind of smells that you have, evokes in people, all people, powerful, primitive, creative urges."

Waiting on the subway platform to catch the train back to what passes for real life, revel for a moment in the wonder. As one visitor puts it, "At Coney, even if you don't like the people you're with, even if you wasted your money on the dumb games, even if it wasn't the most glorious day, the bright colors and flashing lights will fool you into thinking you're having a good time."

—Steve Zeitlin

**PLACE MOMENT:
JILL BRESSLER,
CONEY ISLAND BOARDWALK**

"The Coney Island Boardwalk on a cold November day when a bundled few seek their solace by the shore while they stroll silently down the wooden path, past concession stands and amusement rides that have been put to bed until summer. Once I listened to a man play trumpet to the waves."

Urban Palate

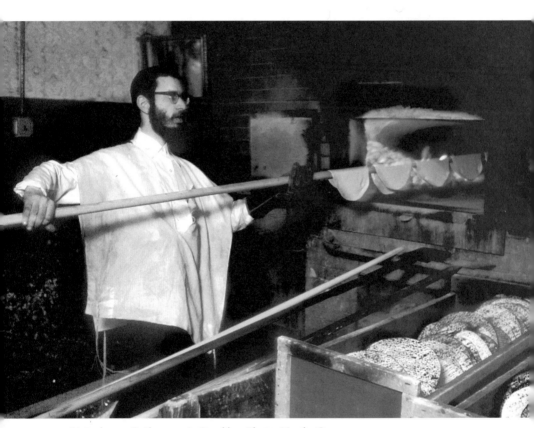

Matzoh goes in the oven in Brooklyn. Photo: Martha Cooper.

Crushed ice and fruit juice yield a classic piragua in East Harlem. Photo: Martha Cooper.

Stroll through any neighborhood in New York and you will be overwhelmed by aromas. In Jackson Heights, Queens, beneath the clatter of the elevated 7 train tracks, the hot-oil sizzle of samosas, the bite of curry, and zest of cardamom and fenugreek mingle in the air. On the Lower East Side, the air is redolent with the yeasty scent of bialys and bagels, the fruity crumble of rugalach, and the tang of pickle vinegar. In Little Korea, in midtown Manhattan, each corner yields a new sensual experience: cabbage, fish, dumplings doused with soy sauce, egg cakes hot off the griddle and slipped into a wax paper bag. But like many of the mainstays of our experience of a city, food is inextricably bound up with identity—and particularly family and community identity. For recent immigrants and native New Yorkers alike, the aromas of familiar foods provide a powerful tie to their cultural heritage, and traditional styles of cooking often remain part of their repertoire long after other customs fade.

On the fourth floor of the Sears department store in the largely West Indian neighborhood of Flatbush, Brooklyn, employees gather around the Formica tables of the staff cafeteria. Motivational posters line the walls, a vending machine hums in the corner, and planters of fake poinsettias hang from the ceiling. Despite appearances, however, this isn't your typical employee café. Instead of the lingering odor of hamburgers or fried chicken, the scents

PLACE MOMENT: JACQUELYN COFFEE, CITY ISLAND

"Sitting at the end of a pier on a Saturday afternoon, sated with beer and lobster, tossing leftover French fries to the gulls, watching the jets bank for their final approach to La Guardia through a bloodshot sky with Manhattan glimmering in the distance. New York never looks any better."

Russ & Daughters' aromas are a "combination of smoke, salt, pickle, and sweet," says Mark Russ Federman. Photo: Martha Cooper.

of baked patties, pungent fish stew, and jerk chicken emanate from the steam tables. As employees receive their orders from the friendly West Indian staff, then hunker over their Styrofoam plates heaped with rice doused with piquant sauce, many are transported back to their islands a thousand miles away.

Aromas are inextricably bound up with place, and aromas of food, especially, convey the feeling of belonging. When Chinese Americans emerge from the Grand Street subway stop after a long day at work, they are embraced by the perfume of oranges and oolong tea and sponge cakes, the stench of fish splayed out on crushed ice, the heavy sapor of hot oil, and the gentler waftings of steam from dumpling carts. As they wend through the teeming markets, the sidewalks splashed with crushed ice and fruit rinds, it's like crossing the threshold into home.

Mark Russ Federman, the owner of Russ & Daughters, a renowned appetizing store on Manhattan's Lower East Side, attributes part of the success of his family's fourth-generation business to the power of smell. "Russ & Daughters has a smell that is unique among all specialty food shops," he says. "That smell is the first sensation as you open the door. . . . It is the combination of smoke, salt, pickle, and sweet. That combination is derived from the various products like smoked whitefish and salmon, pickled cucumbers and tomatoes and salt cured herrings, and the sweet aromas of halvah, rugalach, and chocolate jelly rings. One of the great perks for me, as the owner of Russ & Daughters, is to see the great sense of joy experienced by those who enter our store and are taken by the smell. How many times have customers said, with humor suffused with nostalgia, 'If only you could bottle this smell!'"

Even for native New Yorkers, whose familial connections to ethnic communities may have faded with generations, smell can take them back. At the Lexington Avenue Candy Shop, an old-fashioned soda fountain on the Upper East Side, New Yorkers can still order a coffee malted made with a puff of malt powder, or ice water served in a paper cone. The simple sensations these treats evoke can transport customers to their childhood identities, swinging feet from a dime-store stool, sucking up an extra-thick milkshake through a straw.

PLACE MOMENT: WUN KUEN NG, CHINATOWN

"On any day, the fresh vegetable and fruit stands crowd the sidewalks of Mott Street and Mulberry Street. The lively fish tanks and herbal ingredients could make even the greatest skeptic healthy. The only place where anything moving can be bought and made into a scrumptious feast. Stacked like the grand pyramids on the Nile, the array of pearly-white-emerald-green baby bok choys, orange fragrant papayas, yellow fleshy mangoes, red salmons, elegant lemongrass, plump lemons, bursting green and red peppers, and solid Asian pears, each with its name and price written in black ink on wooden panels, would make any chef's pots and pans sing. There is always an occasion to cook Chinese food naked."

Pete Benfaremo, the King with his crown. Photo © Harvey Wang.

The Lemon Ice King of Corona

How do you eat an ice? You pinch the pleated paper cup between your thumb and index finger, feeling the stifled chill seep through. You bolster your bottom lip against the edge of the cup, reach across the top with your upper lip, and pull a curl of ice into your mouth to shiver against your teeth. When you're ready for the next bite, push in the bottom of the cup; the ice will glide smoothly up, slightly melted around the edges, ready to be smoothed off the top once again. In between bites, nibble on the edge of the cup, crimping it with your teeth, invoking the Dixie-cup snacktime of schooldays. Eating an ice is a timeless art, requiring no spoons, no napkins, nothing other than a little dexterity—and, perhaps most important, an appreciation of the ephemeral nature of life's simplest joys.

52–02 108th Street at Fifty-second Avenue, Corona, Queens

(718) 699–5133

Hours: Every day 10:00 a.m. to 11:00 p.m.

Public Transit: 7 train to 103rd Street. Then take the Q23 bus at 104th Street and tell the driver your destination. Or walk along Roosevelt Avenue to 108th Street, turn right, and walk about twelve blocks to Fifty-second Avenue.

THE KING'S COURT

Peter Benfaremo, the Lemon Ice King of Corona, Queens, knows all about fleeting pleasures. "You're here today, you don't know whether you're going to live or die. Who knows? See, I'm always ready for my Maker. You have to step back a little, take a look. You'll see that there are things going on today that you can't fathom. That's philosophy, you know. I'm not a philosopher." Of course, you don't get to be the Lemon Ice King just by making ices. You have to possess a certain savoir faire to wear the crown—even if your crown is a worn cotton cap and your palace a glassed-in corner shop in Queens, nestled between an Italian pork store and the Classic Dental Spa, "Emergencies Welcome" scripted on its awning.

For years, customers have been enjoying their ices in William F. Moore Park, just across the street from the Corona shop, which boasts, along with the requisite benches, a 9/11 memorial plaque, and struggling trees, an authentic boccie court. On summer days, bystanders can observe the local Italian men playing boccie, keeping score with pins on a wooden board painted red, white, and green. During the winter, drifts of dead leaves collect in the corners of the court, and a radio in the adjacent garden shack blasts Christmas music from a local station. The court is festooned with paper lanterns, and a set of shiny grills has been set up nearby; Pete says the locals host barbecues there. A nearby tree bears a cross and an ever-changing array of testimonials to the neighborhood's latest dearly departed. Men hunch over the chess tables, savoring sandwiches from the *salumeria* across the street (the sign boasts a king of its own: the King of Italian Specialties). Indeed, saturated in a memory-making Corona flavor of food and fun, William F. Moore Park has become a requisite part of the lemon-ice-eating experience.

A SIMPLE PLEASURE, A SIMPLE RECIPE

Peter Benfaremo, or Pete, as he is affectionately called by his fans and staff, has been in the ice business since he came out of the army, in 1945; his father, a bricklayer by trade, had started the business only a year earlier. The shop used to be next door, smaller, and they hand-cranked the ice in tubs. According to Pete, the Board of Health won't allow that now, and he makes all twenty-five flavors electrically. Lemon, of course, is the perennial favorite, with peanut butter (studded with real peanuts) a close second. Lemon, chocolate, and orange ices are also offered in a sugar-free variety, one of the many acquiescences Pete has made to changing times. But his recipe remains classic: sugar,

Lemon ices cool off a summer night. Photo: Martha Cooper.

water, and flavoring. (Life's simplest pleasures, indeed!) The Benfare-mos used to sell ices only in the summertime, but now they do a brisk year-round business, though of course it's notably slower in cold weather.

As a boss, Pete is as curmudgeonly as they come, and by the nature of the business his staff appears and disappears as quickly as a lemon ice. But his employees are as loyal as his patrons, and some even send their children back to get a taste not only of the ices but of working for the King himself. "I love you, Pete," chimes a counterboy. "This guy's like a father to me."

Evidently, however, Benfaremo's laissez-faire attitude toward his own mortality does not carry over to his attitude toward mixing flavors—much less "scooping." Few things can oust Pete from his chair, eyes ablaze, like an unwitting customer asking for a scoop—or, worse, two scoops in the same cup. "We don't scoop! We *shovel!* You can't mix!

SISTER SITE:

WILLIAM F. MOORE PARK,

A K A SPAGHETTI PARK

52–02 108th Street at Corona Avenue, Corona, Queens

Public Transit: 7 train to 103rd Street. Walk from there, or take the Q23 bus at 104th and Roosevelt Avenue and tell the bus driver where you want to get off.

Built in the late 1910s, and officially named for the neighborhood's first casualty in World War I, the park is better known by its local nickname—Spaghetti Park—and for its location, across the street from the Lemon Ice King. The park's treasure is its clay-and-sand boccie court, where players from all over the city gather in the evening to play— aided by the lights installed in 1979 that make it the only nighttime boccie location and a beacon to older Italian gentlemen who love to play. Although boccie takes center stage, the park quietly hums with couples strolling or sitting on benches, enjoying ices from the Lemon Ice King, and the older men playing chess and checkers.

Why would you want to mix it? The second scoop is going to get all messy from the first flavor. You don't like it? Screw you! Too bad. Look at the sign!" He hurls an emphatic finger toward the hand-painted sign: WE DO NOT MIX OR EXCHANGE ICES. Pete clarifies, "We don't use what you think that we use when we put it in the cup. Our manner of giving out the flavors is different. Say a guy wants cherry and lemon. So you give him cherry and then you go and put the lemon on top of it—the lemon's going to get red." He demonstrates by palming a paper cup, wrenching open a freezer door, and plunging his arm deep into the frost-smoky depths. It reemerges bearing a metal paddle; there's a separate shovel for each flavor. With rhythmic thrusts of his shoulder, he works the ice to loosen it, kneading it like a potter warming up his clay. Then, with a turn of the elbow, he lifts a thick curl of ice onto the paddle, swabs it across the opening of the cup, then plunges it in again.

He drops the second shovelful on top and curls it around itself with a flick of the wrist, making a "hood." It is in the merging of the first and second scoops in the hood that the blasphemous flavor-mixing is bound to occur.

Pete presents the dainty cup between his thumb and forefinger, proud but spent. These days, the kids do most of the shoveling—and most of the tireless, patient explaining that retains the Lemon Ice King's untarnished integrity. He notices a head bobbing on the other side of the order window and whistles shrilly, "Got to keep an eye on the front!" "Oh yes, Capitán!" salutes one of the counterboys, and, putting down his card deck after another futile attempt to start a game, he scurries toward the window. To another kid Pete barks, "Start breaking those boxes up!" On the other side of the window, the tentative head queries, "Could I get a scoop of chocolate and a scoop of peanut butter?" Pete grips the edges of his chair, poised for the inevitable confrontation. But "We don't mix," explains the counterboy, gently but firmly. "Oh." A puzzled pause. "Well, then let me have one of each." Pete relaxes his grip on the chair, another battle won in the name of authentic ice. "I'm very optimistic. Why does God make me stay here? I must be doing something right."

THE LEMON ICE KING'S EMPIRE

Ices are not the only product Pete sells: At a certain point he decided candy apples might add an extra bite to his business. First-time visitors might be surprised to note that the glass windows of the Lemon Ice King shop are decorated not with pictures of ices or a roster of flavors but with tidy glass boxes housing rows of candy apples in bright red and green, some dusted with nuts or coconut. Only a few are edible; the others are decoys. "They're made of wood!" Pete exults with his trademark mischievous grin. "Crazy people buy them." In addition to the apples, the shelves along the inside of the store are lined with large glass jars of nuts, and a vase holds a dusty bouquet of American flags and pinwheels. The going rates for these accessories are scribbled in fresh ballpoint ink below the faded ice price list: Evidently, they are also a recent addition. Pete brushes their presence aside as he might a hovering mosquito on a sticky summer day, dismissing them as grudging concessions to the unpredictable allegiances of his clientele.

In a compromise with the changing times, the Lemon Ice King

opened an outpost in Pennsylvania Station not too long ago: one stand at either end of the Long Island Railroad concourse, each consisting of a plain freezer case with a plastic sign above it, and each fenced in by a soft-pretzel rack and a popcorn stand. Their clientele consists of harried commuters looking for a portable train-ride snack, rather than the lazy summer locals dawdling on the Corona street corner, reminiscing about ices past. As royal as he may be, Pete is, after all, a businessman. "Now they're so many people making ices, there's one on every corner. Every candy store, every pizza parlor, hot dog stand, they all got ice!" Yet he scoffs at his loyalists, who insist the Penn Station ices "aren't like

William F. Moore Park, boccie's Madison Square Garden. Photo: Martha Cooper.

home": "Why not? We sell it all over, California, Florida. Everyone wants to buy it. What are we in business for?" The price list for ices ranges from one dollar for the smallest paper cup to twenty-four dollars for the multigallon metal vats that ship regularly across the United States. In short, business is thriving.

Pete cites his accolades with a pride dampened only by years of being able to take it for granted. He admits he has boxes of articles at home, claims that people come to interview him every other day. Most recently, his Corona shop was, appropriately, featured in the opening credits of the sitcom *The King of Queens*. "You know, when you're known, you're known." Then he qualifies this with the Benfaremo mantra: "Listen, nobody can tell the future. There are only two things that are sure in this world:

PLACE MOMENT: CARA DE SILVA, SPAGHETTI PARK

"Spaghetti Park, in increasingly Hispanic Corona Heights, especially at dusk when the vanishing Italian American life of the city, still visible here, is caught in the glow of the park's lanterns as though preserved in amber. Men still speak Italian as they play boccie, and on the recently inaugurated Italian Day, the park's outdoor kitchen—replete with fridge, sink, stove, and deep fryer—was scheduled to produce *zeppole* for every celebrant in this tiny green bastion of resistance."

that's death and taxes. I mean, what do I care? I'm eighty-one years old, what am I going to complain? I'm here." A sly grin creeps over his face, "Unless I'm with my girlfriend, then that's something else." Peter Benfaremo stares out beyond his rows of dusty candy apples to the placid Queens street, and one gets the sense that he always sees puddles of sticky-fingered sunshine sizzling on the summer pavement.

—Caitlin Van Dusen

Coney Island Bialys and Bagels

2359 Coney Island Avenue, Sheepshead Bay, Brooklyn

(718) 339–9281

www.bialys.com

Hours: Every day 5:00 a.m. to 11:00 p.m.

Public Transit: Q train to Avenue U. Walk west (crossing numbered streets in descending order) along Avenue U about five blocks and turn right onto Coney Island Avenue.

Taped to the front of the cash register in Steve Ross's shop is a tattered Soup to Nutz cartoon in which one character asks the other, "What's a bialy?" His friend, holding aloft one of the palm-sized, Frisbee-shaped breads, replies, "If a bagel and an English muffin got married, this would be their baby." Steve's is the oldest bialy business in New York City; the product of another marriage: the gastronomic instincts of Bialystock, Poland, with the mineral-rich water and hearty appetites of New York City.

Standing in front of this modest outpost, it's hard to imagine the welcome that awaits you. Just open the door and smell the air, redolent of yeast, warm dough, and the sweet-and-sour tang of baking onion. A glass case displays wire bins of bagels and bialys in over forty varieties from the traditional to the avant-garde. A hand-printed card touts the new low-carb bagels, and a handy chart informs Weight Watchers: "Regular bialy: 3 points. With lite cream cheese: 5 points." A Snapple case, cardboard racks dispensing phone cards and Alka-Seltzer, and a few shelves of sundry goods complete the scene. At the back of the store, though, the deli facade gives way to a wooden counter dusted with flour and poppy seeds, an ancient iron bialy cutter caked with dried dough, an industrial-sized mixer, and the heart of the operation: a brick-lined oven with rotating racks, from which canvas-covered boards of golden bagels and bialys are pulled with giant wooden paddles to cool in fragrant heaps behind the counter.

INSIDE THE BAGEL AND BIALY

Steve boils his bagels, whereas many of his competitors steam them instead, a shortcut that increases quantity but deprives the bagels of the moisture and chewiness that are the earmarks of a master bagel. In the trade, boiled bagels are known as "water bagels" and steamed bagels as "rack oven bagels." The boiling process, Steve explains, pulls the starch out, making the dough softer and ensuring a longer shelf life. "We've perfected our formula," Steve proclaims. "But walk any block and you'll find three or four stores selling bagels. So I've got to try and stay a step above everybody else." That said, with a wistful laugh, he describes his attempt to cash in on the breakfast bagel fad with a Bac-O-and-egg bagel, made with real eggs and the popular kosher imitation bacon bits. "Customers came in and said, 'Oy, you're making bacon. It's no longer Jewish!' So I stopped making them. But it was a delicious bagel."

"Delicious bagel" is not a phrase that comes easily to Steve. A self-described bialy man, he makes no secret of his allegiance. "If you eat a good bialy with butter, you'll never eat another bagel." Even the mention of the word elicits a hunger in his eyes, and in his lap his fingers begin to stir almost imperceptibly, as if pressing into a round of supple dough. "I mean, I grew up making strictly bialys; we didn't get into bagels until the seventies. But my kids, they're not into bialys. The new generation doesn't know what a bialy is," he laments. Perhaps because of his loyalty to his Bialystock roots, Steve continues to offer only two varieties of bialy: traditional, with onion or garlic in the center; and cinnamon raisin, as a weekend special.

FIRST PERSON: MIMI SHERATON, *THE BIALY EATERS*

"Given the random fickleness of fate, I conjecture that one day an unbaked pletzl fell onto a bakery floor and was stepped on with the heel of a shoe. Not wanting to waste anything, the frugal baker topped it with onions and poppy seeds, baked it, tasted it, and proclaimed a eureka moment in bread history."

Not surprisingly, Steve has firm opinions about how to eat bagels and bialys. "Bagels: you slice them in half and make yourself a sandwich. People nowadays eat bialys the same way, but the traditional way was never to slice a bialy. What you did was turn the bialy over and on the

In search of the perfect bialy. Photo: Martha Cooper.

bottom you put your butter or your cream cheese. You ate it as if it was a topping. I got only one customer that does that now; he tells the clerks, 'Steve knows how I want it.' I tell my customers, this is how you're supposed to eat it. But everybody slices."

Like all true craftsmen, Steve ardently guards trade secrets. He pontificates on the relative ash content of different brands of flour as readily as on the merits of liquid versus powdered malt. And he won't reveal the source for the blueberries in what has become one of his signature bagels. "It took me about six months to find a decent blueberry," he confesses. "These are fresh blueberries. They hold their shape. A lot of the stores, the blueberries they use make purple dough. But my bagel only has a little tint of blue.

"New York is the only place you can get a true bialy," Steve avows. "A lot of bagel stores that do wholesale out in New Jersey make their own bialys, but they make them out of bagel dough." Bialys have more yeast than bagels and no sugar, and their baking methods differ too. Bagels are rolled, placed on a board, set aside while the dough rises (or "proofs"), then stored in the refrigerator, where they can rest for up to five days. Behind the massive doors of the walk-in refrigerator at Coney Island Bialys and Bagels is a "waiting room," where uncooked bagels rest in abeyance, some wan and bare, others studded with raisins, others topped with sesame or poppy seeds.

Bialys, on the other hand, are prepared and baked the same day. The dough is cut into thirty-six round balls at a time, collectively called a *teiglach,* using a bialy press. The dough balls are allowed to proof in a box, then stretched into their signature disk shape, and the depression in the middle is filled with onion or garlic before baking. Finding a qualified bialy stretcher is no easy task these days. "It can take as short as one week to learn bagels. To get the speed, that comes with time. Now with bialys, I saw someone learn within three weeks, but it usually takes a month and a half to two months to learn it. People don't have that commitment. They want it right now."

Steve's bagels are baked on metal "boards"—metal sheets covered in canvas—in the five-hundred-degree brick-lined oven outfitted with shelves that rotate along a track, like the cars on a Ferris wheel. The oven, a family heirloom, is kept running twenty-four hours a day, as is the store. Even when the window grates are down, and Coney Island Avenue is so quiet you can hear the clicks of the streetlights changing, the oven continues to creak around on its ancient hinges. Inside, simple rounds of flour, yeast, salt, and water are transformed into golden loaves, steaming up the windows and filling the air inside with a veil of flour dust.

BAGELS IN BIALYLAND

Steve Ross is a third-generation bialy maker. His grandfather Morris Rosenzweig immigrated from Bialystock, the Polish city that gave the bialy its name but where, according to the food historian Mimi Sheraton, the tradition does not survive. Morris started the business in East New York in 1920, moving it to its current location in the 1950s.

The business was strictly wholesale and strictly bialys, which were first delivered around Brooklyn by horse and buggy. In 1960, Steve's father, Donald Ross, took over, and Steve himself began to apprentice before he was ten, working his way up the ladder by grinding onions, packing bialys, and sweeping floors, stealing moments in between to clamber around on the jungle gym of flour bags in the store's basement.

Coney Island Bialys added bagels to its name in the early 1970s when Steve's father saw bagels being made and sent his brother-in-law out to learn the trade. Looking to expand their wholesale business, the family even experimented with new bagel-cutting machines but, dissatisfied, gave up after a few years and returned to rolling bagels by hand. By the late 1970s, says Steve, mass marketing by Lenders and the addition of bagels to fast-food restaurant menus brought bagels into the mainstream. "I knew a lot of people who went into the business then, and as fast as they went in they went out," Steve recalls. "Everything looks a lot easier until you realize you've got to be up at three o'clock in the morning, and you don't get home until three or four in the afternoon if you're lucky. My kids tuck me into bed at night." Steve recalls a time when he and his wife were at a gala affair and, in tuxedo and ball gown, were called back to the store to fix a broken oven. "I've slept on flour sacks, I've slept in the car. These are all part of owning a business. It's a hard business, but it's done very well for me and my family."

THE BIALY MAN LOOKS TO THE FUTURE

Coney Island Bialys and Bagels is one of only three bialy businesses left in the city, along with Kossar's, on Manhattan's Lower East Side, and Bell's, in Canarsie, which is wholesale only. In the bialy's heyday the Ross family was baking a thousand dozen bialys each day, and on Saturdays and Sundays lines of customers stretched out the door. Now the ovens churn out only a few hundred dozen bialys each day. Ask Steve why and his answers indicate that he's given it a lot of thought. For one thing, orders from local organizations have declined. If civic life is contracting, as many claim it is, then this is one more sign: the Democratic clubs, men's clubs, sisterhoods, temples, and churches that used to order regularly from Coney Island Bialys and Bagels no longer do. On

Heather, Steve, and Bryan Ross. Photo: Martha Cooper.

top of it, the costs of ingredients and utilities—like the enormous amount of water he needs for the kettle—are rising, though Steve still charges a mere forty-five cents a bagel.

Steve has also seen his clientele change. "I've got every ethnic background coming in here: Russians, Asians, African Americans. At one time the bialy was known as a Jewish food; my father used to call it the Jewish soul food. Used to be years ago there was a commercial for Philadelphia Cream Cheese: 'Spread your Philly on a bagel,' and underneath was a caption: 'What's a bagel?' Now you know everybody knows what a bagel is."

Steve is always eager to describe what happened when he tried to transport his operation to Washington, D.C., where in 2001 he was featured at the annual Smithsonian Folklife Festival on the National Mall.

"I ended up with a pot, a Chinese wok-scoop to pull the bagels out, and a pizza oven to bake everything in," he recalls with a chuckle. In the days leading up the festival, he was interviewed on the radio and mentioned that the one thing he worried about was the lack of New York City water in D.C. "New York water has always been the best tasting. It's the consistency: just the right mix of rainwater and Hudson River water." The interview came to the attention of New York City's water commissioner, and she arranged to ceremoniously truck down gallons of New York City water to the Ross family tent at the festival.

Despite the shifts in local business, his wholesale business ships bialys to fans and nostalgic customers as far abroad as Nigeria and Great Britain. Yet Steve seems skeptical that his children will pick up the business in his wake. His daughter comes in during the holidays and some weekends, but at age sixteen her ambitions are elsewhere. Steve isn't concerned, though; he still has plenty of time to fulfill his mission of whetting the Big Apple's appetite for bialys, hot out of the oven, dusty with flour and spiked with crisp, caramelized onion, and served—unsliced—with butter on the bottom.

—*Caitlin Van Dusen*

SISTER SITE: KOSSAR'S BIALYS

367 Grand Street, Lower East Side, Manhattan

(212) 473–4810

www.kossarsbialys.com

Hours: Monday through Thursday and Sunday 6:00 a.m. to 8:00 p.m.; Friday 6:00 a.m. to 3:00 p.m.; closed Saturday

Public Transit: F train to Delancey Street or East Broadway.

Kossar's is located next to the shrunken but still thriving Jewish enclave on the Lower East Side. Established in 1936, the current shop is mostly a factory, with a small retail counter out front. Like Coney Island Bialys and Bagels, Kossar's also does a big Web-order business. The writer Laura Silver is a devoted Kossar's customer and recommends a trip there "anytime except the Jewish Sabbath, when they're closed. The whole place is covered in a fine layer of flour. The onion and garlic smell will snare you in from anywhere on the Lower East Side. Learn the names of bread shapes you never imagined. Bulka is my favorite."

Sahadi's Specialty
and Middle Eastern Foods

The scent of coffee grounds mingled with cardamom, dunes of semolina flour and vermillion paprika bulging from glass jars, the tang of an olive melting in your mouth: few places tantalize like Sahadi's Specialty and Middle Eastern Foods. As if the aromas could carry that far, this mainstay of Atlantic Avenue's Middle Eastern shopping strip in downtown Brooklyn draws customers from surrounding neighborhoods and throughout the city.

187 Atlantic Avenue, Boerum Hill, Brooklyn

(718) 624–4550

www.sahadis.com

Hours: Monday through Friday 9:00 a.m. to 7:00 p.m.; Saturday 8:30 a.m. to 7:00 p.m.

Public Transit: 2, 3, 4, 5 trains to Borough Hall or M, R trains to Court Street. Walk south on Court Street from four to six blocks (depending on the exit you use) and turn right onto Atlantic Avenue.

YOU WANT FIVE OUNCES OF PEANUTS OR A TWENTY-POUND BAG?

Customers come to find ingredients for a Middle Eastern meal and also for bargains on bulk-rate olive oil, grains, and spices. Sahadi's regularly stocks 150 varieties of cheese (including five types of feta), several dozen varieties of olives, and twenty-four olive oils, in industrial tin vats and svelte glass bottles with sprigs of herbs suspended inside. The most thrilling section of the store for most customers is bulk foods. Pass under a brick archway strung with baskets and you're faced with over one hundred brimming containers of roasted and raw nuts (pistachios, almonds, cashews, even the bright red candied Chinese peanuts called crecre), glass jars of dried fruits (bananas, strawberries, cherries, dates, apricots), and bins of rice, oats, and flour. Alongside are sacks of herbs, dried vegetables, and spices (including sumac and a special flavoring made from cherry pits). Racks are stacked with fresh-baked bread, from traditional round loaves and baguettes to sheetlike Afghan handkerchief bread, which folds into quarters and can be used to pick up fingerfuls of hummus and tabbouleh. There are candied treats worthy of the *Nutcracker:* Turkish delight, halvah, pastel-colored Jordan almonds. A refrigerator proffers thick Greek yogurt, kefir, and fresh cheeses. In the back of the store is the prepared foods counter: baba gannoujh, tabbouleh flecked with parsley and cherry tomatoes, grilled chicken, kibbeh, and swirling vats of what is reputed to be the city's best hummus.

In the middle of it all, the fabled red ticket machine spits out paper numbers to lines of customers while blue-aproned employees scoop and weigh and pour. "It gets a little hectic around the holidays," one worker remarks," but for the most part we all get along great." There are fifty employees of Sahadi's Foods, working in the Atlantic Avenue store and the wholesale warehouse in Sunset Park, Brooklyn. The wholesale business probably brings in more revenue, but it's Atlantic Avenue's old-fashioned market atmosphere that gives the company its reputation. At heart, its owner—Charles Sahadi, affectionately known as Charlie to customers and staff alike—is committed to the in-store shopping experience: seeing the lentils weighed and measured, feeling the heft of a loaf

**FIRST PERSON:
ABDEEN JABARA, QUOTED IN
*A COMMUNITY OF MANY
WORLDS: ARAB AMERICANS
IN NEW YORK CITY***

"While growing up in a small northern Michigan town in the 1940s where our family owned and operated a grocery store, I first came into contact with the Arab settlement in Brooklyn. From time to time my parents would order different ingredients for 'Arabic food' from Sahadi's or Malko Brothers on Atlantic Avenue in Brooklyn. I remember well the cartons arriving and the excitement that we had opening them to get the spices and grains, the *tahini* and *halawah*, which were not available to us except from cities in downstate Michigan. . . . Despite our isolation from any Arab community and the fact that we rarely traveled away from our home town, I had a sense that New York City was a lively and copious center of Arab American life."

Charlie Sahadi, a "grocer at heart." Photo: Martha Cooper.

Sahadi's helped transform Atlantic Avenue into a Middle Eastern cornucopia. Photo: Martha Cooper.

of bread in the palm, smelling the cheese, sampling the olives and dried apricots. He also savors the thought that in a bulk foods market a customer can buy five pistachios or a bushel, enough flour to bake a cake or enough to stock the cabinets for a year. Thus the customer is given the opportunity to try new flavors and foods virtually risk free, satiating exactly the type of gastronomic curiosity for which Sahadi's exists.

When Sahadi's expanded its floor space in 1985, Charlie's oldest daughter, Christine, a finance major at New York University, suggested the family add a prepared foods section. Charlie decided to let her give it a try, just as his great-uncle had with his father. So, with faith in the increasing appeal of ready-made food, Christine attended classes at night and worked during the day in the store with her mother, Audrey Sahadi, to start up the new department. The prepared foods counter, with its affiliated catering business, is now a success. Still, Charlie stays true to his mission of bulk foods and bulk prices. "I call us an ingredients store. The prepared foods section is really just a way of showing people what to do with the ingredients that we sell."

The secret behind Sahadi's success may well be its affable owner. "There are times I meet customers who knew me when I was born," Charlie remarks. "I like to float through the store, ask 'How's your mother?' And I'm asking because I really care. There's usually a Sahadi on the premises. I don't believe in absentee management. I sweep the sidewalk. I do the bagging at the register; it gives me a chance to talk to the customers. There are no prima donnas here. We don't allow it."

FROM SYRIA TO BROOKLYN

Charlie Sahadi's father came here from Lebanon after World War I. Following a long apprenticeship in his uncle's grocery business in downtown Manhattan, he started Sahadi's Importing Company in 1941, two blocks from his uncle on Washington Street near Rector, near the now long-gone, but once-bustling, Washington Market. The area already was an important settlement for fellow Arabic-speaking immigrants from the Syrian province of the Ottoman Empire (including what is now Lebanon) who had been coming in force since the 1890s. The rest of New York called this "Little Syria." Smaller colonies had already spun off, including an important one in South Ferry in Brooklyn, spanning today's neighborhoods of Brooklyn Heights and Cobble Hill.

Sahadi's moved to its current location in 1948, perhaps in pursuit of customers, but certainly because construction of the Brooklyn Battery Tunnel forcibly relocated Little Syria. "I was four years old," Charlie recalls. "I have the smallest recollection of banging nails into the wall, putting up the shelves. Everything was in wood." From those first nails, a family institution was born: Today, Charlie's brother, wife, son, daughter, and son-in-law work in the store, and they will no doubt press hammers into the hands of their children.

By the time Sahadi's arrived in Brooklyn, the colony was already transitioning from a mixed residential and commercial community to one primarily commercial. Many considered it the principal Middle Eastern commercial quarter on the entire East Coast. Atlantic Avenue was its main thoroughfare. Syrian and Lebanese customers still shopped and ate out in the district and attended church there. This was a primarily Christian enclave, distinct from the Syrian Jews, whose contemporaneous migration brought them first to the Lower East Side and then deeper into South Brooklyn, and different from the largely Muslim influx of Arabic-speaking Palestinians and Yemenites, whose migra-

---

A taste of Damascus Bread and Pastry Shop. Photo: Martha Cooper.

tion to New York and settlement in downtown Brooklyn followed the easing of immigration restrictions in 1965. The bus from Bay Ridge, where many Middle Eastern New Yorkers now reside, stops on the corner right outside Sahadi's. But as downtown Brooklyn becomes increasingly gentrified, longtime customers are being supplemented with gastronomically curious newcomers.

Charlie Sahadi has distinct memories, however, of the days when his business was considered exotic rather than gourmet. "One day in the sixties, I was refilling the nuts in the front of the store and two ladies came in. They walked up and down the aisles, and as they were walking out one said to the other, 'Who would buy in a store like this?' I was taken aback. I asked myself, 'What do we have that is so strange? We have cashew nuts, almonds, walnuts, pistachios.' But those were not mainstream. Nobody was selling bulk in the sixties. That was something that was done in the twenties and thirties." The other destination in New York City for bulk foods in the mid-twentieth century was the predominately Jewish Lower East Side. Charlie insists that not only did he share suppliers with his Manhattan competitors, but with food as a "great equalizer" the two communities managed to peacefully coexist despite potential cultural and political tensions.

SISTER SITE: DAMASCUS BREAD AND PASTRY SHOP

195 Atlantic Avenue, Boerum Hill, Brooklyn

(718) 625–7070

www.damascuspastry.com

Public Transit: 2, 3, 4, 5 trains to Borough Hall or M, R trains to Court Street.

Next door to Sahadi's is Damascus Bread and Pastry Shop, part of a family baking enterprise founded by Hassan Halaby in 1930, in the early days of Brooklyn's Arabic-speaking colony. Fresh pita bread (then called Syrian bread) and savory spinach and meat pies were the bakery's first offerings. Today Damascus specializes in both savories and sweets, such as baklava, bird's nests, and mamool. If you are looking for bakery products such as pita, zhater, and tahini breads, owner Dennis Halaby will refer you to his cousin's Damascus Bakery plant in Brooklyn's DUMBO neighborhood—another spin-off from the original family business.

"I'M A GROCER AT HEART"

Charlie is keenly aware of his competition and frequently peruses the aisles of Zabar's, Fairway, Citarella, Dean and Deluca, and Gourmet Garage, seeing what they stock, what their prices are, who's shopping there, and what they're buying. He admits that he hasn't given as much attention to the store's Web site as perhaps he should, given the growing clout of supplemental online retailing for stores. He also admits to feeling slightly threatened by the increasing predominance of club stores such as Costco, which have begun to stock more specialty and gourmet items. Ultimately, though, he expects that these trends will bring more customers to his store, as they get a taste of his featured ingredients through more mainstream outlets and then seek them out locally. "I try not to fear. I am not any of them; I am me. If I pay the wrong price, I find out where to get a better deal and I try to correct it. I'm an interested spectator and participant. I shop a lot, and I like to see what other people do. If I walk through another gourmet store and I see the shelves are in disarray, I actually straighten the jars out. It's compulsive: You want the labels facing forward. I'm a grocer at heart."

—*Caitlin Van Dusen*

Arthur Avenue Market

"It was my mother's broken heart that brought me to the Arthur Avenue Market in the first place," writes the Italian American poet and performer Annie Lanzillotto. In 1993, her mother suffered an aortic aneurysm while she was making pasta. Annie said,

2344 Arthur Avenue, Belmont, the Bronx

(718) 367–5686

Hours: Monday through Saturday 6:00 a.m. to 6:00 p.m.

Public Transit: 2, 5 trains to Pelham Parkway, then BX12 bus going west to Arthur Avenue.

4 train to Fordham Road, then BX12 bus going east to Arthur Avenue.

Picture this, a woman, like countless women, with a silver pot of boiling water on her stove. Suddenly she falls and breaks into a sweat. "It's nothing," she says, "I just need to lie down." Eight minutes later she is in an ambulance. Six hours later she is on the operating table. There was a hole in the wall of her aorta. Then came the day she was to take her first "daytrip," six months later.

"Hey, Ma, where do you want to go?"

"Arthur Avenue," she said.

I witnessed my mother's weird pilgrimage back to the salamis, back to the Bronx where her father is buried, where her mother first stepped into shoes in this country, where something began, that is not yet finished.

FROM SALAMIS TO CIGARS

Far from finished, Arthur Avenue Market today can still intoxicate visitors with a barrage of smells, the sight of fourteen different types of prosciutto, and glimpses of the friendly staff who seem to

With the help of Mayor Fiorello La Guardia, Joe Liberatore transitioned from peddler to merchant. Photo: Elena Martínez.

peek through the salamis, cheeses, and other foods hanging above the counters.

Walking into what appears to be a nondescript warehouse, it's only a few steps to Pete's Meat Market, owned by Peter Rella and his nephew Mike Rella, from Bari, Italy. Nearby, Mike's Deli was taken over by Michele (Mike) Greco in the 1960s, and in 1992 his son, David, took over the business. Visiting Mike's is like visiting an old-world Italian *salumeria*—the Italian word for deli. In Italy they carry sausages and cheese. Mike's specializes in foods and dishes from Calabria, his family's hometown. They make roughly one hundred pounds of fresh mozzarella every day, and they're the ones that sell fourteen different types of prosciutto. One of Mike's specialties is pizza rustica, filled with prosciutto, sausage, and cheese, a traditional dish eaten at Easter in Italy. The market has changed somewhat since the time when Italian was the only language heard in its aisles, spoken by the merchants and the clientele alike, but the feeling is still reminiscent of those days. Mike Rella says, "It's like you live in your own little town in Italy," and David Greco echoes, "I'm in Italy every day!"

But the market, like Joe Liberatore's houseplants nearby, is planted in the hothouse of New York, and it is replete with the novel juxtapositions of diverse cultures coming together under the same roof. La Casa Grande Cigar Company is a few feet away—an unadorned operation where you can watch the workers hand-rolling cigars. *Wait,* you say to yourself. *What are* cigars *doing here?* But that's the beauty of a real market: the element of surprise.

IS A PUSHCART STILL A PUSHCART WHEN IT'S MOVED INDOORS?

The Arthur Avenue Market is located on one of the main thoroughfares in Belmont, a neighborhood known as the "Little Italy of the Bronx." There is still a village flavor to this part of the Bronx: its two-story homes, well-groomed churches, quiet residential streets, and busy small shops and restaurants draw you in— in that almost imperceptible way villages have of creating intimacy within their boundaries. In the late nineteenth and early twentieth centuries, the area was almost entirely settled by Italian immigrants, many of whom came from Sicily, Calabria, and Campania and were drawn to the Bronx by industrial jobs

FIRST PERSON:
ANNIE LANZILLOTTO, "HOW TO COOK A HEART"

In 1996, Bronx-born performance artist Annie Lanzillotto became the artist-in-residence at Arthur Avenue Market, where she conducted site-specific art with the merchants in a valentine to her Italian American upbringing in the Bronx. She created live scenes in which merchants sang opera and couples began to argue loudly in a mixture of English and Italian, threatening divorce to the astonishment of customers. She also asked the proprietor of Mario's Meat Specialties how he goes about cooking lamb hearts for a booklet laden with metaphor she called "How to Cook a Heart."

Mario: And there's another [recipe]. My mother-in-law told me last night. You make a hole in the heart. She makes it that way.

Annie: A hole in the heart?

Mario: I've had it that way.

Annie: How do you make the hole?

Mario: What you do is you cut the bottom of the heart. You cut. Then you take the hole. And you chop it very, very small.

Annie: You cut like a circle?

Mario: First you cut the bottom. That's the nerves, the fat. You throw that away. Then you turn the heart over. Yes, like a circle, and you—

Annie: You scoop it.

Mario: Yeah. And that you chop, you save it. You put it aside. Get parsley. Get Romano cheese. And garlic. And chop it. You know, grated cheese, and you mix it all together, cheese, garlic, parsley, and pieces of the heart, and you mix it all together and you stuff it that way. You put it back in the heart.

Annie: Like you bury it in the heart.

Mario: Yes. Put them in. Let them cook. About 350.

Annie: How do you know when it's done?

Mario: You know.

Annie: How long does it take?

Mario: It depends on the heart.

---

as well as by the promise of better housing than that available on the Lower East Side and in East Harlem.

Like most of those who lived in New York's immigrant neighborhoods, locals bought their food from nearby pushcarts and open-air markets. In New York City at the beginning of the nineteenth century, peddlers sold fruit and vegetables in the street. Pushcart peddling started on the Lower East Side in the 1860s, reportedly on Hester Street. Soon stationary open-air pushcart markets appeared throughout the city. Requiring little capital or command of the English language, street peddling had attracted twenty-five thousand immigrants by 1900. Most of the immigrant vendors were men, but in the Jewish community on the Lower East Side it was common to see women selling their wares as well.

Thousands of pushcarts thronged the city's narrow streets, generating so much refuse and so many complaints from competing (and taxpaying) storekeepers that in 1938—deep into the Great Depression—Mayor Fiorello La Guardia abolished the open markets and banned the pushcarts. Using funds and labor provided by the federal government's economic stimulus program, the Works Progress Administration, La Guardia arranged to construct indoor municipal retail markets to house the former pushcart vendors. In October 1940, the Arthur Avenue Retail Market opened at its current location. It contained 117 six-by-seven-foot stalls, and the merchants were predominantly Italian.

Sister municipal markets opened on the Lower East Side and in East Harlem. This was not one of La Guardia's more popular decisions. Former pushcart peddlers struggling in tough times could not always afford even the low rents the city charged for inside stalls. And immigrant shoppers, accustomed to such proximity they nearly stumbled over the pushcarts as they walked out their front doors, found the new system less convenient and the goods more expensive.

Joe Liberatore, who at eighty-three still sells at Arthur Avenue, was one of the merchants who successfully transitioned from pushcart to market. Joe was born in Connecticut but spent his childhood in Italy. He returned to the United States as a teenager and settled in the Bronx with his father. In 1936, at the age of seventeen, he started working as a pushcart peddler selling vegetables and fruit, whatever was available: string beans, strawberries, garlic, lemons. A typical day began at two or three in the morning. He would take the Third Avenue el to the Washington Market in downtown Manhattan. The food had to be bought

Mike's Deli at Arthur Avenue Market is inspired by Italian *salumerie*. Photo: Elena Martínez.

fresh daily because there was no refrigeration in the pushcart. Returning to the Bronx, he worked at his cart until seven or eight in the evening, when he would take everything off the pushcart and store any leftovers in his building's basement. He persevered, despite his parents' concern about the harsh conditions of pushcart vending. The hours were long, and the work sometimes backbreaking. Joe remembers having to burn newspapers in a bucket to keep warm in the cold weather.

Then one day, he recalls, "there was a rumor that Mayor La Guardia was going to build a market, and I told my parents, 'Well, if they are

going to make a market, I'll go inside. Otherwise I'll do something else.'"
Joe recalls that some vendors objected to moving and to the increase
in fees: from one dollar for a street permit to four dollars for market
space. For those who survived the change, like Joe, being part of the
market brought benefits, such as being able to close up at six o'clock
when the market closed, and not having to worry about the weather.
Their social status changed, too. "They used to call us peddlers," Joe recalls. "But when the market opened, the mayor said, 'Those people over
there, the poor peddlers, now they will go inside and you're not going to
call them peddlers anymore, you will call them merchants.'" And a
merchant Joe has been, all these years, still ready to retool rather than
give up. Wanting an easier pace as he passed retirement age nearly
twenty years ago, Joe switched from produce to plants and seeds. Check
out his stand at Easter for palm crosses and hand-painted dry gourds,
and in the summer for delicious tomatoes.

IT'S UP TO THE VENDOR

City government under Mayor La Guardia in the 1930s and 1940s
took on all sorts of new responsibilities. The indoor municipal markets formed part of a larger municipal embrace that included public
transportation, public housing, public parks, highways, and more. By
the 1980s, much had changed, and city government hoped to relinquish
some of the responsibilities it had accrued over the years. Vendors in the
Arthur Avenue Market learned around this time that the city planned
to shut down their market because sanitation and maintenance costs
had soared higher than officials wanted to pay. Now it was up to the
vendors themselves to save the place, and they did, forming a co-op of
merchants to manage the building (which remains in the city's hands).
Merchant control, plus a little renovation, repainting, and air-conditioning—with help from Belmont's Local Development Corporation—
has made a big difference. The number of vendors is down to sixteen
from the twenty-five who confronted the closing crisis in the 1980s, but
each remaining vendor has more space, and business seems to be good.

Fewer Italians now live in the area, which means that the remaining

SISTER SITE: LA MARQUETA

Park Avenue between 114th Street and 115th Street, East Harlem, Manhattan

(212) 534–4900

Hours: Monday through Saturday 7:30 a.m. to 9:30 p.m. (individual vendors differ)

Public Transit: 6 train to 116th Street.

East Harlem got its own municipal market in 1936. The Park Avenue Market opened beneath the Park Avenue subway viaduct between 111th and 116th streets. It catered primarily to Jewish customers, but as the neighborhood transformed into El Barrio, the largest Puerto Rican enclave in the city, shoppers dubbed their market La Marqueta. Many of the original Jewish and Italian vendors hung on to their stalls, learning Spanish and adding new types of produce. News, gossip, job leads—all were exchanged here along with food and household goods. Felipe Colón remembers the Saturdays when shopping at La Marqueta meant seeing people from your island hometown and finding out about new arrivals, marriages, births, baptisms—all the facts of community life that keep people knitted together. For Maritza Acosta, La Marqueta meant "cilantro, sofrito, adobo, shouted prices and orders in Spanish—'dos pesos' (two pounds or two dollars)—the sounds of cracking bone with cleaver, and over all, the tremble and roar of the trains overhead."

La Marqueta thrived until the 1970s, when among other troubles a fire in one of the buildings hastened the market's deterioration. Neighborhood loyalty to the market has supported over the years a series of attempted overhauls. One is happening right now and promises to expand La Marqueta back to its queenly four-block-long size. Today, only two blocks of the cinder-block structure are open for shopping—between 113th and 115th streets—and fewer than a dozen vendors are still in business. Customers still come daily, however, for meat and fish (including Caribbean favorites such as bacalao—dried, salted cod), plus fresh farmer's market produce on Saturdays, as well as merchandise such as toys, cell phones, and fancy cake-decorating tools.

merchants, churches, and cultural facilities have to work a bit harder to help people remember the neighborhood's Italian legacy. Now the area is shared by a large number of New Yorkers from Puerto Rico, Mexico, and Albania. But the Italian presence is still palpable, and the food is still great.

—Elena Martínez

Union Square Greenmarket

East Seventeenth Street and Broadway, Union Square, Manhattan

Hours: Year-round, Monday, Wednesday, Friday, and Saturday 8:00 a.m. to 6:00 p.m.

Public Transit: L, N, Q, R, W, 4, 5, 6 trains to Fourteenth Street/Union Square. The market wraps around the north and west sides of the park. Look for Petco and Barnes & Noble on the north side.

Around 9:30 a.m. every Wednesday, Colin Alevras, the chef and owner of the Tasting Room restaurant in the East Village, throws a large, empty blue hiking pack on his back, unlocks his bike, and pushes off the curb outside the restaurant. He is on his way to the Union Square Greenmarket—simultaneously his muse, his exclusive purveyor, his social outlet, and his professional raison d'être. Thousands of us more ordinary cooks join him, all of us beguiled by the chance to buy fully fresh-tasting food from the farmers who actually grow it. Meandering from vendor to vendor among throngs of shoppers in the midst of historic Union Square is a quintessential urban delight.

THE CENTER OF MANY CIRCLES

During peak season at Union Square, shoppers thread their way through seventy different stalls selling fresh fruit, vegetables, eggs, breads, dairy, fish, meat, flowers, and products like maple syrup and handmade pretzels. Not just abundance but also variety—as in thirty different kinds of mushrooms—are the hallmarks of this market. The diversity is driven by demand. Ron Binaghi of Stokes Farm in Bergen County, New Jersey, a fifth-generation farmer, recalls that when

From an urban farm dating back to 1873 all the way to Union Square. Photo: Martha Cooper.

he started at Union Square nearly thirty years ago he only sold tomatoes, eggplant, peppers, and strawberries. Local chefs began to tell him they needed more specialized items like, say, fresh marjoram. Frustrated by the bad taste of produce trucked in from out of the area, they wanted their ingredients grown locally. So Ron set out to supply them. Today he plants more than half of his seventeen acres in herbs. Exchanges between farmers and cooks are replicated by exchanges among the farmers themselves. Although vendors are often too busy helping customers to discuss crops with each other, information is often gleaned just by observing the other stands. Farmer Alex Pathenroth joked that before he joined the greenmarket, biodiversity at his farm meant that once every seven years he would change his crop for a year and then go back to onions for another seven. He now grows three hundred different crops. His launch into biodiversity started at the market when he noticed, "Hey, the guy across from me is growing blueberries, I can grow blueberries."

The market is also a place where strangers talk to each other—about food, about the neighborhood, about the season as evidenced by the displays in the produce stands. "A trip to the Union Square Greenmarket is always fun," Alevras says, "particularly for chefs, who spend fifteen-to-eighteen-hour days isolated in their cave, cooking. In the market you ask what someone is doing with this year's crop of *this,* or if they've found a good source for *such and such.* Every time you turn around there's someone else you want to say hi to, so you stop, drink coffee, stare at a radish and talk. . . and all of a sudden you realize you've been doing it for an hour and a half!" Greenmarket publicity manager Gabrielle Langholtz affirms that, for many, the market experience is as much social as culinary. Proof came a few years back when the city tried to move some stalls to a narrower stretch of sidewalk, igniting vigorous public protest. "Objectively," Langholtz says, "the ordinance still left plenty of room for shopping, but not nearly enough room to linger and talk. One letter said it clearly: 'I'm not just there for the food.' "

**FIRST PERSON:
ELIZABETH RYAN,
BREEZY HILL ORCHARD**

"When each generation of immigrants arrived in the New World, they brought their own varieties of apples until, by the turn of the century, more than a thousand varieties flourished in the United States—golden russets, sheepsnose, smokehouse, maiden's blush, Chenango strawberry, their very names revealing so many exquisite and varied tastes. With the rise of supermarkets, the variety dwindled, until most American consumers today buy a single variety of apple—Red Delicious—and not for its taste but for its nonseasonal quality and its appearance, enhanced by an edible polish made by the same people who manufacture Johnson's floor wax. Apples have lost their sense of 'appleness' and left us with an impoverishment of tastes."

Spend a little time walking among the stands in Union Square. You can feel the commitment of shoppers and producers. "I was here the day I graduated high school," Ron Binaghi recalls. "I sold a bunch of strawberries, went home, graduated high school. Heck, I was here the day I got married! That was a Saturday. Sunday we went to the Poconos for our honeymoon. I told my wife I had to be back on Wednesday to go to market. 'What?' she says. 'You gotta be where?' 'I got market on Wednesday,' I told her. 'We're picking red peppers. Do you know how much red peppers are worth? We gotta get back.' My wife is thinking, *This is what I'm getting into?* As it turns out, I'd have been zero without her. She does all the books, writes the checks. I grow all the stuff. We complement each other: She's more business, I'm more the romantic type."

The whole greenmarket experience ultimately comes through in every bite. As Alevras says, "Union Square is about getting stuff you feel good about from people that you have a relationship with—one that you build up five or ten minutes at a time for ten years. I don't know that everybody can actually taste all that directly, but I think sometimes people can—and they definitely know when it's not there; the dish will just miss. I want to know where the ingredient comes from; it's important. Otherwise, there's no love for it."

HOW TO REMAKE A PLACE

The Union Square Greenmarket is the oldest, the largest, and the most diverse of New York City's forty-two greenmarkets, and it is one of the largest outdoor farmer's markets in the northeastern United States. Barry Benepe, a native New Yorker, art historian, and urban planner, started New York's greenmarkets in 1976 to resuscitate what he called "metropolitan" farmland and farmers (those within a 120-mile radius of New York City) and to bring fresh, good-quality food to the city. Other people around the country experimented with similar ideas in the 1970s, such as legendary chef Alice Waters, who opened Chez Panisse restaurant in Berkeley, California, and pioneered a culinary movement that celebrated seasonal local produce and the farmers who grew it.

Benepe and his associates had urban reform in mind as well. By the

1970s, once thriving Union Square had been devastated—like many other places that became greenmarkets, brought down by disinvestment, the city's fiscal crisis, government policies that privileged the suburbs, drugs, and crime. Most New Yorkers circled around four-acre Union Square rather than risk walking through, making it the kind of place Benepe believed the farmers could help. "Farmers selling produce from their trucks would start conversations, help resuscitate neighborhoods, and brighten the aesthetic of the troubled town." He searched out aid from agricultural specialists at Rutgers and Cornell universities. Together they publicized the new greenmarkets to agricultural agents and associations throughout metropolitan New York and New Jersey, who in turn spread the word to farmers. Benepe and crew did not ex-

The city's oldest and largest greenmarket welcomes you. Photo: Martha Cooper.

pect to attract large wholesale growers. They concentrated on small- and medium-scale farmers, who often did their own marketing, and reached out to part-time and backyard farmers to simultaneously encourage the start-up of new farms.

The first farmers came from all over metropolitan New York. Benepe wrote about them in his now classic 1977 report, *Greenmarkets: The Rebirth of Farmers Markets in New York City*. There were "a number of 'black dirt' vegetable growers from the rich muckland soil areas of Orange County, fourth-generation fruit growers with orchards overlooking the Hudson River, a Chinese vegetable farmer from far eastern

SISTER SITE: STOKES FARM

23 DeWolf Road, Old Tappan, NJ 07675

(201) 768–3931

www.stokesfarm.com

Located in northeastern New Jersey, only twenty-five miles from Manhattan, Stokes Farm was among the original twelve farms that participated in the New York City greenmarket system. It is one of the few surviving urban farms, started in 1873, when Isaiah Stokes bought forty acres of property in Old Tappan, New Jersey. The farm has, over 130 years, changed from a wholesale vegetable farm to a retail-based specialty herb and vegetable producer. The New York City greenmarket system played no small part in this shift in operations. Ron Binaghi Jr., the current operator of Stokes Farm; his wife, Jeanie, the farm's retail manager; Tom Margotta, the greenmarket and farm manager; and Ron Binaghi III, the youngest family member to take fresh food to the streets of New York City, all have the goal of keeping the farm in business for future generations to enjoy. You can find Stokes Farm stands (filled with flowers, garden plants, squash, peppers, heirloom tomatoes, eleven kinds of eggplant, and dozens of herbs) at three Manhattan locations: Union Square Greenmarket, Richard Tucker Square Market, and Tribeca Market.

Their sign reads: "We would like to say thank you to all of the customers who have supported us for the past twenty-seven years at Union Square. Through the cold and heat, hurricanes and subway crashes, you still come down to the market to see what's new, chat or just hang out. We appreciate your friendship."—The Binaghi Family, a sixth-generation farming family

Long Island, a wine grape grower from the Finger Lakes district of western New York State, a honey producer from the southern part of New Jersey and a plant grower from New York City itself."

Ron Binaghi, one of the pioneer dozen, was sixteen years old when the market was established. He recalls: "We used to pull our produce truck in and back up onto the sidewalk of the pavilion. There were vagrants sleeping all over the place. On rainy days it was scary because all the wackos from the park would come into the pavilion for shelter. They would yell obscenities at us. But I was sixteen, so I thought it was cool. My friends always wanted to hear my stories. I didn't realize it was dangerous or could've been perceived as dangerous. It was just cool to come to the city with my dad."

The presence of the Greenmarket farmers and the families, cooks, and neighbors they attracted gradually helped to make the park safer and more active. The city's economic recovery in the 1980s also brought investors to the Union Square area, and new businesses, luxury apartments, and restaurants featuring greenmarket food began to ring the square. In 1985, the city redesigned and rebuilt Union Square, raising the hackles of many by cutting down trees, but at the same time improving visibility and safety. In a separate development, but one that further affirmed the square as a special place, longtime union activists successfully managed in 1998 to have the square declared a National Historic Landmark. Periodic ceremonies, and now an arc of brass plaques engraved with historical images along the square's southern border, recall its role as a center for labor and social protest from the late 1800s through World War II. It was the site, for instance, of the country's first Labor Day Parade, on September 5, 1882. In 2001, after September 11, the square exploded with homespun memorials and protest demonstrations, and it remains a site of resistance with speakers and placards, particularly on the Fourteenth Street side, to this day.

THE MARKET MATTERS

Greenmarket staff in the early years had worked near miracles to get the markets instituted and sites secured for use. No fewer than eight city agencies needed to give their approval, as did numerous political bodies and interest groups. Despite these early successes, for all the ensuing years at Union Square, farmers have been on one-year leases, paying rent for their space to the Department of Parks and Recreation. Binaghi, who also leads the Greenmarket Farmers Coalition, says it left the growers feeling very vulnerable. Finally, in 2004, Adrian Benepe, the parks commissioner and brother of Barry, gave Union Square growers a ten-year lease. "We've parked," says Binaghi. "It's the first time that we've ever had more than one year. The farmers here are breathing a little sigh of relief."

By the way, not all Union Square vendors are farmers. Take Alex and Stephanie Villani of Blue Moon Fish, for example, who met in Union Square. Direct selling to consumers is better business for the Villanis than selling to wholesalers, and it's also more rewarding. Alex, who has been a fisherman for thirty years, never had anyone thank him for a piece of fish until he started working at the greenmarket. "I really appreciate it," he says, "when someone comes by and says, 'Hey, that was a great sea bass.' With wholesaling it just goes in a box and gets shipped out and a week later you get a check and never hear anything more." Stephanie adds, "Another thing about Union Square is that we have customers from everywhere. People from Africa make a stew out of my smoked fish; Italians, West Indians, and everybody else. It's cool to find out all the different ways they like to cook. It's one of the things we like about coming to the city."

—Makalé Faber

Art and Music, City Style

First appearing as unsigned art in public places, the distinctive work of Keith Haring is exhibited and collected by major museums around the world. Photo © Hazel Hankin Photography.

Art and music lovers worldwide set forth on pilgrimages to New York City's cultural temples—the Metropolitan Museum of Art, Carnegie Hall, Lincoln Center, the Brooklyn Academy of Music—only to discover, outside, on the streets, often adjoining the sites, artists of all kinds shamelessly spreading their wares along the sidewalk. In New York, artists perform in the parks, breakdance in the subways, play Jewish klezmer fiddle tunes outside of Broadway theaters, create a stage for pantomime on the broad steps of the public library. The creative cauldron is forever spilling out onto the streets.

In turn, New York City's streets have always served as inspiration for its grand galleries, museums, and music halls. Graffiti artists, for instance, most notably Dondi, Keith Haring, and Basquiat, appear in shows at the Brooklyn Museum and the Whitney. In turn, renowned artists such as Elizabeth Murray, Jacob Lawrence, and Roy Lichtenstein create public art for the subways.

From the late 1940s through the 1960s, East Harlem and the Melrose, Mott Haven, Longwood, and Hunts Point areas of the South Bronx were, according to residents, "a hotbed of Latin music," with percussionists, singers, and dancers moving from playing rhythms on car hoods to performing in local dance halls and theaters, eventually transforming Cuban rhythms into a New York Latin sound in venues like the Palladium in Manhattan. In the 1950s, doo-wop music sung in Bronx alleyways and gospel from the city's storefront churches

PLACE MOMENT: CARA DE SILVA, CENTRAL PARK

"Shakespeare in the Park on a balmy night when the trees of Central Park become the Forest of Arden."

Drumming circles of many varieties resound throughout New York City's parks. Photo © Hazel Hankin Photography.

influenced the music created in the Brill Building, where duos such as Leiber and Stoller, and Carole King and Gerry Goffin, were given cubicles to compose the music for a generation. The folk music scene in Washington Square Park in the 1960s strummed in harmony with the Bottom Line and the Village Vanguard and changed American music with performers such as Bob Dylan.

Hip-hop grew up during the years that followed the burning of the Bronx in the 1970s and 1980s. During the height of the destruction, Latino and black teenagers, like the mambo and salsa musicians before them, held parties and jams in schools, basements, parks, and playgrounds—even in the burnt-out buildings that became their clubhouses. By the early 1980s, hip-hop was "discovered" by record promoters who froze it on CDs and shifted the emphasis away from bragging rights on the street to success in the music industry. Now, the influence of hip-hop is ubiquitous in the contemporary art, music, and fashion scenes.

In Harlem, each Sunday at 4:00 p.m. for the past twelve years with no vacations, a jazz concert clarinets its way down the corridor outside Marjorie Eliot's living room at 555 Edgecombe Avenue, Apartment 3F, in Sugar Hill, summoning jazz lovers from the woodwork for a performance in her home. Begun as a memorial for her son's untimely death, the concerts drew acclaimed musicians such as Cecil Bridgewater and Bob Cunningham who also play the Village Vanguard, the Blue Note, and Carnegie Hall. In 2004, when the drumbeat of the bills loomed larger than the bass fiddle and the landlord threatened to evict Marjorie and her family, the cultural center City Lore devised an old-fashioned rent party to help sustain the tradition. At that celebration, she told the crowd assembled: "The majesty within us is larger than any of us. So I can trumpet this! And not blow my own horn."

In the pages that follow, we trumpet the creative spirit of New Yorkers, whose sounds, like an instrument played in an upstairs apartment, cannot be contained, and whose images paint the drab and faded tenements, the cold tile of the subways, with brilliant swaths of colors, as if, one New York City night, the paintbox burst.

PLACE MOMENT: LAURA SILVER, SOCRATES SCULPTURE PARK

"Socrates Sculpture Park in Astoria, just before dusk, in winter, when the cold, hard sun illuminates rusted beams, concrete blocks, and an eclectic collection of weather-beaten sculptures. Give in to the childlike urge to run and climb. Find the best glimpse of the fading sun. Just don't stick your warm tongue to a cold pole."

The Village Vanguard

178 Seventh Avenue South, at Max Gordon Corner, Greenwich Village, Manhattan

(212) 255–4037

www.villagevanguard.net

Hours: Shows seven nights a week at 9:00 and 11:00 p.m. (12:30 a.m. set on Saturday night)

Admission $20 plus $10 drink minimum (collected with admission)

Public Transit: 1, 9 trains to Christopher Street/Sheridan Square. Walk north (against traffic) about four blocks along Seventh Avenue South to the Vanguard.

1, 2, 3, 9 trains to Fourteenth Street. Walk south (with traffic) about three blocks on Seventh Avenue South to the convergence of Greenwich and Seventh avenues and West Eleventh Street.

"This little old club deserves a birthday of its own . . . a real party for a seventy-year-old grande dame," Lorraine Gordon said of her club. The Village Vanguard, hailed among those in the know as the Carnegie Hall of jazz and the Mecca of hip, turned seventy in February 2005. One would be hard-pressed to find a jazz musician or fan anywhere in the world who does not know of, has not visited or longed to visit, or does not dream of playing and recording in this unassuming little jazz club in Greenwich Village.

Seven decades is an eternity for a club in New York. Ghosts of great jazz artists still hang out in the place, inhabiting the furnishings and shaping its character. "The room . . . has its own mindset, it has vibrations—vibes," Lorraine explains. "And if it doesn't like something, the pictures on the wall jiggle around."

IT'S JUST A TINY LITTLE PLACE

Located in the heart of Greenwich Village on the heavily trafficked Seventh Avenue South thoroughfare, the Village Vanguard entrance is situated beside a pizza parlor and below a nail salon. Their large, colorful neon signs only serve to highlight the Vanguard's light-bulb-illuminated old-fashioned awning and modest sign.

As we open the street-level door, we descend a perilously steep, long, narrow flight of stairs embraced by red walls. This feature of the club is almost as endearing as the tiny, low-ceilinged, wedge-shaped room at the bottom, opening into the front section of the house. The subdued (but not dim) lighting reveals walls lined with photos of performers who have played at the Vanguard, a couple of instruments, and a mural to the right of the low stage with images of the awning, audience, and artists. The mural has changed over time (the first one depicted a rally in Union Square), but, consonant with the passions of the late Max Gordon (the founder and original owner), his wife, Lorraine (the current owner), and the Vanguard's steadfast supporters, the themes remain jazz and social justice.

Follow the photo wall on the left to the tip of the triangle in which the stage is nestled, then around to the balcony (actually, just a raised section up a couple of steps), which runs along the right side of the room. The back section is defined by a large wall mirror on either side, a small bar on the left, and a leather bench along the back. Small round white tables are set close together throughout the room, which seats only 123. Not much has changed since the club opened in 1935. The mirrors, carpets, and tabletops were replaced. The smell of stale smoke is gone. And now there's a "Mingus Light." Apparently, Charles Mingus, in a moment of either pique or enthusiasm, lifted his bass and jammed it into the ceiling, making a hole. "Everybody comes in [asking,] 'Where's the Mingus Light?' Well, it's actually a hole. . . . It's up there [Lorraine gestures to the bandstand]. . . . He took his bass one night and shoved it in. And that's the Mingus Light. We left the framework."

Lorraine Gordon keeps things simple at the club. For thirty dollars at the door you get a night of jazz and a coupon to cover the ten-dollar drink minimum. A simple drink, nothing fancy, no umbrellas. Even though there's a kitchen, there's no food, no noshes, no nothing. As Lorraine notes on the Vanguard's Web site: "We do not serve food. We haven't served food here in twenty-five years. So if someone offers you a hamburger, check the expiration date." The kitchen serves as office, greenroom, and storage room for instruments and sound equipment.

FIRST PERSON: PETE HAMILL,
A DRINKING LIFE

"In the fall of 1957, Jack Kerouac's *On the Road* was published by Viking Press. . . . I read in the *Village Voice* (then three years old and full of surprises) that Kerouac was due in town for a Friday-night jazz-poetry reading at the Village Vanguard. I paid the admission, went downstairs, ordered vodka at the bar, and for almost two hours listened to Kerouac, Gregory Corso, and some other poets. I was thrilled with the flow of words and the counterpoint of jazz, and gazed through cigarette smoke at the remote women, who all seemed dressed in black, cool as ice sculpture."

A WEDGE-SHAPED SOUND

Regulars at the Vanguard have their favorite tables, and all of them claim that their spot offers the best sound quality—a clear sign that it's good throughout. No matter where your favorite spot is, the small space, close-placed tables, and proximity between performers and audience guarantee a uniquely intimate experience with magnificent sound. Indeed, it is the astonishingly pristine acoustics of the place that have kept artists and audience coming back for seventy years. The Vanguard has flourished for so long largely because the acoustics are so conducive to creating an exceptional listening experience for live performance as well as for live recordings. The superior sound quality of the place is attributable to its triangular shape; the tip-of-the-triangle bandstand location sends the sound directly into the house without any of it getting lost.

The club's shape is also an identity marker: There is no mistaking the club in a photo. And therein lies a quintessential New York story. As the *Wall Street Journal* told it:

In 1914, the city tore a nine-block swath through the upper heart of Greenwich Village, to add a subway link between Seventh Avenue and

Twelfth Street and Varick Street. Entire blocks were razed and the corners of buildings were sheared off. By 1917, Village geometry had changed forever, leaving a number of unusual triangular lots along the newly created Seventh Avenue South. In 1921, developer Morris Weinstein hastily erected a thin, cake-slice building on the southern tip of one of those half-blocks (now renamed Max Gordon corner) and began renting space to various businesses, including a speakeasy in the basement that was aptly named the Golden Triangle.

On a frigid December afternoon, as we interview Lorraine, the club is quiet except for the sounds of the staff setting up for the night ahead. But periodically we hear the muffled sound of the 1, 9, 2, or 3 train as it rumbles by under Seventh Avenue South, and we're reminded why this club is shaped the way it is. Musicians love playing the Vanguard because they can hear themselves, and because of their proximity to the audience. "To be in a club and have . . . the audience so close to you, you get the feeling back and forth—how special it is. It adds something to the music, no doubt about it," says Lorraine. Combine these elements with the passion of the participants—artists, audience, and management—and you've got a formula for success measured in terms far beyond the commercial. In his introduction to Max Gordon's book *Live at the Village Vanguard,* Nat Hentoff writes: "[S]erious people . . . were saying things from the stand. . . . You could feel their passion moving out into the room, and as the set went on you might discover more of your own submerged emotions than you thought were there."

A LEGEND IN ITS TIME

This minimalist basement venue in Greenwich Village is the most famous jazz spot in the world. It's the oldest continuously running venue presenting the crème de la crème among jazz artists; more than a hundred "Live at the Village Vanguard" recordings have been issued since 1957, bringing the club's reputation to an international audience.

Max Gordon was not terribly savvy about jazz in the beginning, although he knew what he liked. Raised in Portland, Oregon, he majored in English literature at Reed College. A poet and writer, he came to New York at the age of twenty-three in 1926 and was immediately drawn to Greenwich Village and the city's bohemian intellectual circles. The all-night cafeterias and coffeehouses were meeting places where issues of the world were discussed, social and cultural revolutions were fomented, and poets wrote passionate verses about those issues. They felt they needed someplace besides the cafeterias to gather and talked about opening a poetry club. In 1932, Max did it. He opened the Village Fair, a short-lived endeavor that folded in the wake of a Prohibition sting operation—only months before repeal. But it was the first realization of the kind of place he dreamed of. As he put it: "a quiet, gentle place. . . . You dropped in, met your friends, heard the news of the day, read the daily papers provided by the house. When it got crowded at night, as I hoped it would, and the conversation bristled with wit and good feeling, perhaps a resident poet would rise and declaim some verses he had composed for the entertainment and edification of the guests."

The Village Fair was down the street from the Vanguard. It was a place "where the poets could come and read their poetry and people would throw money on the floor. That's how they got paid; Max didn't have any money," Lorraine says.

Undaunted by the forced closure of the Village Fair, Max persisted. In 1935, he found the basement space at 178 Seventh Avenue South and grabbed it—for one hundred dollars a month. The space had been vacant for two years after the Golden Triangle folded. The new place would be named the Village Vanguard and, indeed, live up to its name. In addition to poetry, Max presented an eclectic mix of skits, comedy, music, and dinner. In the beginning, the method of payment for the artists was much the same as it had been at the Village Fair. Soon after, he brought in blues and folk music. The expanded mix fit right into his dreams of providing a place for the community to gather and artists to be heard.

In keeping with the ambitious name of the club, Max ignored trendiness and took risks, bringing in unknown artists, a multitude of whom went on to great fame. In 1939 he took a chance on the Revuers, a group of young upstarts that included Judy Holliday, as well as Betty Comden and Adolph Green, who, Gordon wrote, were writing politically satirical skits and songs of social and political significance. They were such a hit that they continued to appear at the Vanguard into 1940, until they were snatched away by the Rainbow Room in Rockefeller Center. Within a few years of opening the Vanguard, the then unknown Leadbelly, Josh White, Pearl Bailey (who later gave up the blues for musical comedy), Woody Guthrie, Pete Seeger, the Almanac Singers, the Weavers, and Harry Belafonte became regulars. Comics such as Wally Cox, Mort Sahl, Lenny Bruce, Woody Allen, and the team of Mike Nichols and Elaine May, and absurdists like Professor Irwin Corey—all of them political—all got their start at the Village Vanguard.

Throughout the 1940s, Max presented jazz as part of the eclectic mix

Edsel Gómez and David Sanchez play the Vanguard, 1997. Photo: Ken Franckling © 1997.

of the Vanguard's offerings, including regular Monday night jam sessions beginning in 1942. The Monday sessions eventually morphed into the Village Vanguard Big Band in the mid-1960s, led by Thad Jones and Mel Lewis. Even though Jones, Lewis, and many of the original band members have passed away, the Monday night big band tradition continues at the Vanguard.

In the 1950s, the club's eclecticism increasingly gave way to jazz, and by the 1960s, the Vanguard had established itself as the premier jazz club, not only in New York but in the world. The first "Live from the Village Vanguard" recording—Sonny Rollins Trio, *A Night at the Village Vanguard* (Blue Note, 1957)—started what would become a tradition of excellence in live jazz recording that continues today. There are now

SISTER SITE: 55 BAR

55 Christopher Street at Seventh Avenue

(212) 929–9883

www.55Bar.com

Public Transit: 1, 9 trains to Christopher Street/Sheridan Square.

Hours: 1:00 p.m. to 4:00 a.m.

Shows: Monday through Thursday at 7:00 p.m. and 10:00 p.m.; Friday and Saturday at
6:00 p.m. and 10:00 p.m.; Sunday at 9:30 p.m. No charge for early shows. Late
show prices range between $5 and $15 depending on the artist.

The 55 Bar is a little out-of-the-way place. You could easily miss it as you walk around the corner from Seventh Avenue, one of the Village's busiest thoroughfares, but for over two decades the 55 Bar has been bringing an eclectic mix of artists and great music to Greenwich Village, featuring jazz and blues 365 nights a year. On one visit you might hear a local aspiring musician, and the next the two-time Grammy nominee and former Miles Davis guitarist Mike Stern.

Though the 55 Bar only started its music shows in 1983, this little place, accommodating approximately fifty people, has a much longer, colorful history. The establishment was opened in 1919 by Hyman Satenstein, just prior to the start of Prohibition. Soon after the enactment of the Eighteenth Amendment barring the manufacture, sale, and transportation of alcohol, the bar became a speakeasy. According to Ed Callaghan, who bartended there in the 1960s and recently returned, Hyman bewell over a hundred albums, most of which are still available. Jazz greats such as Dizzy Gillespie, Charles Mingus, Thelonious Monk, Dinah Washington, Miles Davis, John Coltrane, Betty Carter, Sonny Rollins, Dexter Gordon, Stan Getz, Gerry Mulligan, Bill Evans, and so many others got their start at the Vanguard and/or recorded there.

Why change the successful mix of entertainment fare to predominantly jazz? According to Lorraine, television was a primary factor. "Television took away all these artists. Woody Allen started here, right up there. But television took them away, so Max had to make another choice, from the poets to the folk singers to the jazz. . . . So he started to just put in jazz artists. He didn't know them all, either. He got help from other people. Max was not a big jazz aficionado. He knew what he liked;

---

came a bootlegger. After Prohibition was repealed, the bar received a license and re-opened as a legitimate bar.

In the 1960s, the bar was sold to the pianist Bradley Cunningham, who later opened a jazz club, Bradley's, at University Place. While it remained a neighborhood place for locals, it also attracted celebrities who lived in the area, like Erica Jong, Norman Mailer, and Rip Torn. There are even stories of Faye Dunaway and Shelley Winters flirting with the bartenders. The place retained its wild side: They say it's where everyone went after the after-hours clubs closed. Though live music wasn't yet a part of the scene at the 55, many jazz musicians hung out there, especially those who lived in the area, like Zoot Sims, Al Cohen, Pepper Adams, and Gerry McFarland.

In 1981, Peter Williams bought the 55 Bar, and two years later he started featuring live jazz performances. The initial shows were modest—no one received payment, but anyone could play. In 2001, Queva Lutz bought the bar. She has kept up the tradition of live music every night—booking all the artists herself. Don't expect the established musicians to play old standards here. This is where they get a chance to try out new material, or something perhaps more avant-garde, and they know the audience will be all right with it. Queva feels the club fulfills a special role: "There are so many great jazz musicians in the city, and the venues are very limited. To offer a showcase like this helps the music evolve, develop, change, grow." Queva hopes that her club can be a kind of feeder to the Vanguard—a place she deeply admires.

he had great taste. . . . He struggled. It didn't come overnight. It wasn't a super hit. He had to just do it, and people would have to learn and come or not come. But they did. And that's why it survives today, seventy years later. Hard to believe."

CARRY IT ON

Max passed away in 1989, leaving his monumental legacy in the more than capable hands of Lorraine. Despite the pain of losing Max, the club transitioned smoothly. They had shared artistic taste, social values, standards of uncompromising excellence, and a deep love for jazz. They also shared a commitment to keep the music affordable and accessible even in the face of rising costs, and in the public consciousness even in the face of an overpowering commercial music industry. Just as Max was at the club every night of the week, meeting and greeting guests in his informal, unpretentious, warm manner and enjoying the music while making sure all went well, so is Lorraine.

Growing up in Newark, New Jersey, Lorraine had been going to the club since she was a teenager, already in love with jazz and blues. She remembers coming to the club "as a pseudo-customer because we didn't have much to spend and . . . because [Max] had great jam sessions . . . and all these great stars came down here to play. I came . . . with a couple of kids from Newark, and we would stand here at the bar and order a beer and pass it around. We had just enough money for the train from Newark to New York City."

She and Max would not meet until some years later. In the interim, she married Alfred Lion, owner of Blue Note Records, which eventually would become a major jazz label. At the time, though, "it was a nothing label. . . . We were little struggling people making the jazz we loved. . . . Alfred became very famous later on, but we recorded all the things he loved, traditional jazz, boogie woogie. . . . I did recording with him for seven years." In 1946 or '47, years after she had been hanging out at the Vanguard, Lorraine and Max finally met.

"I bumped into him on Fire Island one day," Lorraine recalls. "He was there, and I was a grown-up woman with a husband. He was sitting

Vintage Village Vanguard. Photo: Martha Cooper.

at the table having a hot cross bun and coffee or something. Max was rather well known, and I had never met him personally. So I just went up to him and told him that I knew a wonderful musician, a pianist that we had been recording on Blue Note Records named Thelonious Monk. Well, Max hadn't heard of Thelonious Monk. He looked me over up and down—the shiny yellow bathing suit—you know, it's summer, Fire Island, no shoes, barefoot. 'Sit down,' he said. And I did, and I told him about Monk, who I thought was a genius. Nobody knew Monk [except for] musicians and Alfred, and we recorded him. . . . So he said, 'I just happen to have a date in September.' So I booked Thelonious Monk. I never booked anyone before. . . . That's actually how I met Max."

Monk's first gigs at the Vanguard didn't draw the crowds, and Max told Lorraine she was ruining his business, but Lorraine said: "Mr. Gordon, wait, this man is a genius, you will see." Sure enough, she says, "Years later I heard Max say to people, 'You know, this Thelonious Monk is a genius.' He booked him over and over, and Thelonious got bigger and bigger. That's how I met Max. That's how we had two children."

Lorraine didn't get involved in running the Vanguard—the club was "Max's baby"—but she was there all the time, listening to the music. She raised their two daughters, one of whom, Deborah, now works at the Vanguard. It's a family business.

AND THE BEAT GOES ON

In this city where the economics of sustaining an entertainment establishment or eatery render the future uncertain, the Village Vanguard's history and reputation make for a most positive prognosis. In seventy years of operation, the rent on the Vanguard has been paid without missing a month, and bills, artists, and staff get paid on time. The rent is no longer one hundred dollars a month, but the drinks aren't fifty cents, either. Nor do the musicians get paid with the money patrons throw on the floor. Lorraine's love of jazz, her wit, and her sense of humor keep her young in spirit and energy. She manages the place with a firm hand and books the musicians—most of whom have long-standing one- or two-week gigs year after year—who play the kinds of jazz she loves and who love playing the Vanguard. For six nights a week Lorraine is there, keeping a watchful eye but mostly enjoying the music, the camaraderie of friends and longtime patrons, and the audience as they are engaged by and with the music.

The club is filled night after night, two shows on weekdays and three on Friday and Saturday. "The parents who came when they were kids are now coming with their kids. There are sometimes three generations here . . . a mother and father and a kid, and the grandparents often come. There are lots of young people. . . . It's not rock, it's not hip-hop; there's pure jazz here, and I'm delighted to see so many young people listening to it," Lorraine says. They are the future audience in training.

People come from all over the world to experience the Vanguard.

They seek out Lorraine to let her know where they are from and how they learned about the club. "I hope you're not disappointed. It's just a little place, not glamorous or glitzy," she tells them, but they always assure her it's the music and the experience they came for. They heard about it by word-of-mouth or through the recordings.

What does Lorraine want us to know about the Vanguard? "We are still here. . . . We are supporting what I consider the most cultural music the United States of America has given the world. We have nothing to call our own that isn't adopted from another country. Ballet, opera, theater—it's all beautiful, but it's not our own. . . . But jazz came out of the culture of this country. . . . It was in New Orleans, it was in Kansas City, and the musicians who played were American musicians. Black musicians, white musicians. And that is what we gave the world, and that is what this club wants to keep in front of people."

—Roberta Singer

Casa Amadeo Record Shop

786 Prospect Avenue, Longwood, the
Bronx

(718) 328–6896

Hours: Monday through Saturday 11:00
a.m. to 6:00 p.m.

Public Transit: 2, 5 trains to Prospect Avenue. The shop is just below the
subway exit, where Prospect Avenue intersects with Westchester
Avenue and Longwood Avenue.

Listed on the National Register of Historic Places, 2001

The thing I remember most about my childhood," says Latin musician Bobby Sanabria, "is the music reverberating through the canyons of the projects." From the forties through the seventies, the streets, stoops, and rooftops of the Bronx resounded with Latin music. Once clubs, dance halls, theaters, and record stores summoned music lovers from what seemed like every block, packing them in, competing for their loyalties, entrancing them. What emerged from this musical hothouse were talented musicians, a generation of great dancers, and a popular music that traveled the world in the era of mambo and cha-cha-cha. Today, in the creative crucible that was and is the South Bronx, an enduring legacy remains from this era. You can find it at Casa Amadeo.

LA MÚSICA CONTINUA

Even at first glance Casa Amadeo intrigues. It's an old-fashioned store, impeccably kept up. Through an open front door in fine weather, Latin sounds greet you as you enter. Guitars, maracas, guiros, and claves beckon to aficionados from inside their glass cases. CDs and vinyl line the walls, featuring every style and era in Latin music: *jibaro* (country) music of Puerto Rico, romantic *danzas* and *boleros*, the *son* of

Cuba, the driving sounds of New York City salsa in its myriad styles and voices. Above, home-painted portraits of notable men in Latin music rest ensconced in rococo wooden moldings: the Puerto Rican composers Pedro Flores and Rafael Hernández and the composer/proprietor himself, Mike Amadeo.

What a casual look does not reveal is that Casa Amadeo is a treasure house and a memory bank of Latin music. This status comes in part from its inventory. If you need advice, Mike will help you choose from among his large holdings, and if he doesn't have what you want, he'll find it for you. Customers hunch over the glass cases and bins, examining the choices, holding long conversations with Mike about their tastes or the relative merits of favorite performers. Musicians regularly call from as far away as Puerto Rico looking for material to record or to find a song they recall but can't place. Mike's deep knowledge of the music and its history is a key to his success. So is his shop's welcoming feel, which has long made it a gathering place for musicians and music lovers. Bronx congressman José Serrano is one of those who stops by to sing a song while Mike plays the guitar. The distinctiveness of this small, remarkable shop also comes from its history as the longest continually operating Latin music store in the city.

FROM EL BARRIO TO THE BRONX

Casa Amadeo opened at its current location in 1941. It was then called Casa Hernández and owned by Victoria Hernández. Victoria was born in Aguadilla, Puerto Rico, to a family of poor tobacco workers. She and her brothers Rafael and Jesús all became accomplished musicians. During World War I, Rafael performed all over Europe with James Reese Europe's 369th Infantry Hellfighter military band, the famous African American regimental band that is credited with introducing jazz to Europeans. After his discharge, Rafael, Victoria, and other family members moved to New York City, fleeing the island's poverty and taking advantage of the 1917 Jones Act that gave Puerto Ricans some citizenship rights like migrating (but also like serving in the army) without conferring equal status. Like many fellow islanders, they settled in East Harlem, a k a El Barrio, where Victoria first worked as a factory seamstress.

Still in El Barrio in 1927, Victoria and Rafael opened Almacenes Hernández on Madison Avenue near 114th Street, the first Puerto Rican–owned music store in New York City. The store supported the family and gave Rafael time to write music. He would become one of the most prolific and well-known composers in Latin America. Victoria supplemented the family's income by giving piano lessons to local residents, including a young Tito Puente. Victoria never followed her brother into performing, perhaps influenced by the more respectable reputation of the business side of music, or perhaps satisfied by the truly remarkable feat of being a Latina entrepreneur in her day.

Small music stores, often family run, played vital roles in the burgeoning Latin music scene in the 1920s, 1930s, and 1940s, continuing through the mambo era of the 1950s and the later development of salsa. Major companies like RCA Victor and Columbia Records depended on savvy local owners like Victoria Hernández to act as cultural brokers by helping the companies find musicians for recordings and gauging the community's musical tastes to produce records that would sell. Knowing such stores were well connected, musicians gathered there and waited to be called upon by record companies needing session players or bandleaders from orchestras and

FIRST PERSON/GHOST SITE: ROBERTA SINGER, TIMES SQUARE RECORD MART

"I first started my Latin music record collection when I bought an old Machito LP at the Times Square Record Mart inside the subway station at Times Square. It was located in the Forty-second Street/Times Square subway station, on the mezzanine level, near the stairs to the Seventh Avenue IRT line. People would pay a token to get into the subway so they could go to the store, at a time when Times Square actually catered to the people who live in New York. It was definitely teeny, but it had this huge selection of things you couldn't get anywhere else. They always had these great cutout bins where you could get three for ten dollars. There was this guy named Harry Sepulveda who knew everything. I would send people to him. A couple of times I left my whole paycheck there—I brought home more than I could carry. I was so sad when it closed a few years ago."

conjuntos (musical groups) needing instrumentalists. Ordinary customers flocked to the stores, too. Like the many social clubs organized by members of island hometowns, record stores were among the new institutions that helped ease the pain of transplantation from Puerto Rico. Here the new migrants could find and purchase the sounds of home. Some record stores even produced and pressed their own records right on the premises.

Victoria and Rafael sold their East Harlem store, and while Rafael lived for a time in Mexico, Victoria opened Casa Hernández in the Bronx, in 1941. Crowded and deteriorating conditions in El Barrio were prompting many to look for better housing and job opportunities just across the river in the southern portions of the Bronx. In the decade after World War II ended and commercial flights from San Juan began,

Composer, proprietor, and musical advisor Mike Amadeo in his shop. Photo: Tom Pitch.

nearly half a million Puerto Ricans moved to the mainland—most to Manhattan and the Bronx. By the early 1960s, the city's Puerto Rican population was greater than metro San Juan's.

SISTER SITE: JCR PERCUSSION

948 Ogden Avenue, Highbridge, the Bronx

Hours: Monday through Saturday 10:00 a.m. to 6:00 p.m. (closed Thursday)

(718) 293–6589

Public Transit: 4 or D train to Yankee Stadium. Walk west on 161st Street to Ogden Avenue and turn right.

While Casa Amadeo carries all the music recorded in the Latin music world, JCR Percussion, owned by Calixto Rivera, is where many of the recording artists buy the percussion instruments that form the rhythmic backbone of their music. There is no other establishment like his in New York City. In a small, unassuming workshop not far from Yankee Stadium, Caly, as he is known to his customers, makes his instruments by hand—cowbells, congas, bongos, and timbales, among others. These instruments are the foundation of Afro-Cuban (salsa) music, and before Caly started his business almost thirty-five years ago, Latin musicians were in a quandary about where to get something like a good cowbell. The varied sounds of cowbells provide the forward propulsion that a band rides on in the *montuno* (solo) section of a salsa tune. Many players had to scrounge bells from junkmen or travel to farms in Connecticut to buy them from farmers who used them on— yes—cows. Caly at the time was one of those musicians, and his drive to achieve the right sound motivated him to start making the instruments himself.

Caly doesn't advertise his wares; word of mouth keeps him busy. Musicians come to him from all over the world to place new orders or have broken instruments repaired. The first thing you see upon entering the shop is Caly or an employee working metal to make timbales and cowbells. The far wall is filled with tools and implements used to make the instruments, while hanging from the ceiling are guiros, panderetas (handheld frame drums from Puerto Rico), and other percussion instruments. The rest of the wall space is filled with photos and autographed promotional shots from most of the big names in Latin music. Downstairs is the wood workshop where Caly keeps his lathes and other woodworking instruments for making bongos, congas, and cajónes (small wood boxes played like congas in Cuba). The best part is Caly's welcoming smile when one enters and leaves. "For that," he says, "I never charge."

Casa Amadeo's first owner, Victoria Hernández, lived upstairs in the Manhasset Building. Photo: Martha Cooper.

Mike Amadeo still honors the Hernández legacy by including their name on the store's awning: "Casa Amadeo antigua [formerly] Casa Hernández." Until recently you could also see painted lettering right above the door advertising novedades (novelties) that remained from Victoria's time. In those days merchandise cases filled with music and instruments inhabited the left side of the store, along with a booth where patrons could listen to the latest 78 rpm records. On the right side of the store, dresses hung; until the late 1940s, many music stores stocked a variety of wares in addition to music.

A special music scene was unfolding around the Hernández shop. Building on Cuban music genres and styles, New York musicians began in the 1940s to distinguish their sound with fuller band arrangements, strong jazz influences, and faster tempos. Latin music legends who called the area home at one time or another included the three "Mambo Kings"—Tito Puente, Machito, and Tito Rodríguez—as well as Vicentico Valdés, Marcelino Guerra, Arsenio Rodríguez, Charlie and Eddie Palmieri, Orlando Marín, Manny Oquendo, Ray Barretto, Barry Rogers, Johnny Pacheco, Joe Loco, Joe Quijano, Willie Colón, Héctor Lavoe, and many others who starred in or backed up performances and recordings from the 1930s onward. They rehearsed and jammed in informal places such as apartments and courtyards, on rooftops, parks, and street corners. Conguero Adolfo (Lefty) Maldonado told us how beautiful it was to walk in the South Bronx and hear on every block the sounds of *tun-tun-tun-tun* from the roof. The local musicians also played in more formal spaces such as social clubs, dance halls, after-hours joints, movie theaters, and schools. Percussionist Benny Bonilla recalls that "on weekends I would convince my mother to let me go out, and I would sling my conga over my shoulder and try to sit in with musicians in the seven or eight bars that were only a few blocks from my house on Kelly Street. It was like going to school for me." At sumptuous halls like Hunts Point Palace, and upstairs clubs like the Caravana, new sounds and dance steps like the *pachanga* caught on. Teens danced to jukeboxes at luncheonette/candy stores like El Mambo, owned by Eddie Palmieri's father, and locals lined up for records at places like Casa Hernández.

A TREASURE HOUSE OF LATIN SOUNDS

Mike Amadeo remembers a Christmas present he bought for himself for seventy-five cents in 1948. It was Christmas night, and Mike, fourteen years old and fresh from Puerto Rico, stopped by Casa Hernández with his cousin. They put on some 78s in the listening booth, and then Mike bought his very first record, *Siete besos* (Seven Kisses), by Julito Rodríguez and His Trio. Twenty-one years later he bought the store from Victoria Hernández and renamed it Casa Amadeo. By that time Mike was himself a musician and composer, but he has never regretted switching over to the business side of things. The store and royalties have helped him put two sons through college and kept him in the middle of the music scene, in much the same way as Victoria. The industry has changed, of course, but Mike is still a cultural broker.

In the 1970s, when salsa superstars Willie Colón and Héctor Lavoe decided to record an album of traditional Puerto Rican Christmas songs with salsa arrangements, they called Mike to find the *aguinaldos* that would work best. The album, *Asalto Navideño,* sold extremely well, and it was culturally important because it emphasized the Puertoricanization of popular Latin music. The music that came to be called salsa in the 1970s is based on Afro-Cuban rhythms, but Puerto Ricans, so influential in the New York City music scene, have appropriated it as their own. Musicians like Willie Colón, born and bred in New York and identified as Nuyorican, added the music of their heritage by blending Cuban rhythms with traditional Puerto Rican styles like *bomba, seis,* and *aguinaldo.*

> **SISTER SITE: CASA LATINA**
>
> 151 East 116th Street, East Harlem, Manhattan
>
> Hours: Monday through Saturday 10:00 a.m. to 7:00 p.m.
>
> Public Transit: 6 train to 116th Street.
>
> In 1948, the musician Bartolo Alvarez established Casa Latina, where he sold music and instruments. Inspired as a youngster by hearing Rafael Hernández play at nearby Almacenes Hernández, Bartolo went on to found Alba and Rival Records, recording some of the era's most popular artists. Casa Latina moved to its present location in 1962. Purchased in 1969 by the Rubio family, this is the longest-running music store in El Barrio.

That Mike held on to the store through the burning and abandonment of the Bronx in the 1970s and 1980s is surely part miracle, mixed with business sense, loyalty, and toughness. The last tenant in a once elegant building, he survived days of carting in his own water in buckets and nights of standing at vigilance with a bat (baseball, not music, was his first love, by the way). Today the neighborhood is rebounding around Mike, much of it because of similar can-do efforts by the locals. The park nearby, for example—across the street from P.S. 52, where so many young musicians of Mike's era learned to play—was reclaimed from devastation by local volunteers who call themselves 52 People for

Progress. Every year Mike organizes a night of trios to contribute to the group's summer series of Latin music concerts in the park.

Casa Amadeo is like a one-room schoolhouse for Latin music. When you walk through the door, you're a pupil.

—Elena Martínez and Marci Reaven

Richmond Barthé's Frieze at Kingsborough Houses

As a boy growing up in the Kingsborough housing project in Brooklyn, Will Halsey had no idea that the eighty-foot-long frieze that he played in and around or passed on the way to church was called *Green Pastures: Walls of Jericho,* that it referred to Exodus, or that it was carved by the well-known African American sculptor Richmond Barthé (1901–1989). For him and his friends it was simply "the Wall." At first, friends would say things like "Look at that man, look at that guy's muscle in his stomach. I bet I can get more muscles like that." In the years that

1180 Pacific Street, Crown Heights, Brooklyn

Public Transit: A, C trains to Utica Avenue. Walk three blocks south on Utica, turn left onto Pacific Street, and walk two blocks to Rochester Avenue.

3, 4 trains to Utica Avenue. Cross Utica and walk nine blocks north along Utica to Pacific, turn right onto Pacific, and walk one block to Rochester Avenue.

The frieze is located between the first and second walks at the Kingsborough Houses, bordered by Rochester and Buffalo avenues and Bergen and Pacific streets.

Halsey lived in the project in the 1950s and early 1960s, street gangs bullied the neighborhood—the Corsairs in the project and the Chaplains in the surrounding neighborhood. They would trash each other, but nobody messed with the Wall. Why is that? Because the Wall, Halsey says, "indicates to the people their condition and their liberation—in the same way that 'Go Down, Moses' indicates the condition and the liberation and the transcendence."

BODIES IN MOTION

L ocated between what are known as the first and second walks—there are seven walks altogether in the project—the eighty-foot frieze, made out of either limestone or cast concrete, can be seen clear across the other side of Kingsborough and yet go unnoticed from the outside. Residents express a sense of ownership; the frieze is just for them. A resident of fifty years says that it's been there all of his life, recalling how, as a child, he climbed over the stepped top.

In the first panel of the frieze—measuring eight feet tall by forty feet long—a Moses figure with his right hand outstretched is followed by two elderly bearded men, suggestive of Hezekiah and Aaron. The frieze is stepped on the top side of the wall, and each section has a different number of exiles, leaving two by two, three by three, four by four. "You see," says Will Halsey, "there are two, then he has three, then he has four, then he has five." Then he sings:

> We stepped out of Babylon two by two,
> We stepped out of Babylon three by three,
> We stepped out of Babylon four by four,
> We stepped out of Babylon five by five.

In the second forty-foot panel, a seated drummer faces dancers as he plays music for them. The dancers appear in synchronized motion, each with one arm raised and the other across the body. "If you are dancing, it's transcendence," Will says. A younger resident, pointing out the drummer on the wall, describes it as a tribute to dance and to the soul, as an invitation to be in rhythm with your life. During the 1930s, the sculptor Richmond Barthé joined a modern dance troupe at Martha Graham's studio. "His figures of dancers, lyric portrayals of the body in motion," wrote Romare Bearden and Harry Henderson in *A History of African-American Artists,* "are among his best works, achieving their effects through linear qualities rather than volume and mass."

The faces of all of the figures are carved with African features—broad noses, full lips, and braided hairstyles—casting doubt that this is a traditional interpretation of the corresponding biblical story. Barthé was known for his portrayal of black Americans. "I don't think art is racial," he said, "but I do feel that a Negro can portray the inner feelings of the Negro people better than a white man can." For Will Halsey, living with the artwork day to day, the piece showed that the "African personality could be something that could be elegant, something that could be wise. . . . It filled me up."

Halsey, now a spoken-word artist, discovered poetry at age fifteen or sixteen in the 1960s when poets from the emerging Black Arts Movement performed at his high school. He developed a relationship with one of the visiting poets, Ed Spriggs, who was also director of the Studio Museum in Harlem. After he moved out of Kingsborough, Halsey noticed in one of Spriggs's art catalogs a familiar picture: It was a photo of the Wall, the place he knew so well from Kingsborough. "That's in

"We all called it 'the Wall.'" Photo: Martha Cooper.

Noted sculptor Richmond Barthé's African-inspired figures grace the Kingsborough Houses. Photo: Martha Cooper.

Brooklyn," he said, "where I grew up." But the caption said the Wall was in Harlem at another housing project, sculpted by African American Harlem Renaissance sculptor Richmond Barthé.

PUBLIC ART FOR THE MASSES

Turns out the piece was intended for the Harlem River Houses, built in 1936–1937 as one of the nation's first public housing projects and "reserved," in this era of housing segregation, for African Americans. In 1975, the complex was designated a New York City Landmark. Among the architects who designed the houses was John Louis Wilson Jr., one of the first African American architects registered in New York State. Sculptors were commissioned to create public art for the Harlem project by the Works Progress Administration (WPA) as part of the Federal Art Project that ran from 1935 to 1943. Heinz Warneke (1895–1983), a Jewish émigré sculptor and supervisor of the sculpture project at the Harlem River Houses, insisted that an African American be part of the WPA sculpture team and personally recruited Barthé, who was already well known as an accomplished figurative sculptor. The WPA team developed a number of sculptures, some still standing at the Harlem complex.

Barthé developed his frieze based on the Pulitzer Prize–winning play *The Green Pastures,* an African American theater piece about getting into heaven, written in 1930 by Marc Connelly. This was his first attempt at doing figures in relief. Despite its beauty, Barthé's bas-relief was kept in storage. Apparently it

FIRST PERSON: WILL HALSEY

"You see it every day and don't know what it is. But you are being seeded. The seeds are being planted. . . . I mean, I know the people in the projects know this is somebody speaking directly to their condition, speaking directly to their tradition, and speaking directly to that thing that is going to motivate them. Look at the faces, look at the stoicism on the faces. Even the children are irate. And there are families there. There is a man and a woman. They are holding one another. There are strong women. These were what we were seeing in the projects. We were seeing strong women without men. We were seeing families trying to stay together. This is the condition of slavery. That was what slavery is like. Slavery is destructive of families. Slavery is destructive of your tradition. . . . . I didn't know what Black Art was. But I knew this was it. That's the thing about art. When people see art, they have respect for it because they know that somewhere along the way it's doing something for them. It's a spiritual thing. . . . To me, that's why the Wall has survived."

SISTER SITE:
WEEKSVILLE HERITAGE CENTER,
AN AFRICAN AMERICAN HISTORICAL SITE

1698–1708 Bergen Street , Crown Heights, Brooklyn

718–756–5250

www.weeksvillesociety.org

Hours: Tuesday to Friday 10:00 a.m. to 4:30 p.m.; Saturday and Sunday by appointment only. Call for admission information. Office hours are Monday to Friday 9:30 a.m. to 4:30 p.m.

Public Transit: A, C trains to Utica Avenue, then walk four blocks south on Utica to Bergen Street. Turn left and walk approximately a block and a half.

3, 4 trains to Utica Avenue, then walk eight blocks north on Utica to Bergen Street. Turn right and walk approximately a block and a half.

Across the street from the Kingsborough Projects are four small wood-frame houses—the last remaining residential artifacts of a nineteenth-century African American community. Weeksville was a settlement built in the years of slavery's demise in New York. It was named for James Weeks, an African American from Virginia who bought a parcel of Brooklyn land in 1838. Although unlettered, he played a key role in developing here a thriving settlement of free blacks, whose community building and social and cultural achievements have been rediscovered by the Weeksville Heritage Center and are commemorated at this historic site.

The rediscovery actually started in 1968 when a historian/engineer team on the trail of local black history flew over the area and spotted four small wood-frame houses. It was the oddly situated lane that struck them; it turned out to be a remnant of an even older colonial path called Hunterfly Road, which formed the eastern boundary of Weeksville. Watershed though it was, the astonishing aerial sighting was only one step in a longer and larger community process of uncovering a history that the history books had ignored. The Society for the Preservation of Weeksville and Bedford-Stuyvesant History (now shortened to the Weeksville Heritage Center) became the vehicle.

Enter Joan Maynard to carry on the society's work as its executive director. She dreamed of a black history museum that would provide "cultural vaccination" for children who needed reminding of their heritage and their value to the future. Buying the deteriorating houses, struggling to repair and preserve them, conducting archaeological and archival research, gaining landmark designation from the city and state of New York, and establishing the exhibits and public programs that were the foundation of the society's reputation all took Maynard and her colleagues decades to accomplish.

Today Weeksville's Historic Hunterfly Road Houses are newly restored and operating an increasingly full schedule of school programs, tours, exhibits, storytelling and cultural programs, and community festivals. According to Maynard, who passed away in January 2006, it's none too soon. "We need children of all backgrounds to visit Weeksville. The world has become too small a place to seriously consider selective survival as a realistic alternative, a place where the children of the powerful and wealthy will survive as the children of the poor and powerless perish. Remember, there's some little child here someplace who will change the world. I'm just convinced of it. And they will come out from someplace nobody even knows. God knows, if anybody really understood who those individuals were who would make a difference in the world, they would shoot them down in their mothers' arms. All of our children cannot sing, dance, or play basketball, but they all have history, the richest source of hopes and dreams."

Joan Maynard, founder of the Weeksville Society, before the recent restoration of the historic homes. Photo: Martha Cooper.

was intended to be the back wall of an amphitheater that was never built, and, in the end, there was no room for the frieze at the Harlem River Houses. Instead, it was installed without Barthé's knowledge or approval at the Kingsborough Houses in Brooklyn. (Interestingly, Kingsborough was one of only two housing projects before 1948 designed to be integrated rather than reserved for blacks or whites only.) Barthé was angry with the decision, since he had designed the piece specifically for the Harlem River Houses, but as a federal employee he had no control over his work. He declined to assist with the restoration of the piece some years later.

A LEGACY FOR THE DISPOSSESSED

The frieze forms its own stage," Will Halsey says, "and you know, when you live in the projects, everything in life is a stage. You are always on. As soon as you walk outside, you got to be on. You got to have your face on. Otherwise, somebody is going to come and mess with you." Will's dream is to finish writing an opera about the projects and perform a site-specific piece on the "stage" that so moved him as a young man. Standing in front of the frieze, in the spring of 2004, Will says: "See, that's us with the bags, that's us, the dispossessed. These are the dispossessed; these are the people that have to leave bondage. That's us."

—Jennifer Scott and Steve Zeitlin

Metropolitan
Meanderings

Wavecrest beach bungalows, Far Rockaway, Queens. Photo: Martha Cooper.

L et's get lost," said Brooklyn-born Barbara Rothman to her friend Joanie, in an essay about her childhood. Then Joanie "took a white, crumpled scarf from her pocket and placed it over my eyes." As soon as Joanie was convinced that Barbara couldn't see anything, she said, "Let's go." She took Barbara's hand and led her through the neighborhood. The trick was to see how much Barbara could see without seeing. "Even blindfolded," Barbara wrote, "it wasn't as easy to get lost as you'd think." How could she mistake the stench outside Chin's side door on Cortelyou Road, or "the smell of freshly laundered shirts and linens fused with the aroma of sweet steam" at Lu's Chinese Hand Laundry on Clarendon. She sensed the aroma of garlic at Tony's restaurant on Twenty-third Street. She even recognized the trees on Cortelyou Road, "so full, [they] canopied the narrow street below, allowing the sun to cast but a low, filtered light on my half-blind eyes." The best strategy for exploring New York, of course, is not to keep your eyes closed but open wide, and to use all your senses.

And it doesn't hurt to get lost sometimes. Discovering the city always begins with a journey that leads us, perhaps inadvertently, to places that surprise the soul. Only later do we find ways to make those places our own.

In Manhattan a rambler in Chinatown can hear the strains of

PLACE MOMENT: KAMILLAH, POWDER ROOM ON THE STATEN ISLAND FERRY, FROM THE FILM FERRY TALES

"The ferry is my transition period. It takes me from work to motherhood/ wife and from wife/motherhood to work. And in between I am not Mrs. and I am not Mommy. I am Kamillah, uncut. This is who I am. And behind all that we put on our makeup."

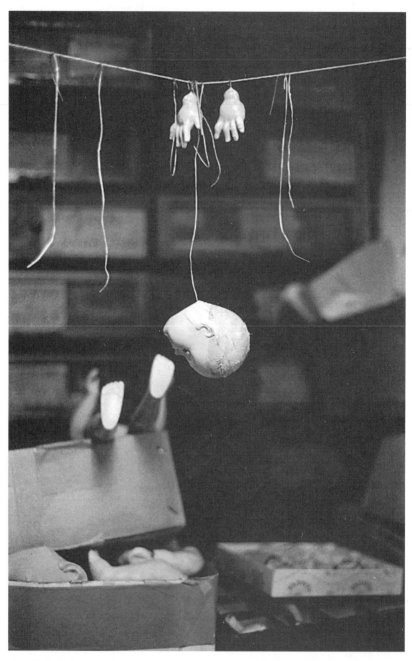

New York Doll Hospital at 787 Lexington Avenue, founded in 1900 and still repairing dolls. Photo: Elaine Norman.

Cantonese opera played by octogenarians led by Auntie and Uncle Leung on any weekday afternoon at the New York Chinatown Senior Center at 70 Mulberry Street. In Brooklyn you can find old matzoh factories and the new Russian bathhouses such as Bania on Coney Island Avenue and Mermaid Spa in Seagate. You can find yourself surprised by the stables of the Federation of Black Cowboys in Howard Beach, Queens, or the quaint Wavecrest bungalows on Rockaway Beach, then stumble upon what is arguably the city's tallest tree in Clove Lakes Park or the world's smallest opera house—the incomparable Amato—on the Lower East Side.

**PLACE MOMENT:
LAURA SILVER,
THE NEW YORK EARTH ROOM**

"The New York Earth Room, Wooster Street, for a view of an underground sans subway tunnels, water pipes, and electric cables. A carpet of rich, dark soil several feet high awaits you. Smell it. Stare at it. Stick your hand in it. Close your eyes, breathe deeply, and pay tribute to what's really beneath New York City."

"I love everyone," a friend told us, "only at varying distances." New York, like New Yorkers, can be viewed from many distances, and the trick is to pick just the right one. From an airplane or a helicopter the configuration of land and water—with the skyline as a third dimension—astonishes. "New York is all about vistas," the folklorist Sheldon Posen once observed.

On the other hand, the folklorist Barbara Kirshenblatt-Gimblett of New York University explains that she is exploring the Lower East Side inch by inch. In this book, we travel all over the city but try to get pretty close up. We feel that blocks in Canarsie and Far Rockaway are as culturally fertile as Manhattan soil, waiting to amaze the rambler.

Quirky Features of the Landscape

New York is a city of individualists—mavericks, iconoclasts, and local characters. Not surprisingly, it's also a city with more than its share of one-of-a-kind local landmarks, places where oddities in the physical landscape seem to rival the diversity in the human flora and fauna. Some of New York's special places of memory, history, and tradition serve to draw together urban communities, reminding us of our immigrant history, or commemorating illustrious residents. Others serve as idiosyncratic local landmarks that make our landscape distinctive, sometimes providing living proof that the city has a sense of humor.

These structures may mean something to a single soul, or to a select group of friends. For instance, "there is a tree on East Seventieth Street between Park and Lexington avenues rooted in front of a creamy colored Victorian mansion," writes Susan Sorenson. "I always walk home via East Seventieth stopping to remember being kissed beneath the tree one midnight when street noise gave way to an indigo air solely resplendent with windy sighs of springtime leaves." Conversely, the clock that straddled the gates leading into the Biltmore Hotel's central court lounge on Madison and Forty-third Street became such a well-known local landmark that no one had to explain the phrase "meet me under the clock."

PLACE MOMENT:

CAITLIN VAN DUSEN,

SECRET STASH OF "TOAST"

"Riding the Manhattan-bound F train as it chugs uphill from Fourth Avenue to Smith–Ninth streets, position yourself near a window facing east and look down: you will see two cement stalls where sand has been pushed into piles in a series of slab formations exactly resembling thick slices of somewhat stale toast. In the winter, a layer of frost laces the upper crusts, like a dusting of bakery flour."

Some local landmarks, like Susan's personal tree or Big Rock in Corona, Queens, are structures created by Mother Nature herself; others may be abandoned ironworks or wooden structures left over from the city's manufacturing eras, and still others the work of guerilla and public artists.

THE INDIAN CAVES

215th Street and Indian Road, Inwood Hill Park, Manhattan

Public Transit: 1 train to 215th Street. Walk three blocks north on Tenth Avenue, turn left onto West 218th Street, and walk 4 blocks to Indian Road. At 218th Street and Indian Road, follow the path into the park. Pass the Nature Center and follow the path to the soccer field until you arrive at Shorakkopoch Rock. Follow the left-hand path up the hill. The Indian caves are a few hundred yards up the hill on your right.

The hills and bluffs at the confluence of the Harlem and Hudson rivers, where the Bronx curls around the tip of Manhattan, form a magical place where quarter-mile-high glaciers seem to have moved with the grace of a sculptor's hand. In 1609, when Henry Hudson sailed up the Hudson to Albany, he encountered the Wiechquaesgecks (a branch of the Wappinger tribe, headquartered at Dobbs Ferry, and members of the Mohegan group of the Algonquin nation). According to some accounts, two tribesmen were taken captive but jumped overboard, one of them drowning. On Hudson's return, they attacked his ship, the *Half Moon,* and six or seven Indians were killed. The Wiechquaesgecks lived in the area until 1643, when they were attacked by the Mohawks and fled the region. But they left numerous archaeological artifacts—pottery shards, weapons, shell and bone implements. In the early twentieth century, archaeological digs near 203rd Street and Seaman Avenue uncovered skeletal remains of a chief, a woman, and a child.

Shell and bone instruments were also uncovered by city archaeologists in and around the park's "Indian caves." Although the caves were deeper in pre-Columbian times, the remaining rock formations help recall that distant age. These Indian caves were not used year-round, but

The Indian caves in Inwood Hill Park, Manhattan. Photo: Martha Cooper.

as a summer camp to harvest an abundance of shellfish, eels, and fish from the nearby river. The caves were much closer to the water at that time, before the landfill projects of the WPA. "Go on a sweltering summer's day," writes New Yorker Dodie Dohoney, "suck up the cool air that gets thrown out from the caves." Sit inside them, and—in your imagination—borrow the eyes of the Wiechquaesgecks.

The city bought the land for Inwood Hill Park between 1915 and 1940. When it was officially opened on May 8, 1926, a thousand children were among the visitors, attracted by the promise that, as the *New York Times* reported, "real Indians were going to take part in the ceremony." As late as the 1920s and 1930s, Princess Naomi, a member of the Algonquin nation, ran a Native American museum and store in the park. Other Native Americans gave tours of the caves, ran a library, and demonstrated native arts and crafts.

Just a few hundred yards from the caves is a small boulder—the Shorakkopoch Rock—adjoining the soccer field. A plaque reads:

> According to legend, on this site of the principal Manhattan Indian village, Peter Minuit in 1626 purchased Manhattan Island for trinkets and beads then worth about 60 guilders. Dedicated as part of New York City's 300th anniversary celebration by the Peter Minuit Post 1247, American Legion, January 1954.

The Indians are said to have planted a tulip tree to commemorate the occasion. The plaque also tells us that the boulder

> marks the spot where a tulip tree (*Liriodendron tulipifera*) grew to a height of 165 feet, a girth of 20 feet. It was until its death in 1933 at the age of 280 years the largest living link with the Reckgawawanc Indians who lived here.

The WPA *Guide to New York,* published in 1939, referred to the "gaunt stump of a huge tulip tree" that marked the spot where the famous trade is said to have taken place.

THE INDUSTRIAL PAST

Gantry Plaza State Park

Public Transit: 7 train to Vernon Boulevard/Jackson Avenue. Exit on Vernon Boulevard, turn left onto Forty-eighth or Forty-ninth Avenue, and walk two blocks toward the water to reach the park.

"We both know what memories can bring," sings Joan Baez, "they bring diamonds and rust." The aging machinery from New York City factories and rail yards brings mostly rust. Rusted gantries, for instance, can still be seen off of Locust Avenue at an old ferry terminal in the Mott Haven/Port Morris section of the Bronx.

Once these structures teemed with life. Manufacturing jobs brought workers from all over the world to the city's shores, and the gantries loaded the barges that supplied the nation. But the city, like each of its residents, has to figure out what to do with elements of its past, when they are no longer used. Just as we find old crusty objects in closets and drawers, the city finds rusting structures by the sides of the rivers, some of them eyesores, some beautiful in their corrosion or decay. *Make something of us,* they seem to cry.

In Long Island City, Queens West Redevelopment and the landscape architecture firm of Thomas Balsley Associates left the two large, corroded gantries standing when they created Long Island City waterfront park. In this commons, less than a decade old, "evocative industrial archaeology—huge, rusting float bridges, once used for transferring freight cars to and from cross-river barges—have been made integral parts of the design," wrote Christopher Gray in the *New York Times*. The gantries, large structures with pulleys and cranes that raised transfer bridges eighteen feet up or down, accommodating hundred-ton cars and topped with corrugated black metal control rooms, become a centerpiece for this lovely spread of parkland. The gantries mark the city's effort to remember, to make something of its past. Once they hoisted freight cars onto barges on the East River from trains that pulled in from Long Island. Then they rusted. Now they are repainted black, and the two giant structures retain the words *Long Island* in bright red letters, repositioned as a gateway to Long Island, giving Manhattanites something to gaze at from midtown, and Queens residents a panoramic view of the Manhattan skyline. At the south side, in a sculpted garden, the designers have left railroad tracks in the ground. Behind them, near the ranger's office and a children's playground, the four black chimneys and a fading sign from the old Schwartz Chemical Company, soon to come down, look back across the river at the Manhattan skyscrapers and office workers who

**PLACE MOMENT:
JACQUELYN COFFEE,
LONG ISLAND CITY
PEPSI-COLA SIGN, ADJOINING
GANTRY PLAZA STATE PARK**

"A wanton red slurve that looks like it flew off from the Folies-Bergère to land on the far shore of the East River, a scarlet shriek of naughty big-city promise."

Whether they drink Coke or Pepsi, New Yorkers love their landmark signs. Photo: Audrey Gottlieb.

replaced the dock workers across the generations. Four elegant piers jut out into the East River, the southernmost used for fishing, with an undulating wooden bench that rises and falls like a wave.

But the change away from manufacturing is still not complete. In South Brooklyn, railroad cars are still loaded onto barges using a pontoon system, run by the New York Regional Rail Corporation. On the other side, in New Jersey, gantries are still used to load and unload. Refurbished and repurposed, abandoned to rust or still in use, the structures that remain from the city's industrial past provide landmarks for everyday New Yorkers who may have no idea what they were used for, continually challenging the city to find ways to interpret them and retain their value for its citizenry.

NEW YORK'S WATER TOWERS

Location: Ubiquitous

Paris has the Eiffel Tower, Pisa has the Leaning Tower, we have the water tower," says Andrew Rosenwach, the owner of the 150-year-old Rosenwach Water Tank Company.

"Once someone points them out to you," writes the folklorist Nancy Groce, "you can't believe how many of them there are. Thousands upon thousands of huge wooden barrels are perched like alien spaceships on rooftops throughout the city. It's impossible to imagine the cityscape without them, but it's also possible that you've never noticed them."

The tanks began to appear in the nineteenth century, when ordinances declared that any building over six stories in height needed 3,500 gallons of water on the premises to assist firefighters. Since the reservoirs in upstate New York are taller than the buildings, hydrostatic pressure ensures that the water flows to the tanks on top of the buildings and maintains water pressure.

Tanks are placed on an iron scaffold on the rooftop. Working on the ingenious principle of the toilet, the tank begins refilling when the water goes below a certain level. Wooden tanks are far cheaper ($25,000) than steel tanks ($65,000), and, given the cost of construction

Notice the "Thinker" atop one of New York's ubiquitous water towers. Photo © Hazel Hankin Photography.

in New York City, that cheap price has made the towers ubiquitous, and New York the undisputed capital of the wooden water tower.

More than half the water tanks in New York are made by the Rosenwach family, which has been at it since 1896. When the Smithsonian Institution featured the folk culture of New York City at its Folklife Festival on the National Mall in Washington, D.C., in 2001, Nancy Groce and her colleague Kathleen Condon brought a crew from the Rosenwach Tank Company to construct a water tower and talk about the tradition. The shop foreman, Kenny Lewis, described it as akin to barrelmaking or shipbuilding: "We're putting together something that has to be watertight, but we have the water on the inside, where the ship wants it on the outside. We're doing the same thing, but we're keeping the water in different places."

PLACE MOMENT:
HEATHER CHAET,
WATER TOWERS

"Atjustthatrighttime—not quite Night, just past Dusk—my grandfather would look up at the trees or out the window at passing homes and announce to anyone, 'Bas-relief!' as if the scene were as pristine and frozen in time as one of those ancient raised carvings. Now I walk along streets in the city atjustthatrighttime. I fly my gaze like a kite up and around the rooftops. In this brief moment, the buildings, each crowned with its water tower, are cutouts, made of black poster board glued to the blueymidnight sky. I hear my grandfather's voice. I whisper to him, 'Bas-relief.'"

In New York, the water towers outnumber the skyscrapers, and from the window of any tall building in Manhattan the vista mingles the two kinds of towers. The wooden barrels all along the skyline seem to be a holdover from another time, a bit of New York's past that steel, glass, and concrete cannot supplant. Andrew Rosenwach once asked his father what the family would do when the water towers were no longer necessary. He answered that there were so many water towers already up that "lifetimes of work would be needed just to take them all down."

THE SHEEPSHEAD BAY FOOTBRIDGE

There's a lot of memories on that bridge," said eighty-seven-year-old Angie Ciccarone, who was born on Twenty-third Street in Sheepshead Bay. A little younger, in his fifties, local advocate Steve Barrison remembers kids diving off the bridge for coins in Sheepshead Bay. But Ciccarone remembers when the boys from Twenty-sixth Street would dive in stark naked. She recalls swimming across the bay with her friends, stopping

Emmons Avenue, Sheepshead Bay

Public Transit: B, Q trains to Sheepshead Bay. Walk south on Sheepshead Bay Road about five blocks, cross Emmons Avenue, and bear left for the footbridge.

Connecting Sheepshead Bay and Manhattan Beach, this wooden footbridge keeps traffic on a human scale. Photo: Amanda Dargan.

at the sandbar in the center, and making a dash for the other side when it started to disappear beneath their feet. And she remembers the boats from all over the area taking shelter in the bay during storms.

PLACE MOMENT:
NANCY ROSENBAUM,
SHEEPSHEAD BAY
FOOTBRIDGE

"On my way to work in the early morning, I cross the wooden planked bridge on my bicycle. Hello, ducks and ducklings. Look, there goes a swan! The boats gleam in the bay. I can't believe that this is Brooklyn, but yes, here we are. Brooklyn's Riviera, they say. Coming off the bridge, I see the men reliably planted on the bay with their fishing poles. They come from all over with their many languages and fish tales. There are Russians, Chinese, Poles, and Puerto Ricans. They tell me that fishing is about patience. Someday I would like to ask them their stories."

Barrison remembers a day in 1979 when he returned from "sowing my wild oats in California after I graduated from law school. As I walked along Emmons Avenue, looking at the fishing boats, the footbridge, and the bay, I realized that this rivaled anything I had seen in all my travels to America's Atlantic and Pacific coasts, the French and Italian rivieras, Mexico, or Venezuela. It's true, the waterfront had fallen into disrepair. The number of fishing boats had declined, and some of the bait and tackle shops had closed." The distinctive contours of the harbor still render the bay a portrait of working-class elegance, with Lundy's seafood restaurant, now a city landmark, on one side, and the residential neighborhood of Manhattan Beach on the other. The footbridge, spanning the bay with a swath of crosshatched wooden poles, helps bring the pieces together on a human scale, and to make the inlet a unique place in the sun.

Constructed in 1880, the footbridge over Sheepshead Bay is one of the rare bridges in New York that does not allow cars. The current bridge, built by the WPA in the 1930s, is both a well-trodden thoroughfare connecting the neighborhood of Sheepshead Bay with Manhattan Beach and a destination in itself, a place to stop, linger, and fish.

Controversy arose in the early 1990s when a group of residents fought to ban fishing off the bridge. The fishing community protested vigorously, and, although casting is now prohibited, the footbridge is still a favorite fishing spot for legions of urban anglers. It remains a delight for mothers and children, and for the elderly woman who, on a cold, wintry day in 2005, parks her car on Emmons Avenue, walks to the footbridge, and tosses day-old loaves of bread into the water, creating a pandemonium of ducks and swans, till you can hardly see the footbridge for the fowl.

GRANT'S TOMB NATIONAL MONUMENT PLAZA

In early 1997, the tomb of Ulysses S. Grant prepared to celebrate its hundredth anniversary on April 27. A number of Civil War buffs and National Park Service representatives decided that one good way to revive the solemnity and the gravitas of this historic monument was to get rid of the whimsical mosaic benches that encircled the tomb in the public plaza on three sides. But the community wouldn't hear of it. Michael Owen Gotkin, a landscape architect and a member of the Morningside Heights Historic District Committee, argued passionately for their preservation "as a fantastic work of urban design and as a proud testament to community participation in the creation of a work of public art." He pointed out that the *AIA Guide to New York City* compared the work to the work of Antonio Gaudí in Barcelona, noting how the benches do not compete with the tomb itself. Members of the community discussed chaining themselves to the benches. The Park Service offered to move them somewhere else, but Taipi Ben-Haim, one of the original project directors, argued that "to take them anywhere would be to destroy them."

122nd Street and Riverside Drive

Public Transit: 1, 9 trains to 116th Street. Walk six blocks north on Broadway, make a left onto Seminary Road, and walk two blocks west.

The semicircular swath of whimsy, all the more striking because it surrounds the Greek colonnade of a historical monument guarded by two stone eagles at the doorway, is a testament to the community arts movement of the late 1960s and early 1970s. The piece was commissioned in 1972 by the Park Service, in part to discourage people from scribbling graffiti on the monument, and in part to commemorate President Grant's founding of Yellowstone National Park a century earlier. It seems inspired by Grant's famous epitaph, inscribed on his tomb, "Let us have

Undulating mosaics envelop Grant's Tomb with a ribbon of color. Photo: Martha Cooper.

peace." It was designed by the artist Pedro Silva and the architect Phillip Danzig and sponsored by City Arts, headed by Susan Klok. Incorporating the energy and imagination of the community, the mosaics were made largely by volunteers, ranging in age from five to eighty-five, in a multitude of styles. An announcement read, "Contribute your design to be laid into a permanent work of art at Grant's Tomb." The only restriction imposed upon each volunteer group was to finish what they started. Although community participation in painted murals was already common at the time, this was considered the first nonprofessional transformation of a national monument.

PLACE MOMENT: TOM GOODRIDGE, GRANT'S TOMB

"When I introduced five-year-old Noah Heckman to the mosaic bench that adjoins Grant's Tomb, he jumped upon it, ran for a couple of yards, and declared, 'It's not only beautiful but you can sit on it.'"

Once compared to an unfolding comic book, the mosaic undulates in a semicircle around the tomb. It appears as a series of interconnected Red Grooms–style sofas. Sometimes the bench itself assumes the shape of a dinosaur or train; other times designs are imbedded in the mosaics. "The serpents," writes Tom Goodridge, a New York City teacher, "morph into curvilinear benches for most of its length. Generally the benches face inward (toward the monument) but occasionally they seem to reverse themselves to face outward to catch the inspiring vista of the park, river, and New Jersey shoreline beyond. At four points the serpent rears up cobra-like into columns with human faces expressing a rather menacing challenge to those daring to pass." The sofa-benches also appear to morph into humans at each end, putting an arm up behind a tree and across the shoulder of the next mosaic form. The mosaics highlight the varieties of things to be celebrated in this world—women's faces, hearts, butterflies, plants of all kinds, children playing, swans, eagles, lobsters, sea horses, buffalo, waterfalls tumbling on rocks, trees, yin and yang ballet dancers, and a chess board on a table. "Its mighty bank of images," Tom Goodridge conjectures, "may have been conjured in an attempt to summon earth's most potent powers to collaborate in a peacemaking that will try the mettle of all those who would fight for the life of the earth and all her inhabitants; transforming ourselves, and slaying the demons that keep us from daring to know one another."

THE MOSAIC TRAIL OF JIM POWER

In tiny shards of mirrors affixed to lampposts, New Yorkers can see reflections of the Cooper Union building, Astor Place, Broadway, and the landmark structures of the East Village. If they get close enough,

From the intersection of Broadway and East Eighth Street, the trail runs east along Eighth Street/Saint Marks Place to Avenue A, then south to Fourth Street, then west to Tower Records on Broadway.

they also see themselves in these mosaic lampposts created by Vietnam veteran Jim Power as part of his Mosaic Trail. The work is almost certainly illegal, but indisputably, along with memorial walls and graffiti, it is New York's longest-lasting guerilla art.

Born in Waterford, Ireland, Jim Power, "the Mosaic Man," came to live in New York City in 1959 at age thirteen. His family settled in Richmond Hills, Queens. He served in Vietnam and moved back to the Village in 1981. In 1985, he constructed his first mosaic around a tree pit in front of the Saint Marks Hotel. In 1988, under Mayor David Dinkins, he was authorized by the Department of Transportation with a one-year renewal permit, but he has continued his work for nearly twenty years.

PLACE MOMENT: GILLIAN FASSEL,
AMERICAN MUSEUM OF NATURAL HISTORY DIORAMAS

"Consider this a plea that the dioramas—the dusty old kudus and bongos in the Hall of African Mammals, especially—never be replaced by anything state-of-the-art or, heaven forbid, interactive. When you can't count on your favorite bar or corner bodega being there tomorrow, it's a comfort to know that the white rhinos are still facing off against that lone porcupine. . . . While it may be true that every metropolis houses its corner of the taxidermic animal kingdom, surely these are a hardier breed to have staved off the constant change that defines this city."

The Mosaic Man, Jim Power, balances on one of his own creations. Photo: Martha Cooper.

Jim's mosaic work is made up of a wide variety of materials: tiles, crockery, colored glass, mirrors, and seashells, some purchased, some donated, some found. It includes abstract design, figurative representations, and a good deal of lettering. He is adamantly against hard drugs and has even inscribed the words *no heroin* into many of his sidewalk mosaics. The miracle is that almost all of his work has remained unmolested.

**PLACE MOMENT:
ERIC MILLER,
JIM POWER LAMPPOSTS**

"The electric lights on lampposts come on at night and go off during the day: Thus they mark and regulate night and day. The attached traffic and pedestrian light signals likewise regulate traffic, telling one to go or to wait before going. . . . Jim Power's mosaic work on lampposts features hundreds of colors! What messages might this send? Certainly not just stop or go! Perhaps it might signal one to pause and wonder, consider, meditate, admire the beauty of it, relax, and think, I have arrived in the East Village."

Jim's work is celebratory, exalting the individual's urge to give of oneself for free. His work is part of the tradition of customizing mass culture in the urban environment. As the folklorist Barbara Kirshenblatt-Gimblett writes, "Cities and mass culture . . . offer a new frontier for exploring the indomitable will to make meaning, create value, and develop connoisseurship under the most exhilarating as well as the most devastating conditions."

His mosaics, Jim says, take "the anxiety out of people's days when they see them. It's not just long miles of lonely streets. It's your home."

**GHOST SITE:
THE TIC TAC TOE CHICKEN**

Formerly located in the arcade at 8 Mott Street between Worth Street and Mosco Street

Amidst the crowds and colorful signs of Chinatown, a walker passing by 8 Mott Street can still see the faint outline on the sign of the Chinatown Fair arcade advertising the "World Famous Tic Tac Toe Chicken." If ghosts can return to haunt the city cathedrals and historic

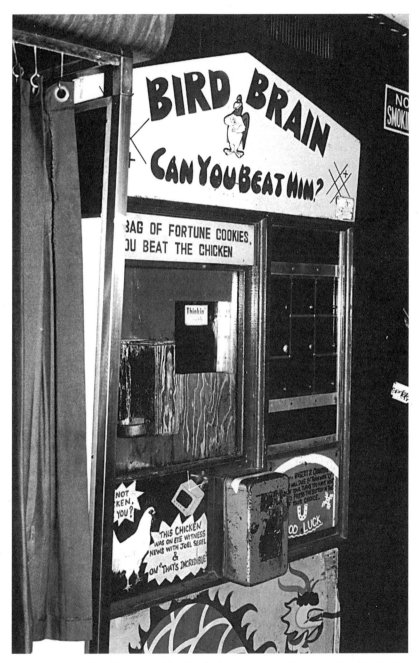

Many a New Yorker felt pretty silly after losing a game to the legendary Tic Tac Toe Chicken. Photo: Elaine Norman.

FIRST PERSON: ELAINE NORMAN

"In the early '90s I remember bringing my brother's ex-wife and her daughter to see Chinatown in the early nineties, and I brought them into this noisy arcade—*ting zing zing*, all those sounds—and I showed them the famous Tic Tac Toe Chicken. Of course, her daughter, Wendy, kept saying, 'Play, play.' Kids were lined up at all the other games, but the chicken was totally free. But as soon as Wendy's mother put her money in, the whole roomful of kids left their games and surrounded us and the chicken. And, of course, she lost. As we left and continued walking through Chinatown, Wendy kept saying, 'My mom lost to a chicken. My mom lost to a chicken.' And her mother kept saying, 'Stop it, Wendy.' But Wendy just wouldn't stop, and finally her mother said, 'I don't know why the chicken had to go first.'"

houses, certainly the Tic Tac Toe Chicken still haunts Chinatown. The chicken, named Lily, was retired in 1998 and never replaced. "Nestled between NBA Jam and a vintage photo booth," wrote Brandon Holley for *Time Out* in 1996, "is the fabled, feathered tic-tac-toe champ of the Chinatown Fair arcade. Her red cage taunts potential opponents with SHE'S NOT CHICKEN, ARE YOU? but promises A LARGE BAG OF FORTUNE COOKIES IF YOU BEAT THE CHICKEN. . . . Inevitably some sucker wanders in, plunks in 50 cents and tries to beat the birdbrain at X's and O's. The chicken takes her turn. She goes behind an opaque red plastic divider (the THINKIN' BOOTH) to make her move, then pecks at the feed that's her reward. Some may tie and some may lose, but it's impossible to beat her." How sad she is gone.

. . .

From the Indian caves to the gantries, from the Empire State Building to Jim Power's mosaics, New Yorkers select bits and pieces of the city's natural and human-made history to orient themselves around, providing the landscape with meaning in their daily lives, creating their own New York.

—Amanda Dargan and Steve Zeitlin

Art in the Subways

Elizabeth Murray, *Blooming*, 1996

Fifty-ninth Street (N, R, W, 4, 5, 6 trains)

Glass mosaic walls on the mezzanine connecting the 4, 5, 6 and the N, R, W; medallions
   on the 4, 5 express platforms

Andrew Ginzel and Kristen Jones, *Oculus*, 1998

Park Place (2, 3 trains); Chambers Street (A, C trains)

Stone mosaic murals throughout the station complex; stone and glass floor mosaic at
   the Park Place entrance

Tom Otterness, *Life Underground*, 2001

Fourteenth Street (A, C, E, L trains)

Bronze sculptures on railings, beams, and columns throughout the station

And more than 140 others . . .

Eye contact. On the subways, a city of eyes darts from one side of the car to another, pretending not to see. Eyes, cognizant of any sign of trouble. Eyes, undressing the person

"Conduct your blooming in the noise and whip of the whirlwind."—Gwendolyn Brooks, quoted in Elizabeth Murray's *Blooming* (Fifty-ninth Street Station)

sitting beside you. Reading the newspaper over your shoulder. At Chambers Street/Park Place, three hundred mosaic eyes—each just over a foot in width—stare out at passengers throughout the length of this downtown A, C, E, 2, and 3 station. Adapted from a photographic study of the eyes of three hundred New Yorkers conducted by the artists Kristin Jones and Andrew Ginzel, *Oculus* reflects the city's diversity and individuality. Eyelashes, eyelids, corneas, and irises are framed in rectangu-

Blooming, 1996, © Elizabeth Murray, Fifty-ninth Street subway station. Commissioned and owned by MTA Arts for Transit. Photo: Rob Wilson.

lar swatches and purposely mismatched, calling into question the powers of observation of passersby. The eyes watch and beg to be looked at. They seem to be watching over those who walk past with a mix of curiosity and caution. The eyes are survivors. They have seen more than they would have cared to. In a subway system that runs nonstop, sleep is simply not an option.

In the early morning half asleep, late in the day half dead, a swath of color from a luminescent mosaic streams through the windows of a rider's bobbing head. Seen on the move, often at stations riders are neither leaving from nor going to, the brilliant images lie in waiting, occasionally bursting through the cracks of consciousness.

At Fifty-ninth Street, workaday travelers can count on Elizabeth Murray's enormous mosaic coffee cups, huge as the craving for coffee early in the morning. At Fifty-third, showcased inside a wall opposite the token booth, subway riders gaze into a mirror of themselves as Ralph Fasanella's *Subway Riders* catches their eye, a reminder of who they are—black and white, young and old, jaded and overeager, thick-legged, sleeping, scrunched in, minding their own business. Each of these riders contains a world, a story of life, a point of departure and a destination. Their lives overlap for a small portion of the journey. Fasanella's portrait is overly optimistic only in the fact that all the people depicted manage to wedge themselves into a seat. "I didn't paint my paintings to hang in some rich guy's living room," says this acclaimed son of a buttonhole maker and an ice-delivery man.

LOWER DOWN, THE SPIRIT LIFTS

Fluorescent-lit, painted, or tiled white, the city's subway stations often come across as undifferentiated space, placeless places, indisputably charm free. While the city's neighborhoods are so distinctive, the underground network that connects them was designed as a functional and clean, more or less well-lighted place. At its inception in the late nineteenth century, the first architects, Heins and LeFarge, who had recently designed the Cathedral of Saint John the Divine, answered to the first engineer, William Barclay Parsons, appointed in 1891. Engineering took precedence over architecture and design. The signage was described as "wayfinding," as if the city said to the subways, simply, *Move me.*

But from the start, the labyrinth was designed to move people through more than space. Both the original architects and the engineers knew that the subway system had to be something more than a people-mover if it were to become "a great public work." Parsons, influenced by the City Beautiful movement, set aside half a million dollars to make the system beautiful as well as functional—with the aim of bringing out the better impulses of civic life.

Heins and LeFarge included in their original proposal ceramic plaques, tablets, mosaics, friezes, and bronze commemorative plaques. They hired the nation's best manufacturers of arts-and-crafts pottery to adorn the walls. The Grueby Faience Company manufactured an image of one of Columbus's ships for Columbus Circle, and a bevy of beavers (recalling the fur-trading industry of the Astor family) for Astor Place. The Rockwood Company's plaques at the Fulton Street station (4 and 5 line) depicted Robert Fulton's steamship, the *Clermont*. For the Wall Street stop on the same line, Rockwood designed an abstract rendering of the wall for which the street was named. And for the past hundred years passersby, consciously or unconsciously, register the cues—wayfinding or inspiration, depending on the day, the time, and whatever else is happening in their lives.

THE RENAISSANCE IN SUBWAY ART

As the stations aged, they grew increasingly shabby, and in the 1970s the system further deteriorated as New York neared bankruptcy. Graffiti was the art of the subways, soon to be all but eradicated by Mayor Ed Koch's administration. As the city recovered, more funds were put into renovating the stations, but it was a simple and sensible law that allowed the luminousness of art to shine down into the sunless underground: In 1982 the "Percent for Art" law was passed by the New York City Council, mandating that 1 percent of the budget for eligible citywide construction projects be spent on artwork for those facilities. Implementation began on September 15, 1983, establishing a procedure for determining eligible projects and an equitable artist selection process. Ironically, the urge to eliminate graffiti gave rise to a renaissance of public art, which, in a second twist, was often inspired by the graffiti that had preceded it. During the Koch administration, Ronay Menschel became deputy mayor and was appointed to the Metropolitan Transit Authority board. She hired Wendy Feuer to administrate an Arts for Transit program within the agency in 1985. A few years later, Sandra Bloodworth, a painter and tireless advocate for populist art, was hired to assist; she took over the program in 1996. Over 140 projects have now been permanently installed along the 722 miles of track.

Life Underground, 2001, © Tom Otterness, Fourteenth Street/Eighth Avenue subway station. Commissioned and owned by MTA Arts for Transit. Photo: Rob Wilson.

And so the 1980s gave birth to a radical thought: "Somebody somewhere cares about how I feel in this place—somebody cares about me," said Sandra Bloodworth. "It's all about how you treat people with respect—it's the ultimate respect to give to your riders." How appropriate, then, that the whimsical temporary work of art at 116th Street/Columbia University on the 1 and 9 trains, Michelle Greene's *Railrider's Throne* (1991), an ornate steel armchair placed on the platform for moments of grand reflection, was made permanent during her tenure.

"It's about place place place place," Sandra Bloodworth exclaimed in a recent interview. "Arts for Transit was never about celebrating new trends in contemporary art. Even Elizabeth Murray, an abstract artist, drew real high-heeled shoes and actual coffee cups to mark and celebrate the Bloomingdale's stop."

METAPHORS FOR WORLDS ABOVE AND BELOW

A ll the works relate to the community, the community of riders and the community above," said Bloodworth. Many of the artworks use words—not, as Bloodworth noted, "because we are publishing poetry on the walls, but because they say something to the riders. Yet, just as poets such as Milton and Dante used metaphor to depict worlds above and below—heaven or hell—subway art, situated on mezzanines and platforms, functions as poetic metaphor for the worlds above and below ground. With a painter's eye and an administrator's brush, Bloodworth and the Transit Authority select and commission a swath of below-ground similes, signs, and metaphors for the neighborhoods and personages who haunt what passes for the real world above.

Some are literal symbols. The mosaics for 110th, 116th, 125th, and 135th streets (2 and 3 lines) highlight the figures who put their Harlem neighborhoods on the map: Adam Clayton Powell, Langston Hughes, Duke Ellington, Billie Holiday, and Malcolm X. In Faith Ringgold's *Flying Home* on 125th Street, Harlem heroes fly above rooftops and over the famed Apollo Theater. Down in the Village, Lee Brozgold's mosaics and tiles honor the rebels of Greenwich Village, from bohemian poets to gay activists. Nancy Speros's *Artemis, Acrobats, Divas, and Dancers* represents Lincoln Center at the Lincoln Center stop on the 1 or 2.

Elizabeth Murray's *Blooming* at Fifty-ninth Street alludes to the local retailer, Bloomingdale's, as she imagines a "blooming dale." Bing Lee's mosaic for Chinatown's Canal Street harbors images from Zen Buddhism, as well as Chinese calligraphy and depictions of export items such as silk, porcelain, and tea, evoking both exotic images of the Orient and the multitude of chatchkes in the Chinatown shops above.

José Ortega's design for Third Avenue and 149th Street uses images of suns, faces, circles, and motifs from the neighborhood's Afro-Caribbean population. *The Open Secret* by Houston Conwill at 125th

Street (4, 5, and 6 trains) suggest scarification designs and other African ceremonial forms, the creation of sacred space, and the community bearing witness to ritual.

In Forty-second Street's *Under Bryant Park* by Samm Kunce, in the tunnel that connects the F, V, and D trains with the 7, the images are open ended. On the Sixth Avenue side, the white-tiled walls are interrupted by rising hills of earthy brown mosaic—and streaks of green appear to break through at certain points, accompanied by a line from Gustav Carl Jung: "Nature must not win the game, but it can never lose." Every rider will interpret this piece differently: A friend suggested that the quotes from

Oculus, 1998, © Kristen Jones and Andrew Ginzel, Park Place/Chambers Street subway station. Commissioned and owned by MTA Arts for Transit. Photo: Mark Kamber, courtesy of the MTA.

Jung and James Joyce alluded to the public library above. Yet this writer thinks of Times Square a block away and the skyscrapers blotting out as much of nature as culture possibly can. As you walk through the tunnel, golden brown roots seem to break in from above, shattering the tile, as if some great redwood tree grew above, taller than the Empire State Building, ready reminder of nature's triumph.

PLACE MOMENT: AMANDA DARGAN, FORTY-SECOND STREET STATION

"When I stand on the platform at Forty-second Street on the 4, 5, and 6, and the train brakes suck in air as they noisily get ready to roll, I always hear the first musical phrase of the song 'Somewhere'—it goes, 'There's a place for us'—from *West Side Story*. I mentioned that to my students, and one of them heard it, too. Somehow that seem appropriate to me here in New York—but of course what I'm hoping is that there's a place for me to sit on the train so I can read my paper."

The metaphors seen through glazed eyes depict not only the world above but the world below. Along the Forty-second Street Tunnel, Kunce's images of the water table and imaginary tree roots suggest what traversing the underground might be like without the subway tunnel. Harry Roseman's *Subway Wall at Wall Street* (2 and 3 trains) begins with lifelike representations of rocks, the "groundwork of Manhattan," as if to show New Yorkers what's really below ground.

Apart from the alligators, that is—because for the gullible and all lovers of New York folklore, the urban legend of "alligators in the sewers" abides. Until recently, walking along the tunnel separating the F beneath Sixth Avenue and the 1, 2, 3, and 9 trains along Seventh, you were accompanied by a line of alligators, no more than a foot tall, crawling along beside you, a realization of the city's most famous urban legend. The folklorist Jan Harold Brunvand traces one possible source of the story to a newspaper report on February 10, 1935, of a single alligator found dead in an uptown sewer. He cites a version that appears in Thomas Pynchon's 1963 novel *V*:

> Last year, or maybe the year before, kids all over Nueva York bought . . . little alligators for pets. Macy's was selling them for fifty cents; every child, it seemed, had to have one. But soon the children grew bored with

them. Some set them loose in the streets, but most flushed them down the toilets. And these had grown and reproduced, had fed off rats and sewage. So now they moved big, blind, albino, all over the sewer system. Down there, God knows how many there were. Some had turned cannibal because in their neighborhood the rats had all been eaten, or fled in terror.

The line of low-lying alligators was a temporary artwork from the early 1990s, and it is gone. But now, also on Fourteenth Street but on Eighth Avenue (A, E, and C trains), Tom Otterness in *Life Underground* imagines a fanciful alligator, head popping out of a manhole cover, with human hands, biting what appears to be a baby's butt. Otterness's whimsical alligator is one of 140 sculpted surprises scattered through the station, including a rider endlessly waiting for a train, and fare beaters ducking under the turnstile as cops await them on the other side.

In "The MTA Song," written in 1948 by Jacqueline Steiner and Bess Lomax Hawes, the hero, Charlie, is said to "ride forever 'neath the streets of Boston" as the "man who never returned." A rider suffering the same fate in New York today would imagine an interesting dreamscape of a city reflected in the art below ground—giant high-heeled shoes, steamboats, and flying folk. But to the riders who divide their time between above and below, the images are wayfinding in the deepest sense. They render the underground a part of this endlessly creative city rather than a placeless netherworld. The work transforms this urban underbelly with sweeps of meaning and color that are now an integral portion of the city's artscape, as valid as its museums and sculpture gardens.

Standing in the doleful wind that blows through tunnels on to the platforms, in the light that sliiiiiiiiiiiiiiiiiiiiiiiides along steel rails, signaling the train's imminent arrival, riders seem to say, *Move me, not only from here to there, but deeply, profoundly*. So run your finger along the colorful mosaics at Forty-second Street, with lines from Jack and Jill and James Joyce emblazoned on the walls. The art is not cordoned off. You're allowed to touch it. "The biggest accolade we can get," said Sandra Bloodworth, "is when someone reaches out and touches the wall in wonder."

—*Steve Zeitlin*

Governors Island

Upper New York Bay

Governors Island is still only partially open to the public, with seasonal ferry service from summer through fall.

Public Transit: R, W trains to Whitehall Street. Walk east along Whitehall against traffic to the East River to catch the ferry.

4, 5 trains to Bowling Green. Walk east along Whitehall Street against traffic to the East River, or follow State Street east until it runs into White-hall, then turn right and walk to the river to catch the ferry.

The Governors Island ferry leaves from the Battery Maritime Building, 11 South Street at the foot of White-hall. For ferry schedules, log on to www.nps.gov/gois.

Listed on the National Register of Historic Places as a National Historic District, 1985

Designated a New York City Historic Landmark District, 1996

New York's smaller islands have always been the city's workhorses. Ellis Island collected the immigrants. Hart Island buried the poor. Blackwell's Island housed the insane. Governors Island manned the defenses. The world is hardly less perilous now than when soldiers first defended New York's harbor, but danger now takes a different form than fleets of invading ships. So, a bit over two centuries after its birth as a fort, Governors Island is being returned to the people of New York. More marvelous yet, we're being asked what kind of place we want it to be.

A WORLD APART

The surprise of journeying to Governors Island begins at the Battery Maritime Building, a lovely false front to some old ferry slips that used to take commuters to Brooklyn. Here's where you catch the ferry to Governors Island. Look for a vaulted porch (with Guastavino

tile under the roof) and forty-foot columns, just north of the new terminal for the Staten Island Ferry. The building is imposing but easy to
overlook amid the unruly comings and goings at the southeastern tip of
Manhattan Island.

Until now, Governors Island was a place apart from New York City
though scarcely eight hundred yards offshore. Today the island belongs
to us all, but, oddly, the sensation of foreign passage still remains. The
feeling comes on in a rush as you walk through the colonnade and down
the long entranceway to the ferry's small dock, past old-fashioned hooks
and hoists and men in harbor uniforms. It continues as the ferry pushes
off, gliding to its destination in all of five minutes. Great views of the
harbor pass by, but in your mind's eye you fill in the scene with the hundreds of vessels and thousands of men that crowded New York's port
when it was among the busiest in the world.

In the future, passenger ferries might once again land on the south
side of Governors Island facing Brooklyn—in Buttermilk Channel,
where favorable winds and a calmer waterway made it easier to dock
small boats. For now, we disembark directly across from Manhattan on
a part of the island whose redbrick buildings housed the federal arsenal
for New York until 1920. Ranger Michael Shaver meets us there in a little open-sided electrically powered car that National Park Service staff
motor around in. Bitter cold wind off the water shoots through the car,
but Mike doesn't wear any gloves. Perhaps time on this island inures
you to the cold, but it suggests how hard winter guard duty would have
been at old Fort Jay or Castle Williams.

Mike is the chief park ranger at Governors Island. His fascination
with history led him to apply for a job with the Park Service after a stint
fighting fires with the U.S. Forest Service. The National Park Service is
a federal agency within the Department of the Interior—the same
agency that manages Yellowstone, Ellis Island, and Gettysburg. Mike's
duties at Governors Island include a little bit of everything, from running operations to giving public tours to computing the payroll.
Rangers now tend to specialize, but Mike happily counts himself among
the last generation of rangers encouraged to be jacks-of-all-trades. "One
of the delightful things about my job," he says, "is that I've been trained
to do so many things. I fight forest fires. I can manage a library. I can

Near Ligget Hall, the Early Bird Memorial honors early aviators such as Wilbur Wright and Ruth Law who flew test flights from Governors Island. Photo © New York State Department of Economic Development. Photo: Bob McGee.

curate a museum collection. I know a little bit about historic preservation, so I can talk intelligently with contractors and architects about the preservation needs of a building. I have a little bit of law and policy. I have a little bit of law enforcement and search and rescue. I can do pretty much whatever needs to be done in a national park."

It's partly up to the National Park Service to help New York transform Governors Island from a military base to a public amenity. The Park Service owns and directly controls twenty-two acres of the island, which were designated a National Monument, but it also helps guide the public through the island's larger landmark district, covering about half of the 172-acre land mass and created in the 1990s when the New York City Landmarks Preservation Commission put this historic area under its protection. Mike describes the island's shape as an ice cream cone. The northern portion—with its historically evocative buildings and landscapes—forms the ice cream. The southern portion, forming the cone, has more open land and fewer buildings that are valued for their architecture or history. So it's the southern part that's available for new development, ball fields, and park spaces. The Governors Island Preservation and Development Corporation (GIPEC), a public development corporation controlled jointly by New York City and New York State, controls all but the Park Service's twenty-two acres of National Monument.

Normally a new park of this size and complexity would take years to open. But since its transition to public ownership in 2003, Governors Island has been opening slowly yet steadily, with the Park Service and GIPEC controlling the pace and encouraging New Yorkers to get used to their new territory. Ferry service from Manhattan to Governors Island now runs regularly from summer through fall, welcoming people to tour selected areas, attend special events, and soak up the sun and views along a stretch of harborfront esplanade. Simultaneously and behind the scenes, GIPEC and the Park Service are stabilizing aging buildings and collaborating with public and private groups on long-term development of the island.

Our little electric vehicle pokes about the island's built and open spaces, with Mike giving a running commentary on the island's history that must grow more fluent and fleshed out each time he gives a tour. It's hard not to catch his excitement. In the middle of gorgeous Upper New York Bay, nearly two hundred acres of island sit and wait for us; views that typically only the rich can afford are offered from every point along the perimeter. Lady Liberty, the Brooklyn Bridge, the downtown towers of Manhattan. Brooklyn's Red Hook waterfront, a huge Saudi container ship idling at dock. Inland from the shoreline are acres of well-tended grass and plane and oak trees. In one tree a pheasant large enough to be seen from the road makes its home. Gracious nineteenth-century homes that housed generations of officers cluster in lovely settings. Strategically placed military structures—some the most innovative of their day—survive intact two centuries after their construction. Acres of open space surround the existing structures, five minutes across the water from some of the densest urban development on earth. Yet somehow, in this world apart, life on Governors Island didn't emulate the big city. Most of the people working on its future hope that it never will.

FROM THE ARMY TO THE COAST GUARD: 1790s TO 2000s

W hat would become Governors Island was a seasonal oystering and nut-gathering grounds for the Canarsee Indians, who lost their access to the island to the Dutch in the 1630s. By the close of the 1600s, British colonial governors had rights to the fertile patch, using it at various times as residence, private hunting grounds, and income-producing rental property. Once named for its nut trees (in Canarsee, *Pagganck;* in Dutch, *Nooten*), the place came to be called "the Governor's Island," and over time simply Governors Island. Military use of the island began in small measure in the mid-1700s, and the massive British occupation of New York during the Revolutionary War kept its defensive advantages for the Crown. When the British fleet sailed into New York harbor in 1776 with over four hundred ships carrying thirty thousand troops, American cannon briefly shot at them from earthworks constructed on Governors Island, providing cover for the retreat of General Washington and his army. So many British ships crowded the harbor that a farmer from Staten Island is said to have quipped that it appeared the forest had returned to these shores (by this point deforestation was well advanced).

After the American victory and the eventual creation of a federal government with the ratification of the Constitution, New York transferred control of Governors Island to the federal government for use as a defensive outpost. By the close of the 1790s, forts were being rebuilt and constructed all around the harbor, funded by the national treasury. With Britain and France still threatening the young United States from across the Atlantic, from the Caribbean, and from the north, south, and west of its own huge land mass, Americans felt nothing if not vulnerable—

New Yorkers perhaps more than most, having recently experienced seven years of occupation. The Army built Fort Jay, Castle Williams, and South Battery on Governors Island, Fort Wood on the plot of land that later welcomed the Statue of Liberty, Fort Gibson where Ellis Island would be built, Castle Clinton at the southern tip of Manhattan, and, to defend other parts of the city's waterways, Fort Hamilton, Fort Wadsworth, Fort Lafayette, and many others. Multiple sophisticated fortifications protected the harbor and the city by the early 1800s, soon proving their worth—though not in battle. During the War of 1812, the British attacked the far more lightly defended Baltimore and Washington, D.C., advancing through the Chesapeake Bay and avoiding New York harbor and its formidable defenses.

Mike's car buzzes across the dry moat and up a grass-covered hillock to star-shaped Fort Jay, as he expounds on the Renaissance-era insights used in its construction. On long, mostly flat Governors Island, the military designers were in effect building themselves both heights and increased surface area for maximum lethality. Mike describes what attackers would face. "First you had to approach by boat being shot at the whole time by cannon with tennis-ball-sized shot. The fort is surrounded by a glacis—it's a

SISTER SITE: COMMANDING OFFICER'S QUARTERS

Designated a New York City Landmark, 1967

Built in 1843, and adapted several times since, this building did indeed house every commanding officer of Governors Island from the time of its construction until the Coast Guard departed in 1996. Officers posted here took part in every war fought by the United States, and many of them, such as Winfield Scott, H. H. (Hap) Arnold, Leonard Wood, and Omar Bradley, are prominent names in military history. On December 7, 1988, the house was chosen as the site for the arms summit meeting between President Ronald Reagan and President Mikhail Gorbachev of the Soviet Union, not long before glasnost, the fall of the Berlin Wall, and the end of the cold war.

Situated in landscaped Nolan Park—where commissioned officers inhabited the most beautiful cluster of homes on the island—the rear of the house has a fantastic view onto Buttermilk Channel, which can seen from its five bay windows and from the back porch. The building is still being used for receptions and ceremonial events and may continue in that role as the new life of the island evolves.

French term for a wide, flat killing grounds—and from the parapet of the fort you've got the angles of the star points giving the defenders

SISTER SITE:
CASTLE WILLIAMS

Designated a New York City Landmark, 1967

Along with Fort Jay and the South Battery (long ago transformed into officers' quarters), Castle Williams was built (1807–1811) to defend New York's harbor from hostile foreign empires. Today, landfill has made its aggressively strategic position harder to discern, but Castle Williams's location on a rocky outcropping of land and its hundred cannons made the fort extremely dangerous to any ship in target range in Upper New York Bay. The round wall was designed to resist penetration by attacking cannon, reinforced by its thickness: eight feet at the bottom and seven at the top. The Landmarks Preservation Commission describes Castle Williams as a "massive bastion forming three-fifths of a circle, with a two-story entrance pavilion filling in the remainder of the form. . . . At the time of its construction, it served as a prototype for seacoast fortifications in America, and it is today one of the best examples of its type in existence."

cover to shoot from both left and right. Remember, the fort isn't protecting anything on the inside; it's protecting the harbor. If you're attacking, you have to make it across open land, through the deep moat— with people shooting across and down at you—and then you have to climb the wall of the fort with ladders. You might make it, but it's going to be a costly exercise. Plus, Fort Jay on the north of the island and Castle Williams on the south, with its eight-foot thick walls, were connected by a trench, so the troops could resupply themselves at will."

By the 1830s, the early forts no longer provided adequate lines of defense for the city, so the Army began to deploy Governors Island for alternative uses. Housing its officer corps was one function. Serving as the region's arsenal was another. As Mike explains, you wouldn't put an arsenal inside an active fort, so Governors Island's increasing use over the second half of the nineteenth century as a storehouse for weapons reflects the end of its days as a fortification. Mike spreads his arms wide, indicating the large fields spreading out on the eastern edge of the island next to its three piers and cobblestone wharf. "We have pictures of this area around 1900 when the arsenal was like a retirement home for an-

Fort Jay, Governors Island, 1982/83. Photo: Library of Congress, Prints and Photographs Division, John T. Lowe, HABS.

tiquated Civil War cannons and ammunition. This whole field was nothing but pyramids of cannonballs and cannons laid out in neat rows outside their carriages." During World War I, the south end of the island was one big rail yard with dozens of warehouses. War materiél and supplies were assembled and stored here until they were shipped to Allied troops in France.

In the 1930s, the officers and men of the First Army were headquartered on Governors Island, and the families of officers began to make their homes here. Tom and Dick Smothers, known to the world as the

Smothers Brothers comedy team, were born at the base hospital in the late 1930s. Former officers' quarters alongside Fort Jay were converted into comfortable apartments. One wonders whether the residents felt more or less secure knowing that there was still a magazine of live ammunition underground, directly beneath their homes. Along with increasing residential use came the rudiments of community infrastructure: houses of worship, stores, a movie theater—even the once lethal glacis was transformed into a golf course.

World War II interrupted domestication of the island. Temporary barracks and basic training for local troops crowded its open spaces, and periodically reporters thronged to the island to cover the induction of high-profile recruits like the boxer Joe Louis. When the task of invading Normandy was assigned to the First Army, its Governors Island headquarters pulled up and moved to Bristol, England, for the duration of the war.

The Army left Governors Island in 1966, but shortly thereafter the Coast Guard moved in, so the island continued its anomalous life as a military base in the middle of New York City. Mike says that the city's tough reputation in the 1960s made some families consider a posting on Governors Island "arduous duty,"

SISTER SITE: GOVERNORS ISLAND, LIGGET HALL

The barracks at Ligget Hall (1930) housed the entire Sixteenth Infantry Regiment, all 1,375 men. They ate together, trained together, lived together—that is, all the enlisted men did. The officers were housed in a separate U-shaped building attached to one end. Designed by the firm of McKim, Mead and White, Ligget Hall was a Georgian-style model barracks, one-quarter mile long, that at the time of its construction was the longest military building in the world.

It is said that Mayor Fiorello La Guardia wanted to site his new airport right here (with the runway extending southward toward the harbor entrance). Not happy with the city's intended intrusion on their island, the Army chose this spot for Ligget Hall, neatly precluding the mayor's plan and sending the airport to Queens. At least that's the story. What's certain, however, is that a number of early aviators used this area of Governors Island for their test flights. Wilbur Wright flew from here to Grant's Tomb and back in 1909, and Ruth Law, one of the most famous aviators of her day, alighted at Governors Island after a distance-record-breaking nonstop flight from Chicago in 1916.

but after interviewing former young "Coasties" who grew up here, he's concluded that the children of Coast Guard families liked their unique habitat. The Army had constructed its own elementary school on the island in the 1930s, P.S. 26, and the Coast Guard built one in the early 1970s. Two decades later you could still see a movie at the base cinema on a Friday night for a mere two dollars, or drop by the bowling alley and the Burger King. The 1990 Census reported about three thousand people living on the island, with another two thousand commuting back and forth each day. Until the Coast Guard left the island in 1996—eager to cut the expensive base from its budget—Governors Island stayed a separate sphere. Where else in New York could a daily ritual at sunset bring human movement to a stop? Each day at dusk the sounds of a bugle playing retreat poured forth from speakers installed around the island. As the flag was lowered, all the island's occupants stopped in their tracks, faced the garrison's flagpole, stayed quiet, and stood still.

A "CENTRAL PARK" FOR THE HARBOR

New Yorkers moved quickly to reclaim Governors Island from the federal government after the Coast Guard left. Federal property that is no longer wanted gets "surplused," and other agencies are asked if they would like to step in and take over. Usually there are no fees involved, but efforts to balance the budget persuaded Congress to try to sell Governors Island for several hundred million dollars. Putting a price tag on the island complicated matters for New York City but had the unintended benefit of keeping the island off the surplus auction block and away from other agencies—who were not that interested anyway.

In the meantime, groups outside the government started to organize to save Governors Island for the people of New York. The first alert came from the National Trust for Historic Preservation to New York's own Regional Plan Association (RPA), a private group that since the 1920s has concerned itself with planning for the New York metropolitan region. Excited by the possibilities of a great new public space for New York, RPA galvanized a new consortium of individuals and groups to turn their attention to Governors Island. "What's the public interest on

Governors Island?" is the question these concerned citizens began to ask themselves and others. Interesting answers emerged, and as things turned out, many of the principles developed in these early planning meetings have been adopted in the agreement for Governors Island.

Deed restrictions require that—in addition to the National Monument—a minimum of forty acres of the island be dedicated as new park land. At least twenty of those acres will be contiguous. Another twenty acres will be used for educational purposes. The beautiful esplanade with views onto the harbor must stay intact. The island must stay in public ownership. No private housing is allowed. Designating the northern area as a national and a city landmark district also means the buildings and grounds in that stretch must be preserved.

Reaching an agreement took enormous effort on the part of many people. The late Senator Daniel Patrick Moynihan clinched a deal with President Bill Clinton for the island on a helicopter ride the two happened to take over New York City. Moynihan must have made a convincing argument, because by the time they landed Clinton had agreed to sell the island back to New York for only one dollar, as long as its future use served the public interest. A combination of local and national politics prevented the deal from being struck, although Clinton—at the urging of Congresswoman Carolyn Maloney—did establish the twenty-two-acre National Monument as one of his last acts in office. It took a few years and some new sympathy for New York after September 11, 2001, but President George W. Bush, Governor George Pataki, and Mayor Michael Bloomberg finally realized Clinton's promise in April 2002 when they announced that Governors Island would be returned to the people of New York for the sum of one dollar.

The story isn't over yet. All along, the citizens coalition called the Governors Island Alliance, with staff support from the RPA, has been organizing and advocating for public-spirited uses of the island. Places for play, recreation, education, the arts, and public affairs are all being talked about. But ultimately the decisions about the island's future will be made by its two managers, the National Park Service and GIPEC. The big tension, of course, is how to spur the kind of development that brings in revenue without giving away the island to private interests. One bad idea that's already been eliminated: casino gambling. The deed restrictions are one protection against a giveaway, but the Governors Island Alliance is encouraging New Yorkers to pay attention to what is being proposed.

Will Governors Island be a "Central Park for New York's harbor," as its citizen promoters suggest? Come visit the island, help create new ways of using its terrain, and log on to the websites of its planners to make your own hopes for the island known: Governors Island Alliance, www.rpa.org/govisland.html; National Park Service, www.nps.gov/gois. This is a place where you can envelop yourself in the city and escape from it at the same time.

—*Marci Reaven*

Urban Nature

An East Harlem casita—one of the small huts in the style of old-fashioned Puerto Rican country houses that transform vacant lots across the city into social clubs and community gardens. Photo: Martha Cooper.

O nce," writes Michael Gold in his memoir, *Jews Without Money*, about the turn-of-the-century Lower East Side, "Jake Gottlieb and I discovered grass struggling between the sidewalk cracks near the livery stable. We were amazed by this miracle. We guarded this treasure, allowed no one to step on it. Every hour the gang studied 'our' grass, to try to catch it growing. It died, of course, after a few days: only children are hardy enough to grow on the East Side."

The city's most pristine and natural parks, of course, are not located in midtown Manhattan or on the Lower East Side. According to Michael Feller of the Natural Resources Group at the New York City Department of Parks, they are in northwest Staten Island, places like Saw Mill Creek Preserve and Sweet Bay Magnolia Preserve. But most of the city's parks, even the most natural, juxtapose ancient marshes and woodlands with man-made embankments and roadways. Inwood Hill Park in upper Manhattan is part of New York's ancient rocky shoreline. In the park, the rock shelters used by the Indians still fascinate New Yorkers, but those caves, once by the water, are now half a mile inland. The WPA filled in the marshland and created the Hudson Barge Canal nearby. In fact, by realigning the waterway,

PLACE MOMENT: JENNIFER FURL, PARK AVENUE TULIPS

"The median on Park Avenue, somewhere in the Fifties, on a spring Sunday, probably after Easter. Sit next to thousands of tulips, bright pink or maybe yellow, all planted inches apart by people in the middle of the workday, when hardly anyone notices. The taxis will drive by on either side, but you can sit there with the tulips and look down the street at Grand Central together. Smiling that it is now the proper season to sit outside again."

Tree experts argue whether this Staten Island "Colossus," a 119-foot tulip tree in Clove Lakes Park, is the tallest tree in New York City or whether the title belongs to another tulip, the Queens "Giant," in Alley Pond Park. Photo: Elaine Norman.

construction shifted Marble Hill from Manhattan to the Bronx, leaving its political designations still split between the two boroughs.

Similarly, Pelham Bay Park in the Bronx displays an ancient, rocky New England shoreline and vestal marshes—but, in fact, there is no Pelham Bay. It's now an enormous WPA-constructed parking lot for Orchard Beach. And on the other side of the pristine park is a late 1960s housing complex, Co-op City. Alley Pond Park in Queens appears forever wild, but it's ecologically challenged by cloverleafs—and not the natural kind but from the Grand Central, Long Island, and Cross Island expressways. Throughout the city, the Parks Department works to undo the concrete hard-edge shoreline favored by the WPA and restore the natural shore.

PLACE MOMENT:

ED ROSENFELD, JAMAICA

BAY WILDLIFE PRESERVE

"In view of Manhattan to the west, Kennedy Airport to the east, lies the Jamaica Bay Wildlife Preserve. Over the waving marsh grasses I observe the crossing paths of a great white ibis, its long neck downward bent at the head as it rises in flight, and the Concorde, echoing the great bird, its crook-necked cockpit down as it rises in takeoff."

"Very little of Central and Prospect parks is natural," says Feller. "They're, in a sense, bonsai trees on a grand scale. But to give [their designers Frederick Law] Olmstead and [Calvert] Vaux credit, the parks are so well done that they come to represent an idealized nature." In New York City today, very little of what passes for nature is natural. It seems to be that pinch of the natural sprinkled amidst the urban that makes us love it all the more. In the subway tunnel connecting the F and V trains to the 1, 2, and 3 on Forty-second Street, a line from Goethe is inscribed in mosaic on the walls, commenting on nature in New York: "Even the unnatural is natural."

Community Greening:
La Casita Rincón Criollo,
Magnolia Tree Earth Center,
Liz Christy Bowery-Houston
Community Garden

The South Bronx, Bed-Stuy, and the Lower East Side: In all three places in the 1960s and 1970s, charismatic and visionary individuals led neighbors and compatriots on campaigns to green their communities. Using the tools of nature, they transformed bleak streets and rubble-strewn lots into places that were healthy, safe, and beautiful. Much of what they achieved is still here for us to enjoy.

LA CASITA RINCÓN CRIOLLO

158th Street and Brook Avenue, Melrose, the Bronx

Public Transit: 2, 5 trains to Jackson Avenue. Walk one block west to Cauldwell Avenue and turn right. Walk six blocks north to East 156th Street and turn left. Walk three blocks to Brook Avenue and turn right. Walk two blocks to the casita.

Casitas are small houses surrounded by gardens created to recall the look and feel of the Puerto Rican countryside. One of the city's oldest and largest, Rincón Criollo, occupies city-owned land that was abandoned and strewn with garbage before neighborhood people reclaimed it in the late 1970s. Since then, neighbors have used their corner to gather, garden, hold community events, and pass down musical and cultural traditions. Today, the casita still thrives but, caught in the too-frequent urban conundrum of good causes competing for the same scarce space, will move down the block to 157th Street and Brook Avenue to make room for low-income housing.

José (Chema) Soto is credited by his fellows as the inspiration behind the beautiful casita. One day he had had enough of the sights of destruction that daily greeted him in his neighborhood, known more than any other part of the city for its scope of devastation in the sixties and seventies. Choosing a vacant lot he passed regularly with his daughter, he plunged in and began clearing debris. Other residents joined him, and soon around fifty people found themselves taking care of land they did not own. Inspired by a casita Chema saw in East Harlem, they created a little home of their own in the Bronx, and called it Rincón Criollo (Downhome Corner).

The two-room casita is built from recycled scrap lumber and other found objects, painted aquamarine, fronted by a deck, and surrounded by fruit trees and gardens of flowers and vegetables. As in Puerto Rico, a clean-swept small yard without vegetation, known as a *batey*, surrounds the house and is separated by a fence from the gardens. There is a kitchen with running water and a ramp for visitors in wheelchairs. The casita is peopled and run by its members, who range in age from young adults to seniors, and who maintain their membership and welcome by adhering to group standards of proper behavior. The casita is a place for urban gardening, hanging out, and mounting formal and informal gatherings. It's also a place where music and dance—particularly the important Puerto Rican musical traditions of *bomba* and *plena*—are played, danced, and taught. Both *bomba* and *plena* are percussion based and are rooted in West and Central African traditions blended in different degrees with Euro-Iberian and indigenous music and movement. *Plena* became known as *el periódico cantado* (the sung newspaper) because its lyrics narrate and comment on community goings-on, gossip, and political news. Early on, it became a forceful tool for labor and community organization and activism.

The folklorist Joseph Sciorra has thought deeply about the importance of New York's casitas. He writes:

The New York casita and *batey* are an attempt to evoke a specific place

Rincón Criollo: The intergenerational nature of *la casita* fosters the passing down of cultural traditions. Photo: Martha Cooper.

and time, that is, Puerto Rico of the recent past. The re-creation of a tropical, pre-industrial landscape in the northern, urban environment is achieved through close attention to detail. At Rincón Criollo, the bottom halves of tree trunks are painted white, in keeping with practices and aesthetics common throughout the Afro-Caribbean. A functioning outhouse, once common to poor people's homes on the island, stands behind the casita in a yard where chickens, ducks, rabbits, and (until it was confiscated by the American Society for the Prevention of Cruelty to Animals) a goat are kept. It is this constellation of culturally significant objects that gives people a sense of being home.

Sciorra then quotes from Chema, translating from the Spanish:

> This piece of land resembles Puerto Rico because it has a Puerto Rican–style house, a Puerto Rican–style garden, and a Puerto Rican–style latrine. Because of this, many people call it 'the link.' In no other place are you going to feel as though you're in Puerto Rico. And here you see the same things as over there, like tomatoes, peppers, eggplants, *plena,* and the exact same house. Look! The bottom of the house is made entirely from bamboo, which you find in Puerto Rico. And here everyone enjoys whistling like the *coquí* [an island tree frog]. There is nothing more Puerto Rican than the *coquí.*

And there is little of more concern to city officials than the thought of permanent squatters on city-owned land. The legal status of Rincón Criollo has been in contention since its beginning, along with hundreds of other green oases created in what Sciorra called "life-affirming responses to the political negligence and economic tyranny that reduced the South Bronx (and other poor neighborhoods) to rubble." For a few years the city's GreenThumb program regulated the unofficial use of city land. But Mayor Rudolph Giuliani did away with GreenThumb when he tried to do away with the city's community gardens—many of them started, like Rincón Criollo, in grassroots efforts to reclaim abandoned and dangerous lots. When the mayor's plan was stopped in the courts, many of the gardens gained official status and caretakers. Rincón Criollo was not among the victors, but its tenacious supporters seem able to keep the garden going. As casita member José Rivera once said about adapting Puerto Rican traditions to the South Bronx, "You've got to keep on inventing."

FIRST PERSON: STEVE ZEITLIN

"When I visited Rincón Criollo some years ago, I met a woman there who grew up in Puerto Rico. She recalled how when she first visited the outhouse in the garden and whiffed that overwhelming stench, 'it really took me back.' I was overwhelmed by the transformative powers of memory!"

MAGNOLIA TREE EARTH CENTER

677–679 Lafayette Avenue, Bedford-
Stuyvesant, Brooklyn

(718) 387–2116

Hours: The magnolia trees are always
on view, but to visit the center or its
gardens, call for an appointment
and event info.

Public transit: G train to Bedford Av-
enue/Nostrand Avenue. Walk east
along Lafayette Avenue about two
blocks. You'll find the center just
after crossing Marcy Avenue.

Designated a New York City Landmark,
1970

June is a good time to visit the center to see its magnolia grandiflora trees blossom in full glory. Large, white, and lemon-scented, the flowers are what distinguish a grandiflora, also known as a southern magnolia. The taller of the two trees was planted by local resident William Lemken around 1885 and brought here as a seedling from Georgia. The magnificent grandiflora is not supposed to grow as far north as Brooklyn, but this one did, protected from our cold winds by three nearby buildings whose cellars also warmed its roots. The old magnolia and its younger sister (planted years later by Delta Sigma Theta sorority and Congresswoman Shirley Chisholm) now adorn a respected center for education about the environment.

The lovely flora may be visible above ground, but the center has its roots in people power. You can tell that from its mission: environmental justice. Advocates for environmental justice are forging a new frontier in civil rights, asserting that poor and minority Americans have suffered far too long from a disproportionate share of health-damaging environmental dangers located within their communities. Let us all *share* the dangers we have to live with, they argue, and let us all share in the greenery. Once that happens, who knows? In the interest of a sustainable planet, we might be motivated to find more responsible uses for land and renewable resources.

A quest for equity and people power guides the center's future and accounts for its past. In the mid-1960s, Hattie Carthan (1901–1984) grew increasingly distressed by the continuing downward spiral of her neighborhood. Her conviction that local residents could make a difference led her into activism, and her lifelong love for trees led her to focus on tree planting and to discover the miraculous Lafayette Street magnolia. At first her neighbors thought trees might be beside the point in a community ravaged by racism and poverty, but Carthan persisted, and her energy and good ideas won increasing support within the neighborhood as well as outside of it. She recalled to a *New York Times* reporter the letter she wrote to the city's new mayor, John Lindsay, in 1966 inviting him to a barbecue. "I wrote a long love letter to Mayor Lindsay inviting him to our party, and one day the phone rang, and it was the mayor, and he asked if he could come to our barbecue." With the mayor as a friend, the spotlight shone on Mrs. Carthan's T & T–Vernon Block Association. T & T stood for Throop and Tompkins, the avenues that border Vernon—a name the group used "like it was dynamite," she once explained. Soon the Parks Department was calling

Magnolia Tree Earth Center: landmark of perseverance. Photo: Martha Cooper.

to offer help with tree planting and conservation, supporting a campaign that eventually planted over fifteen hundred trees in the area. When Carthan took up the cause of the magnolia in 1968, various city agencies were prepared to listen. What threatened the venerable tree was a plan to knock down the brownstones that protected it to build a new housing development (a project sponsored by Model Cities, a former federal program to benefit low-income communities). To quell Carthan's objection, the development's architect suggested that her group build a new wall. But walls cost money, so Carthan and the Magnolia Tree Committee engaged neighbors—young and old—in fundraising, and reached out to citywide groups. In the meantime they politicked.

A big victory came in 1970 when the New York City Landmarks Preservation Commission declared the tree a landmark. Most landmarks are buildings, but there are rare and unusual designations such as the Cyclone roller coaster in Coney Island and the cast-iron watchtower in Marcus Garvey Park. There is even one other tree: a weeping beech planted in 1847 in Flushing, Queens, by the nurseryman Samuel Parsons. With landmark designation secured, the magnolia would be protected from purposeful destruction. What puzzled the commission was how to protect the tree while not opposing the new housing going up next door. The commission's regulatory guidelines sought to protect the tree from construction damage, but would a new wall really protect it? Would any change in the surrounding structures alter the microclimate and doom the plucky magnolia? Luckily for the tree, the size of the housing development shrank, and the old brownstones were saved. Not one to rest on her laurels, Carthan now asked for the buildings, too. "Just saving the tree was not enough," she later explained. "What about those buildings? I said to myself we are going to have a Bedford-Stuyvesant botanical garden here, a nature center, right here." Flexing her political savvy and muscle, Carthan bargained down the price of the buildings, and Antenor Adams, who lived in the neighborhood and owned a McDonald's franchise, put up the cash.

The Magnolia Tree Earth Center has been operating for decades as a full-service community environmental organization with a wide range of programs, housed in the original brownstones with the magnolia trees out front. Older children and teenagers take hands-on classes here in horticulture and environmental subjects, and staff members bring the center's expertise into local schools. An Urban Tree Corps operates from the center and continues to beautify the neighborhood. Art exhibits and special workshops are available to the general public. Young adults take advantage of minority career training programs in subjects related to the center's mission.

"I was born poor, I live poor, and I'm going to die poor," Carthan told the New York City Planning Commission when asking it to set a modest purchase price for the brownstones that protected the magnolia. "I don't beg. But these are for the community."

LIZ CHRISTY BOWERY-HOUSTON COMMUNITY GARDEN

Bowery and Houston Street, East Village, Manhattan

www.lizchristygarden.org

Hours: Saturdays noon to 4:00 p.m., year-round; Tuesdays 6:00 p.m. to dusk, May through September; Thursdays 1:00 p.m. to 6:00 p.m., May through September; and often when someone is gardening.

Public transit: F train to Second Avenue. Use Second Avenue exit. Walk one block west along Houston Street. The garden entrance is at the corner of Bowery and Houston.

One of the city's marvelous incongruities is the location of luscious Liz Christy Garden at the corner of Houston and Bowery—one of Manhattan's least attractive crossroads. Enter the garden and Houston Street almost disappears from view. Concentrate on the turtle and fish pond, the beehive, the little nook with the Buddhist altar, and traffic sounds miraculously diminish. This is New York City's original community garden. Over two thousand varieties of plants, shrubs, and trees grow in some 7,500 feet of green space through all four seasons. The garden is surrounded by a high iron fence, but the gate is often wide open—and the public is invited.

The garden's founder was an artist who lived nearby, Liz Christy. (She died prematurely in 1985, at which point the garden was renamed in her honor.) Like Chema Soto, Christy tired of seeing an abandoned, junk-filled blot on the local landscape, and one day in 1973, challenged by a local mother to do something about it, Liz did. She organized friends who spent about a year cleaning up almost eight feet of trash dispersed around the lot, and together they started the Bowery-Houston Community Farm and Garden.

Donald Loggins, who helped build the garden and is still involved today, recalls their early interactions with the Sanitation Department and the police. "When the Sanitation Department saw us they thought,

Liz Christy Garden offers an oasis of natural beauty to both visitors and passersby along Houston Street in the East Village. Photo: Elena Martínez.

Great job! They came by and threw our bags in the back of their sanitation trucks and were really nice about it. Once we got down to ground level, we had to dig through about two feet of rock and rubble. Then we needed topsoil. That's when the Police Department got involved. There was a police stable over on Varick Street where about fifty to sixty horses were producing a lot of manure. We couldn't afford fertilizer at that point, so we said, 'How about giving us the manure?' One of our gardeners had a little truck, so we'd go over to the stables once or twice a week and fill it up with tons of manure. The police loved us because the manure smelled to high heaven and we got rid of it for them."

The second year planting started: not only trees, shrubs, and flowers but also vegetables, which the gardeners distributed free to local residents. After a while the plantings became more ornamental, in part because, due to high lead content in the soil from surrounding pollutants, the gardeners felt their produce might not be safe to eat. According to Loggins, the switch since then to unleaded gas for cars has alleviated the problem to some extent, so a few gardeners grow food again—tomatoes, a little corn, peach and apricot trees, and "delicious grapes"—but most of them prefer to grow flowers.

To convey to new gardeners the accumulated knowledge about growing conditions at Bowery and Houston, the group publishes a wise and funny compendium of facts about the place, complete with answers to frequently asked questions like "Yes, we get honey from the bees," and "No, we don't have killer bees (yet)." The authors encourage gardeners to take advantage of a "microclimate pleasantly modified by a number of favorable circumstances," thus supporting a long growing season for dahlias, gladiolus, calla lilies, snapdragons, and agapanthus. "Winter is slightly milder," the writers explain, "because we're located near the ocean, in the middle of a big city, and protected from cold north winds by high brick walls. These walls also act as solar collectors to release warmth at night."

What distinguishes this garden's story from many others is that Liz Christy and her gardener compatriots didn't stop with this one project. Calling themselves the Green Guerillas, they forcibly brought their case for community greening to devastated places around the entire city. Their methods were unorthodox. Take seed grenades, for instance. Abandoned lots lay everywhere, but many were not so easy to enter. So Liz and friends filled balloons, condoms, old Christmas ornaments, and other conveniently throwable receptacles with fertilizer and seeds, and over the fences the seed grenades went! Donald Loggins remembers everybody's amazement when in the middle of a vacant lot flowers burst forth. "There's a halo effect," he says. "If you have something nice, people want to make it even nicer. If it looks like garbage, people are going to throw more garbage in there. So once flowers started sprouting, people said, 'Oh, let's put some more flowers in there.' " Also, the seed grenades were fun to throw and felt a bit like civil disobedience, advancing the Green Guerillas' political mission. Although urban farming had been done before (perhaps best known are the Victory Gardens of the World War II home front), the idea of appropriating abandoned land for community gardens was new in the early 1970s when the Green Guerillas started. On the surface their mission was all about gardens. Just below the surface lurked the radical idea of bringing into the public domain land that once had been privately held but now had been callously abandoned.

The message struck a chord. Between seed grenades, press coverage, and word of mouth, news got around that the Green Guerillas could help start other gardens, and soon Liz was packing her little Datsun full of tools and seeds and responding to calls from all over the city. The urban gardening movement grew, helped by the labors of volunteer gardeners throughout the five boroughs, and a myriad of public officials, experts, and politicians such as Congressman Fred Richmond of Brooklyn, who sponsored the first federal program in urban farming and gardening, and President Jimmy Carter, whose 1977 walk in the rubble of the South Bronx spurred the release of federal money to help devastated urban areas.

**FIRST PERSON:
EDGARDO VEGA YUNQUÉ,
*MENDOZA'S DREAMS***

I returned to the apartment, drank
Seven straight shots of rum and tried
To figure out how many empty lots
There were in New York City, Philadelphia,
Newark, Boston, Hartford, Chicago, Gary,
and all the other places where the people
struggled and sweated and cried and
fought to extricate themselves from the
bonds of oppression.

Three decades into the movement, both the Liz Christy Garden and the Green Guerillas are established organizations that continue to provide leadership. Both welcome new gardeners and guerillas, for, as the garden's orientation brochure so aptly states, "In the dog-eat-dog world of Mother Nature, the weeds usually win."

—Marci Reaven

The Flower District

Twenty-eighth Street between Sixth Avenue and Seventh Avenue, and Sixth Avenue between Twenty-seventh Street and Twenty-eighth Street, Chelsea, Manhattan

Hours: 6:30 a.m. to 1:00 p.m. or later.

Public Transit: C, E trains to Twenty-third Street. Walk north (with traffic) along Eighth Avenue to Twenty-eighth Street, turn right, and walk to Seventh Avenue.

F, V trains to Twenty-third Street. Walk north (with traffic) along Sixth Avenue to Twenty-seventh Street.

R train to Twenty-eighth Street. Walk one block west (against traffic) along Twenty-eighth Street.

1, 9 trains to West Twenty-eighth Street.

To familiars, it's "the flower market" or just "the market"; to the rest of us, the Flower District. Clustered mainly along Twenty-eighth Street are cut-flower stores, plant stores, and foliage (leaves and branches) stores. Add silk- and dried-flower stores, plus floral supply houses, and you have one of the last specialty commercial districts left in Manhattan.

EVERYTHING IN ITS PLACE

Seasonal flowers on display adorn the sidewalks of Twenty-eighth Street. Palm trees, ficus, and other leafy trees huddle together in mini jungles that advertise their respective vendors. The stores might be homely little structures, deep and narrow, with well-worn wooden or linoleum floors, but they're filled with color and fragrance. "Smells like a funeral home in here," jokes a man who runs a flower shop in Tribeca, as he walks into New Concept to make his purchases. Customers walk away with packages wrapped in brown paper or have larger orders delivered to them. Deliverymen load up vans on the street. Now and then, props for a film set drive by; today's set is an entire landscape of waist-high swamp grass.

The sellers refer to flowers as "product." In this tactile, visual business, many florists and designers still like to come to the market for their product. They want to see what they're buying for weddings and funerals, hotels and restaurants, corporate meeting rooms, building lobbies, concert halls, and churches and synagogues, as well as for classes in floral design and the private homes of wealthy patrons lucky enough to refresh their flower vases weekly. Retail florists buy flowers for their stores and also buy for customers with special requests. Photo stylists buy flowers for their photo shoots and, along with freelance floral designers, sometimes rent the upstairs spaces along Twenty-eighth Street, helping local storeowners pay their bills. Not everybody needs to see his or her order, however. At Empire Flowers a phone order comes in from Puffy (a k a Sean Puffy Combs, Puff Daddy, and P. Diddy), who wants his standard order of thirty white calla lilies. Soon after, Puffy's florist comes in to pick them up.

Retailers and designers need to build rapport with individual salespeople in the market if they're going to expect quality. "And if your salesman's not gonna give you quality, you're going to go to a different salesman," says one buyer. "So you have to develop a relationship of trust here." To avoid going to the market every day, florists might ask their salespeople to select and deliver the flowers for them. If they are displeased they can send the flowers back, provided they do not abuse the arrangement.

Dried-flower stores coexist on the street but keep to themselves. They don't even buy regularly from their cut-flower neighbors, because drying now takes place in special drying houses or right on the farm, using a new process that retains the flowers' natural colors. Farmers grow flowers specifically for drying, then cut, freeze-dry, and package them by the hundreds to sell to places like the flower market.

In addition to fresh, dried, and silk flowers, stores in the district also sell many varieties of trees, potted and hanging plants, and floral supplies such as ribbons, vases, pots, baskets, note cards, corsage boxes, flower tubes, and more.

First encounters with the market can overwhelm both buyers and sellers. Old hands swear that presently one learns to recognize the order that uniformly prevails: seasonal flowers in one section, local flowers in another, Dutch flowers in yet another, with those a day old or more separated from the lot. Roses are grouped together; so are sweet peas, lilies, and orchids. Dutch flowers are considered of better quality than flowers from South America, so even if a store carries the same twenty varieties from both the Netherlands and South America, neither mixing nor proximity is allowed. The Dutch mums will not be near the South American mums. An observant newcomer can quickly pigeonhole the stores as well, because many merchants carve out special niches: tropical flowers, foliage, top end, middle of the line, out of season or hard to get, and so on.

By grouping the vendors and buyers together in one extended place, the market fosters the opportunities and networks that help commerce to flourish. But as in all specialty worlds, you need to learn the rules. Rose Edinger, a floral designer, remembers her first days on the job: "I had my first large job as a floral designer, but I really wasn't well versed about anything. I went down to Twenty-eighth Street to scout out the vendors. I had never been down there before. I was not in the business. I knew nothing about the trade. If you think that I knew the names of the flowers, you got to be kidding. I didn't know anything but to go down there. So I walked into a supply store—Central—and spoke to Harry. I said, 'I don't know what I'm doing. Do you think you could talk me through this?' And he did. I was really surprised. And then he said, 'Why don't you go next door? They're nice guys.' Next door was Mutual, so I went in. I took a look around. It's very busy, and I figured, okay, I'll go home and do my math, figure out how much I need by multiplying the number of flowers by the number of tables or arrangements. I'll come back tomorrow.

"The next morning I knew that I had to get down there early because everybody said that the market opens at four o'clock. (Now I know that if you get there by six thirty or seven you're fine.) I said to my husband, Henry, 'Would you come down with me the first time, because it's four o'clock in the morning and I don't really know what I'm doing.' And he said, 'No problem.' We had a car and were both pretty energized by the novelty of all this. We got down there at about a quarter to five, and it is still dark. We turned the corner from Seventh Avenue going east on Twenty-eighth, and we couldn't move. These humongous trucks had

One of the great things about the Flower District is that you know when you've found it. Photo: Martha Cooper.

come from the airport to deliver the flowers. They just took over the whole block. Finally we weave through and rush over to Mutual, but there's no parking, because of these big trucks. Henry stays in the car, and I go in with my list. But I'm too early. The flowers, instead of being on the shelves, are all in boxes because they're just coming off the trucks. So I go back outside and sit in the car with Henry and wait." Rose laughs. "He never came with me again.

"For me the whole place was a turn-on. When I began in the 1980s there must have been forty vendors, so there was lots of running around, seeing what people had, comparing prices. And I still love that aspect of it. It's thrilling. Like a child going to a candy store—you want one of everything but you have to stick to your list. I don't care if I'm buying flowers for you or for me. It's fun."

WHERE THE FLOWERS COME FROM

Generally, the flowers positioned outside of the stores are local. This used to mean grown in the tri-state area but now includes all points reasonably accessible by truck—such as New Jersey, the Carolinas, or Maine. Other domestic flower sources are Florida and California, along with Hawaii, which supplies tropical varieties, as do the West Indies and Costa Rica. From overseas come the flowers of South America and the misleadingly-named Dutch flowers, which might be from the Netherlands but also might be from France or New Zealand. What makes them Dutch is their point of purchase: the world-famous Dutch Flower Auction. This is a very fast kind of auction invented long ago by a Dutch farmer to protect highly perishable commodities. Dutch flowers are still auctioned in the Netherlands, but the "decreasing-price" format of Dutch auctions now extends beyond the worlds of flowers and produce. Some sellers make deals with particular growers to be the exclusive representative of their product in the market. And overseas growers in, say, Hawaii or the West Indies try to get their product into the market by wooing buyers, even flying them out to their respective countries for a tour.

For vendors and aficionados, it is important to know who the growers and suppliers are. Different farms offer different qualities of product. The distinctions may not be visible to the layperson but are obvious to professionals. The better flowers also have a longer shelf life. Regulations governing the growth and care of South American flowers are less strict than those for Dutch and tropical flowers. Considered of lesser quality, South American blooms are cheaper. But even among Dutch flowers there are nuances in quality and these are reflected in the cost. Hothouses and a global buyer's market mean you can buy almost anything you want all year round—even a few precious Dutch tulips in the middle of summer, a very difficult time to produce bulb material.

PURCHASE OR PERISH

Flowers are perishable. With the exception of orchids, they are shipped without having their stems in water tubes. One thing European growers do to prolong shelf life is to treat flowers with a sulfur solution called STS. This both retards the maturation of the flower and slows down its sensitivity to ethylene gas. (Fruits, vegetables, and flowers produce ethylene gas within their tissues as they ripen and age.) When flowers get delivered to Twenty-eighth Street, they have been cut and out of water for two to four days. With luck they may be sold immediately, but they could linger with a wholesaler for two to three more days before purchase by a retailer, whose display might be several days old before a consumer takes the flowers home. So flowers that we call "fresh" might be six days old.

Wholesalers hold on to flowers as long as they can by keeping them in the refrigerator at night. This trick works for a couple of days. But as Rose Edinger explained, "Remember they're selling perishables. They need to get rid of them. And they need to get some money back." Therefore, it is possible to bargain with wholesalers when the flowers are not as fresh as they once were.

Sometimes, peddlers buy old flowers from the wholesalers. Brian Luebcke, the owner of Empire Flowers, gives the example of a fellow named Gene, "who you'll see across the street on Thursdays and Fridays. He buys out everything old in the market. And then he sells them all day long. He probably makes a good living."

HOW BUSINESS IS DONE

The flower market is a high-pressure, physically demanding work environment. Gary Page of G. Page & Co. jokes that the reigning occupational tradition is "tired." People in sales often deal simultaneously with walk-in customers, with orders coming in over the phone, and with local and overseas growers placing orders for new product. Gary wears a many-pocketed vest every day to use as a temporary filing system for receipts.

Most business in the Flower District takes place before 11:00 a.m. Photo: Martha Cooper.

Stores open to the public at about 6:30 a.m., but business may have started three hours earlier. The busiest time is from about 7:00 until 11:00 a.m., and the wholesalers close up by 1:00 p.m. The stores that also do retail business stay open through the late afternoon.

Most flower prices quoted are by the stem, not the bunch, and some stores sell by the box only. The more you buy, the lower the price should go. Bargaining is not unheard of. Customers pick out flowers and leave them in a bin or on a shelf. It's as though they are sold, but the customer can still shop around and see if these items can be found more cheaply elsewhere. If so, the shopper might come back to the first place and ask if the vendor will match the better price. If not, there is no obligation to buy. Some customers may schlep their purchased product back to their own stores, but a small army of delivery vans owned by flower-market vendors or hired from independents also makes deliveries around the city, generally up until about noon.

The market has an annual revenue of about $120 million and employs about three hundred people, including salespeople (who work in the store itself, often buy the flowers, and try to secure new clients), "setup guys" (who set up the flowers for display in the morning, put them away, or "knock them down," in the afternoon, and condition them to enhance their appeal), packers (some flowers need to be kept cold with ice, and others are very delicate and need to be padded); and drivers (for the stores that do deliveries). There are no real unskilled laborers in the store. Setup guys, for example, need to learn a lot about flowers. As Brian Luebcke, who has worked as a driver, a setup guy, and a salesman, explains: "There are certain ways to take care of each item, and it's completely different. You wet this, you wrap it in newspaper, and you put it away. This you never wet 'cause it's gonna mold. And this has to go in water every single day even if it's fresh, as opposed to ginger that doesn't have to go into water for five or six days. It doesn't. It's a real sturdy flower. Then there are things like sweet peas from Holland and cymbidiums and amaryllis, which are just real delicate. Those have to be picked up, brought into the refrigerator, and placed down like a baby. Pom-poms you throw on the shelf—you literally just pick up the box and throw it on the shelf. So that's something that you have to learn. If you're taught the wrong way, there's gonna be damage, there's gonna be losses."

ONE HUNDRED YEARS OLD AND COUNTING

Some say the Flower District's days on West Twenty-eighth Street are numbered; others question whether the market can even stay in Manhattan. A wholesale cut-flower house owned by a family named Pennock may have been the first to move onto the street in 1903. Before long, others joined it—many of them also family owned, like Associated and Harry Vlachos, which still operate on Twenty-eighth Street. The heyday for the market was in the 1940s and 1950s, when approximately seventy-five vendors operated between Twenty-sixth and Thirtieth streets along Sixth Avenue, and then up and down the streets between Broadway and Seventh Avenue.

Mitchell Vlachos's father started his wholesale business in the late 1920s. "Some of the dealers in those days," Mitchell says, "were representatives of local greenhouse producers. Certain large greenhouse growers would have a location on Twenty-eighth Street in the market for their own product. Then there were specialists—people who specialized in lily of the valley and different types of lily. Thomas Young was strictly orchids; he was around the corner. William Doyle, he was violets. But gradually, business went to houses that were more diversified."

Diversity hasn't prevented the market from shrinking in recent years, however. Some of the pressure has come from new vendors who, in one way or another, are cutting out market middlemen. First came competition from independents bringing flowers directly to the florists in small trucks. A market regular describes a typical scenario: Someone rents a tractor-trailer and drives to a Miami wholesaler who has a load of roses; the fellow buys them off the wholesaler for ten or twelve cents a stem, drives them back to New York, skipping the cost of air freight, then skimps on wages to the guy making the bunches, and finally sells the roses from the truck or deli for $8.99 a dozen or two dozen for $10. More recently, independent wholesalers with refrigerated trucks pick up flowers directly from the airport and drive around selling product to retail florists. They skip the burden of paying rent on Twenty-eighth Street altogether. Adding to the truck-sales competition are Korean-owned vegetable markets with their streetside flower displays. (Wholesaler Mitchell Vlachos disputes this notion, seeing each Korean vegetable store as a "billboard for flowers.") And now, Internet sales and Federal Express deliveries mean florists can buy even closer to the source of production if they wish.

But more than methods of doing business have changed. So has the real estate. Aggressive buying of local land parcels for luxury residences began in the 1970s and ultimately contributed to the area's being re-zoned from manufacturing/commercial to residential/commercial in the mid-1990s. Some of the flower businesses were forced out, and others sold their buildings for high profits. Those that stayed now struggle with the continually inflating rents and diminishing sales. Making matters more difficult, residents of the area's new fancy lofts and apartments who are annoyed about traffic congestion and early morning noise from delivery trucks bring nuisance complaints to the community board and the city council. Flower sellers fear that local politicians will privilege the con-

FIRST PERSON:
GARY PAGE, FLOWER DISTRICT

"Flowers are the jewels of nature. They're like the most beautiful, dressed-up women of any time, all the time."

cerns of residents over businesses because it's the residents who vote them in and out of office.

A number of Flower District wholesalers created the Flower Market Association in 1999, hoping to find ways to keep the market intact, even if the wholesalers must move en masse. Sustaining an association among businesses in competition with one another is not always easy. Looking out for one's own well-being needs to be balanced against hanging together for the common good. The strengths of the market seem to be the quality and variety of the product and the critical mass of stores, selling all the things a florist or designer might need in one centralized location. Brian Luebcke believes that one reason designers still need the market is that they need to buy in specific quantities. "A designer might need a hundred and seventy-five yellow roses, three hundred red, twenty-five white, and seventy-five green. They can't call up somebody in Miami and order that. The party people can't buy direct as easily as a florist can." Plus, as Rose Edinger points out, Twenty-eighth Street still provides specialty product like gardenias, stephanotis, and varieties of foliage that can't be bought off the trucks. The association's leaders hope to make sure they can remain a destination—somewhere—and regrow and modernize the market to make it competitive again. Quaint may not compensate for cramped.

Tom Lunke, an urban planner and former member of Community Board 4, believes the city should go out of its way to help the flower market survive and thrive. "The reason people move into Manhattan in the first place is for that sense of place. People are always looking for that connection to their environment: 'You know where the flower market is?' 'Yes.' 'I live near there,' or 'I work near there.'" He also wishes the city's planners would indulge in some creative thinking that could help sustain mixed-use neighborhoods by altering traffic patterns, say, to work around the Flower District's delivery hours, creating mixed-use buildings that reserve the lower floors for flower industry businesses, and requiring that new residential construction install window and wall buffering against the predictable sounds of commercial activity.

Such concerns are not limited to the future of the Flower District. Rezoning for luxury residences, combined with a lack of support or downright hostility toward the city's remaining commercial and industrial zones, is helping to drive industry and jobs from the city. Nearly 7500 small firms still make things in New York City. One way to support them is to log on to Made in NYC (http://madeinnyc.org) and find out more. And next time you hire a floral designer, buy local. Support the Flower District!

—Ilana Harlow and Marci Reaven

Fishing around New York

SHEEPSHEAD BAY FISHING BOATS

"Few people believe when they see the fish in that tank," says Bill Fink, an educator who's teaching kids how to fish off the Battery, "that kids just caught them right here in Lower New York Bay. I don't know where they think they're from, but they live right here." Take a boat ride for fresh air and fish from Sheepshead Bay or

Emmons Avenue between Twenty-first Street and Twenty-eighth Street, Sheepshead Bay, Brooklyn

Public Transit: B, Q trains to Sheepshead Bay. Walk south on Sheepshead Bay Road about five blocks to Emmons Avenue. Turn left onto Emmons and walk about three blocks to the beginning of the ten piers.

throw a line over a seawall anywhere around town. You may well catch more than a great view.

The city's waterways are tidal. Four times a day, a six-foot tide floods in or ebbs out from the shores of Gotham. Fresh water mingles with the salty ocean, creating brackish water that striped bass, American shad, and other species need to spawn. The East River, actually a tidal strait, connects Long Island Sound to the Hudson River and is a major passageway for fish traveling from one body of water to the other. The Hudson drains a watershed that reaches to the Adirondacks. Its underwater canyon extends many miles out to sea. Marine life thrives in this confluence of rivers, ocean, and sound.

The Party Boats at Sheepshead Bay

Fishing in New York? Ask a person who has even a passing knowledge of fishing in the city and you might hear something like "Oh, you mean the party boats at Sheepshead Bay?" That's what the vessels are called

Not distracted by a partially submerged car, a man fishes by sunset at World's Fair Marina, Flushing, Queens. Photo: Audrey Gottlieb.

that dock at Sheepshead Bay piers and take New Yorkers out to deeper waters. But even they are one of the city's best-kept secrets. A party boat captain recalls sitting at a table at Welcome Back to Brooklyn Day and talking to Brooklynites who never heard of Sheepshead Bay. "They had no idea there was a fleet of boats in Sheepshead Bay. Lived here all their lives and never knew it. . . . We're the largest fishing fleet on the East Coast and nobody knows we exist."

The area off south Brooklyn known as Sheepshead Bay feeds into the Rockaway Inlet, which is the opening into Jamaica Bay. It's not far from the barrier beaches of Long Island known as the Rockaways and is a natural harbor in which to berth vessels. With quick access to the inlet,

Jamaica Bay, the Atlantic, Sandy Hook, and points south or north to the Narrows, the boats from Sheepshead Bay (named after the sheepshead fish) range along many of New York City's most productive fishing grounds.

Along the ten wooden piers, the gaily painted fishing boats pull in and out on a tight schedule of full- and half-day fishing trips, plus all-night cruises for bluefish—a journey nicknamed "the all-night blues." (Some visitors actually believe there are blues concerts on the waterfront when they see the signs.)

The cost of a fishing trip varies from about thirty dollars to seventy-five dollars. In twenty-five minutes the boats reach the Atlantic or drop their lines in Jamaica Bay, the Hudson River, or the sea off Coney Island. They go where the fish are—fluke, bluefish, stripers, blackfish, sea bass, porgies.

The variety of fish is matched by the ethnic diversity on the party boats—Chinese, Koreans, African Americans. "It's a League of Nations on every boat," said Ann O'Driscoll, who used to refuel the vessels several times a week. "Language barriers disappear the moment the boat pulls out to sea," says George Richford, the captain of the *Pastime Princess*.

There is no rest for the weary down at the piers. At six in the morning the all-day cruises pull out. Late in the morning the criers begin hawking the half-day afternoon fluking cruise. (Fluke is a close relative of flounder.) In the early afternoon the fluking boats pull out, and late in the day, one at a time, they chug back in, blowing their seafaring horns. ("That's the *Brooklyn*," said O'Driscoll, cued by its distinctive blow.) Then begins a flurry of fish sales as locals come down to the piers to buy fresh seafood. By early evening the criers begin hawking the all-night bluefish trips; at one, two, or three in the morning the all-night blues pull in, and work begins cleaning the boats to prepare the next day's sail.

Tenfinger Piers

Sheepshead Bay, originally an area of the township of Gravesend, was first settled in the early 1800s. It was a village by the water where New Yorkers came for day trips or for the season to be by the sea. In the latter half of the nineteenth century, Canarsie Pier on Jamaica Bay was the center of party boat fishing; individuals or groups could pay a fare for a rod, bait, and a trip to productive local fishing grounds. In the late 1870s, with improving public transportation, business shifted toward Sheepshead Bay. Trolley service was installed from Prospect Park all the way to Emmons Avenue. A hundred thousand people would flood adjacent Coney Island on busy spring and summer weekends. Party boat fishing became one of the area's popular activities.

"Talking about fishing reminds me of the fact that Sheepshead Bay is the best point within 25 miles of this city to go for a day's sport with the finny tribe. . . . I can leave my home on Henry Street and in an hour's time be sitting in a boat hauling in fish."—A well-known church sexton, *Brooklyn Eagle,* June 19, 1887

The party boat fleet contained all manner of ships, including triple-decker boats that accommodated hundreds of anglers. People came early on the weekends to ensure a spot on their favorite boats, which left the docks with capacity crowds. On November 5, 1897, the *Brooklyn Eagle* reported: "Mr. William Patrick of Emmons Avenue, Sheepshead Bay, called at the *Eagle* office today with the good news to fishermen that cod, hake, and ling are running in great quantities into the bay from the ocean through the Rockaway Inlet. . . . The run will probably last a month or six weeks." Later that month, the newspaper reported record catches of cod: "Never before in the memory of the oldest fishermen along the shores from Bay Ridge to Sheepshead Bay have there been so many codfish in local waters. . . . Pretty near everyone that ever fishes is going fishing."

After 1929 and the onset of the Depression, many fine yachts were refitted as fishing party boats. Wealthy yachtsmen had to sell at fire sale prices to raise cash. During the 1930s, the WPA deepened the Sheepshead Bay channel, allowing it to accommodate larger fishing boats year-round, and, in 1936, built what are called the Tenfinger Piers (replacing dozens of rickety structures) protruding into the bay along

Emmons Avenue. In the 1940s, navy surplus vessels from the war effort were sold off at scrap metal prices. A new generation of party boats came from that surplus.

The quantity and diversity of fish species populating local waters kept party boat fishing popular for generations. Walter Wiegand's father started small in the business, driving people from Yorkville in Manhattan to Sheepshead Bay for a day of chartered fishing. Eventually he acquired a boat, the *Flamingo,* which Walter ran with him, upgrading twice. The *Flamingo III* is now run by his son Bob. As Walter remembers: "When I was growing up, the captains of the Sheepshead Bay party boats were like celebrities. You almost wanted to get their auto-

Fishing off the Coney Island pier. Photo: Elaine Norman.

graphs. And you didn't have all the sophisticated weather forecasting and positioning equipment in those days. It was more a situation of iron men and wooden ships.

"Sheepshead Bay was like a Mecca for fishing. Boats would sail every day. Literally throngs of people would come, and they'd sail early. Many a day you'd see five hundred, a thousand people standing on the dock on Sheepshead Bay because they got down late and couldn't get on a boat anymore—all the boats had already sailed.

"That's a thing of the past! There's no such thing as capacity crowds now. Every year it seems someone can't make it and goes out of business. You hate to see it, but you think maybe that will bring more business your way, but it never seems to work out that way. A lot of people made a living from the business over the years, but nobody retired rich from it. This fishing business gets in your blood like a drug and you want to keep doing it, but it's not easy to make a living. As far as my

FIRST PERSON: BILL MCCORMICK

"Sometime in the very early 1900s, my grandfather received a beach bungalow in the area of Staten Island known as Ocean Breeze. He had done some work for Thomas Adams, the inventor of the Chiclet, and the house was his recompense. When I was a child in the late forties through the early seventies, my family would pack up and leave the apartment in the city sometime in mid-June and spend our summers on the beach. The community consisted of row upon row of small houses surrounded by a big saltwater marsh, creeks, and a small inlet coming in from New York harbor.

"My uncle and father would spend a good amount of their free time catching crabs and fishing. As a youngster it was my job to catch the bait. The creeks that twined through the area were small and tidal, but they held a significant amount of baitfish known as 'killies.' The art to catching them was fairly simple. I would be sent over to the creek with a milk bottle that had a few pieces of bread crust in it. Tie a string around the bottle's neck; drop it in the water and wait for it to fill up with the 'killies.' In no time I would have a small pail full of bait for our trips to the inlet to catch crabs or bluefish.

"Most of my early summers growing up, I was involved some way with the local waters (learning to swim, to row a boat, or to cast off the beach for the schools of bluefish). But catching the 'killies' as a small kid was my favorite memory."

grandchildren are concerned, I hope they get a good education to prepare themselves for the outside world."

Business remained relatively strong through the postwar years.
There were many fishing clubs around town, often centered at the local
bar and grill, and business was steady. Beginning in the 1970s the situation slowly changed. The growing popularity of other pursuits and of
weekend sports on television cut into the business. Increased regulation
passed to protect fishing stocks limit the catch that can be legally hauled
in. Though the fishing can still yield a good catch, certain popular
species have disappeared, such as whiting and cod.

The Sheepshead Bay party boat fleet lives on despite its diminishing
numbers. It's still the largest fleet in the Northeast. Although certain
species are highly regulated, others remain in abundance. Bluefish and
striped bass are plentiful in season. So too are porgies, sea bass, herring,
and weakfish, to name a few. Other species like flounder and fluke have
strict size limits, which aren't easily met, though they are very actively
fished.

But denizens of the bay love to talk about the old days. "What do you
think of Sheepshead Bay these days?" Brodie, a former first mate on the
bay, was asked. "You take a tall Pall Mall," he says, holding the unfil-
tered cigarette between his thumb and forefinger. "When I was a boy,
Sheepshead Bay was about like this cigarette. Now," he says, moving his
fingernail about to where the filter would come to, "now, it's down to
here." Yet the fishermen still come, and the fish still bite.

'ROUND EVERY BOROUGH, FISH

Fishing from Sheepshead Bay boats
represents only a segment of the fish-
ery of New York City, which has well over
five hundred miles of coastal boundary.
Any corner of the city's marine system
has the potential to hold fish, from the

"You see a lot of weird things in
New York besides the people.
There's a lot of weird fish,
too."—Robert, New York City
fisherman

seemingly inhospitable Gowanus Canal in Boerum Hill to the backwa-
ter canals of Gerritsen Beach or even the semicomatose waters of New-

One of the last bait and tackle shops left on Sheepshead Bay. Photo: Elaine Norman.

town Creek. These offshoots of the major water passages attract the same species that swim the faster flowing river waters. Old wooden piers all over town have collapsed or are unusable as a result of marine worms boring through them—worms that, ironically, can only thrive in relatively clean water. Those same pilings attract breeding fish species, as well as fish seeking to eat their smaller brethren or even the tasty worms eating through the pilings.

Off the Marine Parkway Bridge going to the Rockaways a fisherman boasts: "This bridge is real productive late in the fall. I mean you can come here, still find fluke, you go on the other side, you got some nice big sea bass. You've got your flounders in your wintertime. That guy up there takes a nice keeper of bass in the fall. He's always up here. He gets at least one a week. Tuesday I had over forty fluke. I'm serious. But I only kept like seven. You're only allowed to keep six."

Even commercial fishing still takes place. An eeler in Jamaica Bay Wildlife Preserve says: "I tell people I'm a commercial fisherman, and they're mystified. They don't even think that exists anymore. The pay isn't that great, but you get all the advantages of being a fisherman—being free, being able to be with my father. I'm always with my father if we're working. We go hunting together, we go fishing together, and it's a great thing in itself. We have a really tight bond. We're basically lost without each other. I never came into this expecting to get rich. I always came into this with the expectation that if I can pay my bills and in the future feed my family, and have money left over to get a few things that I want, I'm a happy man." A professional clammer on Staten Island reports that "for clams to reproduce and self-generate, it doesn't get any better than Staten Island." At one time, plans were afoot to bring hydraulic dredges into the bay and remove all the clams to a spot on Long Island. The clammers fought the plan in court, and now about three hundred men make all or part of their living on the clams. "I talk to friends of mine," the clammer says, "cops, firemen, regular people who I just run into every day, and they can't believe that there's clams coming outta these waters. I try to explain to them that the clams they're eating are probably these clams. Outta these beds are probably 25 percent of New York shellfish."

The reputation of city waterways is undeservedly bleak. "When I was a kid," said one New Yorker recorded in the documentary *Gotham Fish Tales,* "you couldn't step your foot in the Gowanus Canal for the fact that your foot might not come back. Yeah, I'm shocked you're fishing here." But the Clean Water Act of 1973 mandated major reform of sewage treatment and industrial waste across the nation, and New York City has reaped great benefits. Incrementally but steadily, water quality has improved. The most eloquent testimony to the success of the act is the fish themselves—all 250 species—that pass through or inhabit the city's waters.

THE LURE OF FISHING

"Once you get hooked on fishing, it's worse than drugs, I guess. It's a natural high. [He laughs.] You can never get enough."—New York City fisherman

"You know how a drug addict shoots dope? I shoot saltwater."—Brodie, Sheepshead Bay

So many reasons to fish: fresh air, relaxation, a good meal, camaraderie, spiritual fulfillment. A man on Ninety-sixth Street thinks about his stomach. "I like 'em, I eat 'em. I ate one yesterday. I had a nice blue one. . . . If I catch a twenty-five-pounder, I am not going to throw it back in the lake. I am going to take it home, clean it thoroughly, and I'm gonna eat it."

On Sheepshead Bay an Eastern European immigrant thinks about the fresh air: "I am coming here for fresh air. I'm coming here and spending the time. I work in the industry, the textile industry, and on the weekend, I had to come—when I didn't work on Saturday, I needed to come in from Manhattan. When the wind touches my body, I relax. If I didn't get that relaxation, to relax, then the whole week I feel I missed something."

For others it's not the relaxation but the excitement. "It's the chase after the fish," says Philip from his Roosevelt Island spot. "It's having the opportunity to engage the fish in its native terrain that makes it exciting." Another fisherman describes the feeling of being a predator, seeing the food chain in action: "Wild America in New York, unbelievable!" Fishing is also about humor and camaraderie, captured in this exchange on Canarsie Pier:

Rob: I understand there is a very good run of gefilte here, around Passover.
Gene: The gefilte fish are very good, except you have to fish them with nets because they come in bottles. If you use just a plain hook it doesn't work.
Rob: I see. So do you usually catch them in the Passover season?
Gene: Yes, we pass over them most of the time.

—Robert Maass,
director of the documentary *Gotham Fish Tales,*
www.gothamfishtales.com

City Spirits

Under the Brooklyn Bridge on the holiday of Tashlicht, Jews empty their pockets of bread and dust to symbolically rid themselves of sin for the new year. Photo: Martha Cooper.

New Yorkers search for God in crowded places. They seek out places within places to lift the spirit and awe the soul— and they find ways to situate those sacred spaces in relation to other spiritual realms such as the holy city of Mecca, the Haitian world of Les Invisibles, or heaven and hell.

Since Dewitt Clinton proposed the New York City street grid in 1811, all structures in Manhattan above Houston Street are laid out along east-west streets and north-south avenues. A noted exception is the mosque at 201 East Ninety-sixth Street. The first building erected as a mosque in New York City, built in 1989, it was turned at an angle to face Mecca, in Saudi Arabia. Complex formulas of longitude and latitude were necessary to position the entrance to the mosque so that a traveler setting out along the earth's surface would travel the shortest distance between the Islamic Cultural Center and Mosque on Ninety-sixth and the Great Mosque in Mecca.

In country towns and villages, there is plenty of room to set churches and holy places apart; in a dense urban setting, where space is perennially contested, sacred spaces need to be continually reimagined and re-created. For the holiday of Sukkoth, Jewish New Yorkers build temporary four-sided structures with greenery-covered roofs to commemorate the temporary shelters Jews lived in while wandering forty years in the desert. A stroll down Eastern Parkway in Brooklyn during the holiday reveals New York City–style sukkoth—wooden structures built not in open yards but on the small balconies up and down the wide apartment houses that span the avenue. In Queens, Sikh temples crop up in basements and next to bus stops. The Sikh *gurdwara* was once a synagogue in Richmond Hill, and the Gita Temple in Corona was created from an old supermarket.

Sacred places intersect with sacred time. During Tashlicht, Jews scatter ashes under the Brooklyn Bridge. At Easter, Catholics enact incidents in Christ's journey on the way to the crucifixion by carrying a cross and processing in front of particular homes; in 1989 and 1990, according to the writer Wayne Ashley, parishioners of Saint Brigid's Parish enacted each of the Stations of the Cross by processing to sites of violence and vice in their Lower East Side neighborhood.

Synagogues and churches in the city's neighborhoods tell the story of immigration and the changing needs of society and culture. In the Bronx, the story of Irish and Jewish immigration and migration is told in the religious symbols still visible on Puerto Rican churches and old vaudeville houses, themselves now changing with new waves of Dominican and Mexican immigrants. Some churches and congregations find ways to accommodate the different waves of immigration simultaneously, in the spiritual present. At Saint Dominic's Church in the Morris Point neighborhood of the Bronx, according to congregant Elizabeth Gonzalez, a writer, the congregation celebrates three Virgins at different times of year: the Virgin of Providence from Puerto Rico on November 19, the Virgin of La Altagracia from the Dominican Republic on January 6, and the Virgin of Guadalupe from Mexico on December 12. At the

FIRST PERSON:

THE REVEREND DEACON EDGAR W. HOPPER

Deacon Hopper is working to preserve the haunting and historic "slave gallery," the formerly segregated seating area above the balcony in Saint Augustine's Church, built in 1828 on the Lower East Side, as a potent reminder of how entrenched racism was in the fabric of everyday life in New York.

"When I sit here, I'm overcome with sadness knowing that persons of my race were subjected to this kind of thing. I'm also overcome with sadness knowing that this happened within the confines of a Christian church. But by the same token the space itself is a testament to the endurance of man under less than civil conditions. The very fact that I'm a part of the Episcopal Church as a member of the ordained clergy is evidence that we stayed and didn't reject Christianity—that we were able to find something to carry us through in the Gospels."

Deacon Edgar W. Hopper stands in the once segregated seating area known as the "slave gallery" in historic Saint Augustine's Episcopal Church. Photo: Robert Maass.

FIRST PERSON: DEANNA EVANS

DeAnna Evans, a high school student, wrote this on a visit to the "slave gallery."

They think they have controlled my worship

By hiding me away from my God

But while I'm swaying, holding onto my
master's baby instead of my own

With my clothes sticking to me in this intense heat. . . .

With the preacher talking about a God who
probably can't see me

I'm gonna praise Him

No one will control my worship

No one shall deny me my God.

celebration of the Virgin of Providence, Puerto Rican *bomba* musicians perform; at the Virgin of Guadalupe's, a Mexican mariachi band. The celebrations draw diverse residents of the neighborhood to church, creating common ground for these three immigrant communities, at the same time linking the workaday Bronx to a time of miracles when, in 1531, a "Lady from Heaven," who became the Virgin of Guadalupe, is said to have appeared to a poor Indian at Tepeyac, a hill northwest of Mexico City.

Kehila Kedosha Janina Synagogue and Museum

Hyman (Hy) Genee's curiosity was aroused when he read that Isaac Dostis would give a slide show on Greek Jewry at the City University of New York. Was Dostis related to the fellow who attended Kehila Kedosha Janina many years before? Hy, the synagogue's longtime president, wanted to find out. He attended the slide show and talked to the mysterious Isaac (who, sure enough, was the old congregant's son). Beginning with that meeting, they embarked on a mission to revive their "Romaniote" heritage—a rare branch of Judaism, hanging on by a thread in the little synagogue on Broome Street.

280 Broome Street, Lower East Side, Manhattan

(212) 431–1619

www.kkjsn.org

Hours: Religious services: Saturdays from 9:00 a.m. Museum: Sundays 11:00 a.m. to 4:00 p.m.; will open during the week by appointment.

Public Transit: B, D trains to Grand Street. Walk east on Grand to Eldridge Street. Turn left onto Eldridge and walk one block to Broome Street.

F, J, M, Z trains to Delancey Street/Essex Street. Walk one block south on Essex, turn right onto Broome Street, and walk about four blocks.

Listed on the National Register of Historic Places, 1999

Designated a New York City Landmark, 2004

A GREEK JEWISH PLACE ON THE LOWER EAST SIDE

Two stories high, faced with light-colored brick, newly cleaned and shining, the synagogue stands apart from its commercially focused neighbors, mostly food-related enterprises serving the far-flung businesses of Chinatown. It's easy to spot the symbols of Judaica adorning

The recently renovated and landmarked exterior of Kehila Kedosha Janina. Photo from *Before the Flame Goes Out,* by Vincent Giordano.

the synagogue's facade. More elusive are the architectural references to far-off lands—to a part of the map we once called the Near East.

Hy agrees to meet us at the synagogue on a Sunday. Come any time, he says. "I'll be there all day." The entrance vestibule is tiny, crowded with stairs that lead up to the women's balcony and down to the kitchen and activity room. (As in other orthodox forms of Judaism, women and men sit separately for services.) Directly ahead are dark wooden benches that face the raised *bema,* the platform from which services are conducted. Behind the *bema* along the back wall stands the ark—the *ehal*—covered with an embroidered velvet cloth. This is where the Torah scrolls, containing the written form of Jewish law, are stored. The whole room is long, narrow, and rather dark, its furnishings far from fancy. It seems to take after its tenement-building neighbors, and for that reason, perhaps, it feels like home.

**FIRST PERSON:
MOISE SOULÁM**

"When I arrived . . . in America ten years ago, I dreamed of money-growing trees. Now I see that you labor night and day, and the first of the month rolls around all too soon, with the landlord demanding the rent. . . . Jews in Turkey think that here trees sprout money—*dolares*—but in truth, this is the country not of *dolares,* but *dolores*—of woes."—*El Luzero,* a newspaper of New York's Sephardic community, 1924

When we walk in, Hy is busy helping a small group of children and adults make their way through a sung prayer. Lacking a rabbi, Hy and other lay leaders conduct the services and read from the Torah. Rather than disturb them, we follow the sound of voices from above. Men and women of various ages and complexions sit in chairs surrounding the big cutout space in the middle of the floor. Traditionally, from this perch, the women look down at the *bema* and witness the services. But at Kehila Kedosha Janina, the second floor also serves as the synagogue's museum, and these folks are clearly visitors.

Arrayed along the walls are exhibit panels bearing maps, photographs, and text. "Learn about a people you never knew existed," reads the brochure text. "Discover a lost tribe just around the corner." Nearby are free-standing cases showing traditional clothing, religious objects, and the stuff of Greek Jewish life in New York and the northwestern city of Janina, or Ioannina, capital of the Epirus region of Greece and hometown to the synagogue's original congregation. The exhibits are simple but professionally done, created to educate congregants and visitors about Romaniote Judaism. Congregation members, of course, had been practicing their faith all along, but over time, and with the ruptures of immigration, war, and genocide, the Romaniote minority in New York had forgotten why they practiced the way they did.

The visitors here today are surprisingly diverse; in fact, it's hard to imagine where they are from. They're listening to a kind-looking man tell a story in heavily accented English. It's World War II and Elias Hadjis and his family have just run from Volos to escape from the Nazis. The Greek deportations to the death camps had begun. "I remember that night," Elias says. "I'll never forget in my life. We slept in a barn, some on the top, some on the bottom; we slept with the hay. My mother cooked a big soup—*pasuada*. All thirteen of us ate from one pot, with a spoon she had. A silver spoon from her dowry, so she took it with her when we left. I asked her many years back when we started making the museum, 'Mom, what happened to the silver spoon?' 'We lost it,' she told me. We lost it.'"

As Elias finishes his story (he survived the war hiding in Piraeus, helped by partisans, for his father fought with the Resistance), the identity of the visitors becomes clear. It's a class in Greek American community life, taught by Dan Georgakas, a professor at Queens College. No wonder the group is so wonderfully mixed. From immigrant Queens to the immigrant Lower East Side.

Downstairs, Hy banters back and forth with Marcia Haddad Ikonomopoulos, who runs the museum, and a few other congregants. They decide the menu for the upcoming board meeting: feta and kashkavel cheese, hard-boiled eggs, and bourekas (small pastries with savory fillings). They talk over the recent bar mitzvah at the synagogue attended by 140 well-wishers. (The ceremony marks a thirteen-year-old's formal entrance to religious life.) And they worry about their diminishing numbers. From week to week they struggle to attract the minimum of ten men they need to form the minyan and hold the prayers. Members have held services here for over seventy-five years, and they are trying to hold out for one hundred.

TWO MILLENNIA IN THE MAKING

On September 17, 1927, one week before the Jewish New Year, Hy's parents and fellow Greek Jews from Janina opened their brand-new synagogue: Kehila Kedosha Janina, the Holy Congregation of Janina. The congregation itself was not new. For two decades already Lower East Side Yaniotes (people from Janina) had been operating a burial society and holding religious services in rented rooms. Building their own structure marked their settled status and their improving incomes. The lingerie business had helped. At one time on the Lower East Side, Hy estimates, about forty Greek Jewish–owned stores sold pajamas, stockings, and the rest. Today only one is left: Elethia, whose name means "true."

It was not at all uncommon to organize a congregation around a place of origin. In fact, Jews all over New York City had done just that, and as a result, synagogues once dotted the landscape. Small, tightly knit groups structured religious and secular life. What distinguished Kehila Kedosha Janina from many of the others was its Greek identity (Polish, Russian, and German were far more common) and its identification with the Sephardic Jewish tradition of Spain and Portugal rather than the Ashkenazic tradition of Central Europe and Russia. That identification changed in the 1990s when Isaac Dostis rediscovered the Romaniote roots of the congregation's distinctive traditions.

Sephardic Jews had lived for centuries on the Iberian peninsula under Spanish and Portuguese royal and ecclesiastical rule until the year 1492, when King Ferdinand and Queen Isabella brutally expelled them. Where the Jews would go was of no concern to the Catholic monarchs, who the same year commissioned Christopher Columbus to sail in search of a new route to the Indies. Jews would have no place in the soon-to-be-enriched Spanish empire, but the forced sales of their goods would refill the coffers of the Spanish monarchs and help to pay for the New World conquests to come.

Many of the exiles fled to lands that were part of the Ottoman Empire surrounding the Mediterranean Sea: to the areas we know as the Balkans, Greece, Turkey, Syria, and Egypt. The Ottoman Empire was

Torah scrolls at Kehila Kedosha Janina, saved from a synagogue in Ioannina, Greece, plundered by the Nazis. Photo courtesy of City Lore.

rather new when the Sephardic Jews arrived, its Turkish leaders having only that same century consolidated their rule. Forced to leave their material goods behind, the Sephardic Jews carried into exile their culture (including their language, known as Ladino), their memories, and their learning and skills. Their enormous migration swelled and came to dominate pre-existing settlements of Jews that extended throughout the lands now controlled by the Ottoman Turks. Jewish links with Greece date back to the territorial conquests of Alexander the Great (356–323 B.C.), and Jewish settlements continued to exist in the cities of the Hellenic world and later Roman and Byzantine empires. These native Greco-Roman Jews were known by the name Romaniote. It was the Romaniotes of Ioannina, Greece, who were particularly successful at preserving their community and tradition for centuries—until the Nazi Holocaust.

In the 1910s, Jews of all traditions as well as many Christians emigrated en masse from the Ottoman lands to the United States, propelled here by all manner of human and natural disaster. The Lower East Side Tenement Museum—located only a few blocks from Kehila Kedosha Janina—records an upsurge of what then were called Greek and Turkish (or Oriental) Jews living in the apartments at 97 Orchard Street during these years. Go on a tour of the museum and you'll see the re-created apartment of one of these families, the Confinos, who emigrated here from Kastoria, Greece, in 1913.

Whatever distinctions may have persisted between Sephardic and Romaniote Jews in the old world, once here, the differences seemed to lose clarity—especially given the Romaniotes' small numbers. Isaac Dostis recalls: "I myself am Romaniote, but I remember growing up in the Lower East Side completely puzzled about my community's identity. I thought Kehila Kedosha Janina was a Sephardic synagogue. It wasn't; it was a Romaniote synagogue from Ioannina. My friends were Sephardic; I lived in a Sephardic neighborhood. If I was Sephardic too, why didn't I know Ladino, the language of the Sephardim? I remember the awkwardness, the discomfort, of being more aware of what I wasn't than of what I was—Romaniote."

Isaac's discomfort motivated his curiosity. Helped by books like *The Jews of Ioannina* by Rae Dalven and his own exploratory trips to Ioannina, he began to peel away the layers of confusion and shed light on the complex story of the worldwide Jewish Diaspora and on emigration and settlement in America.

PASSING IT ON TO THE NEXT GENERATION

Cognizant of their status as the last practicing Romaniote synagogue in the Western Hemisphere, the congregants of Kehila Kedosha Janina have embarked on a sophisticated campaign to preserve their heritage. They are educating themselves and others about Romaniote and Greek Jewish traditions by organizing cultural initiatives such as cooking classes and group excursions to Greece, by publishing a synagogue newsletter, and, of course, by operating their museum. Thanks to the Sisterhood of Janina—still active after three-quarters of a century—they are following the Jewish admonition to take care of the needy. The congregation's good works include restoring the old Jewish cemetery in Janina, which was severely neglected after the community was decimated in the Holocaust. They are struggling to keep the congregation intact and pass down Romaniote customs such as a distinctive wedding blessing, a particular way of reading from and storing the Torah, and special Greek chants for reciting the liturgy. They are also preserving and renovating the synagogue itself. First acknowledged as historically significant by the National Register of Historic Places (1999), the building is now legally protected by its designation as a New York City Landmark (2004). Its facade has been beautifully renovated—a huge expense for a tiny congregation, but with friends like the architect Leonard Colchamiro (who did the work without charge) and supporters in New York's preservation community, somehow the bills are being paid.

It's a complicated business to balance past and present, but the members of Kehila Kedosha Janina believe they have this mission to perform. Their reasons are many, but in part it's about being the last of a line. "One of our Torah scrolls comes from a synagogue in Ioannina that was destroyed by the Nazis during the Holocaust," Isaac Dostis explains. "The mayor of Ioannina, Demetrios Vlachides, saved the scrolls and returned them to the few survivors after the Nazis were defeated. Our countrymen sent one of the scrolls to Jerusalem and one to us, encased in a beautiful *tik,* as an offering of thanks to God for the survival of the old synagogue and for their lives."

—Marci Reaven

Masjid At-Taqwa

More than twenty years ago, former members of the Na-tion of Islam founded Masjid At-Taqwa in what used to be a corner bar where illegal drugs were sold. Today the *masjid*—whose name roughly translates as "mosque

1266 Bedford Avenue/1184 Fulton Street (second entrance), Bedford-Stuyvesant, Brooklyn

(718) 622–0800

Public Transit: A, C trains to Nostrand Avenue. Walk one block west on Ful-ton Street to Bedford Avenue.

of prostration for God-Consciousness and piety"—attracts over a thou-sand worshippers for Friday afternoon prayers and anchors the economic and social revival of the surrounding community.

Five times daily on the streets of Bedford-Stuyvesant, calls to prayer reverberate from a loudspeaker mounted on the roof of the mosque. "God is great, God is great. Come to prayer, come to success. There is no God but God, and Mohammed is the messenger." The muezzin's live chanting in Arabic begins before dawn. Some neighbors set their clocks by the calls. Others walk to the mosque or say their prayers where they can. The calls are so beautiful, says Sister Subhanah Wahhaj, even those who are not Muslim ask to learn about the faith.

The imam and congregation welcome visitors to the mosque. Fridays after one o'clock in the afternoon will be crowded; other days and times, less so. Dress as you would for a visit to any house of worship.

A PLACE OF REFUGE AND COMFORT

Masjid At-Taqwa is a large and humble storefront covered in var-nished natural wood and forest-green panels. The men enter the mosque from Fulton Street. Women and young children enter their separate prayer section, the *masula,* from Bedford Avenue. Prior to prayer, members use the mosque's *wadu* for washing hands and feet. African American, Bangladeshi, Egyptian, Malian, Moroccan, Nigerian, Pakistani, Senegalese, and Sudanese Muslims all worship here, a diverse congregation drawn from the surrounding neighborhood. Prayer is chanted in the common language—English. Mostly the congregation is male, with about a thousand men and a third as many women—a ratio reflected in the number of prayer sections, with three for men and one for women. Even on crowded days most worshippers can squeeze in, but when the space overflows, as on holy days, they spill out onto Fulton Street and spread their prayer rugs on the sidewalk.

Imam Siraj Wahhaj is not only the congregation's spiritual leader; he also runs the mosque. He leads daily prayers and the weekly Friday sermon and often conducts full days of teaching and counseling: Arabic, Islamic studies, marital counseling, premarital counseling, leadership training, and more. Sometimes he is called upon to testify for female congregation members whose employers object to their traditional dress—the *hijab* being the full-body covering, the *kimar* just the headscarf. The imam notes that his name, Siraj Wahhaj, comes from the Koran, meaning "we sent them a bright light." "Not that I'm that bright a light, but I could be a little, little, little light," he adds with a smile. Imam Siraj always imagined that he would become a teacher, but as a young man attending New York University, he expected to teach mathematics, not religion. Math and painting portraits were the two passions that in his youth consumed him for hours, but Islamic law views portraiture as vying with the creator; thus the imam no longer paints. What energy he once devoted to charcoal and watercolor he now devotes to his large and growing community.

FROM SHOOT-OUTS TO AN ISLAMIC MARKETPLACE

In 1981, the imam's family and a small group of others left the Nation of Islam—the Black Muslim organization—on the first day of the holy month of Ramadan to form their own mosque. They had no build-

At Masjid At-Taqwa, the community extends outward from the mosque. Photo: Martha Cooper.

ing, so they bought an abandoned one from the city at auction. "This area then," he remembers, "was really, really rough. Really rough. We had shoot-outs every day." Drug trafficking plagued the neighborhood, and though the imam and mosque leaders attended community meetings, nothing seemed to change. So the mosque's male members set out to clean things up. Brother Ali Abdul Karim recalls that one day a burst of gunfire ricocheted through a window of a nearby restaurant. "That was the last straw."

Imam Siraj picks up the story. "January 21, 1987. We had a big rally, monster rally, thousands of people, and we talked with the police beforehand about closing down the crack houses. There were fifteen crack houses on this block alone. In the past when they closed down a crack

During Ramadan, the walls of the city's mosques cannot contain the prayers. Photo: Martha Cooper.

house it would open again after only a day. But this time when the police made their raids, we sent in our men after them. We mounted patrols in front of those crack houses for forty days and nights. I'm talking twenty-four hours a day. When customers came by, we told them, 'No more, it's closed.' If a drug dealer came by, we escorted him out of the community. We had brothers marching around the block on patrols. We had brothers driving around. And occasionally the police would come by. Between all of these things, the crack houses stayed shut."

The congregation's discipline and bravery couldn't help but attract attention. What followed was awards from politicians, appearances on the *Geraldo* show, invitations to speak, visits from delegations of Muslims from abroad, and interviews with media from all over the world. But the congregation's real effort has gone into setting down roots. Releasing themselves from the grip of drugs and violence freed the members to raise their families in safety and build their community anew. Today, merchants and vendors do business in the mosque-owned stores on either side of the building, as well as on outdoor tables set up year-round on the sidewalks. Customers can find prayer rugs, *kufis* (Muslim skullcaps), ankle-length attire for males and females, Islamic books and tapes, oils, and more. The mosque itself owns five stores in the neighborhood, and congregation members own about another thirty, including halal restaurants and a halal bakery. (Halal foods are prepared in a special process sanctioned by Islamic law.)

The revived street life has been healthy for residents but also for important visitors like gypsy cab drivers. During the years of drugs and crime, these drivers suffered robbery after robbery. After mosque members kicked out the dealers, they gave the cabdrivers stickers for their car windows identifying them as friends of the mosque. The robberies almost ground to a halt. Since gypsy cabs serve low-income neighborhoods that city-authorized yellow cabs often do not, drivers and customers both won.

PLACE MOMENT: TAHANI SALAH, ATLANTIC AVENUE MOSQUE

"There's always a moment for me when I'm getting close to our family's mosque on Atlantic Avenue, for the five o'clock prayer on a winter's day, and as I'm approaching, I hear the soothing rhythmic call to prayer, just as I see the sun setting over the building. It's as if the sun is going down just as the light of the *salah* is rising."

CREATING A SENSE OF PLACE

As the mosque prospers, the sights, sounds, and fragrances of Islamic devotion are coming to define the landscape. A sign atop the mosque facing Bedford Avenue shows an elaborate, full-color rendering of the building's facade as it will appear in the future, once sufficient funds have been raised for renovation. The imam and congregation hope for the day when the mosque's growing membership will have comfortable spaces to pray and to study, a traditional Islamic dome will rise above Fulton Street, and the muezzins with the loveliest voices will call to ancient prayer the faithful of Brooklyn.

—Marci Reaven

Ganesha Hindu Temple

45–57 Bowne Street, Flushing, Queens

(718) 460–8484

www.nyganeshtemple.org

Hours: Monday through Sunday 8:00 a.m. to 9:00 p.m. Visitors are welcome for holiday and festival celebrations as well as daily prayer and worship.

Public Transit: 7 train to Flushing/Main Street. Walk three blocks to Bowne Street, turn right and walk eight blocks to Forty-fifth Avenue. Or take the Q27 bus from Main Street to the Bowne Street stop, where you will see the temple to your left.

Intricately carved, broad, and made of stone, its structure rises majestically, if surprisingly, over the small, detached houses of Bowne Street. Built in a South Indian style, the architecture of Sri Maha Vallabha Ganapati Devasthanam—or Ganesha Temple—seeks no match or blend with its neighboring structures. Its distinctive appearance instead marks a sea-change in the history and culture of Queens, and the coming of age of one of New York's newer immigrant groups.

YOU CAN SEE MUCH MORE THAN MEETS THE EYE

The temple's gate is always open, welcoming regulars and visitors seven days a week from early morning until night. Up decorated steps, across a courtyard where shoes are neatly set aside, and through the front door, the temple opens up into a large rectangular space for devotion. In alcoves along the walls, statues of Hindu deities repose, with the most prominent shrine dedicated to Ganesha. The son of Lord Shiva and the goddess Parvati, Ganesha represents, with his elephant's head and human body, the "universality of creation." An important deity in Hinduism, Ganesha is the remover of obstacles. Devotees pray to him each morning upon waking to ensure that the day goes well. Dr. Uma Mysorekar, the Temple Society president, corrects a mistaken impression that the presence of multiple deities means Hinduism reveres more than one god. "We believe in a Supreme Reality, in God as one," she explains. "By perceiving the Lord in these different forms it is possible to get better rapport with God. Before one can worship God as a formless entity, we need visual ways. I can sit across from Our Lord and cry on his shoulder."

In this spacious area for prayer and ritual, empty of the rows of seats common to other houses of worship, practitioners perform religious rites that are both individual and collective. Acts of art and beauty abound. Fresh flower garlands made by priests and devotees adorn the prayer areas. Floral rangoli designs made with brightly colored rice flour embellish floors throughout the temple, protecting its sacred spaces from evil influences. Painted scenes from Hindu cosmology convey meaning while they ornament the walls. "Spiritual hunger is fulfilled right here in this place," Dr. Mysorekar tells us. "The rituals and chants made here literally enrich the walls with spirituality, creating vibrations which devotees can feel."

Consecrated in 1977, the temple provides an important venue for the teaching of Hindu beliefs and traditions to the younger generation. Conveying this vast body of knowledge in a social milieu where, unlike in India, Hinduism is a distinct minority faith, is an enormous challenge. But the scholar Madhulika Khandelwal writes in *Becoming American, Being Indian* that Indians are among the immigrant groups trying most assiduously to keep their religious traditions intact, and on the whole, few Indians are questioning their faiths or converting to

FIRST PERSON: INDIAN RESIDENT OF QUEENS, QUOTED IN *BECOMING AMERICAN, BEING INDIAN*

"In Bombay, our neighbors were Gujaratis, Punjabis, and South Indians. Here, they are Chinese, Koreans, and Hispanics. We continued our family traditions amidst diversity there, and we will do the same here. I do not see much change in our life in the United States. Maintaining our traditions was the most important goal for us there, and it continues to be the most important here. Here we just have to try harder."

different religions. That said, Hinduism is also known for its internally diverse structure and for eschewing the kind of centralized dogma that characterizes some other of the world's major religions. Khandelwal explains that Hinduism has no single sacred text or clerical order, leading many to call it a culture or way of life rather than an organized religion. She describes Hinduism not as a revealed religion but as the evolution of a variety of cults and beliefs: "Throughout its history, Hinduism's response to other forms of religion has been to add new layers, and the meaning of Hinduism accordingly often lies in new adherents' perceptions of it." Ganesha Temple itself has evolved to meet the changing devotional interests and practices of its worshippers—some of whom come not from India but from Guyana,

SISTER SITE: JOHN BOWNE HOUSE

3701 Bowne Street at Thirty-seventh Avenue, Flushing, Queens

(718) 359–0528

Public Transit: 7 train to Main Street. Walk two blocks east on Roosevelt Avenue. Turn
   left onto Bowne Street and walk a block and a half.

Designated a National Historic Landmark, 1961

Bowne Street, where Ganesha Temple is located, is named for John Bowne, a religious dissenter who converted to Quakerism upon moving to Flushing from New England in the mid-1600s. The governing charter of Dutch American Flushing promised "liberty of conscience" to settlers, a precedent that dissidents appealed to in 1657 when they drew up a document called the Flushing Remonstrance to protest hostile treatment. Governor Peter Stuyvesant had been heavily fining and harassing Quakers, and for the crime of holding Quaker meetings in his home, arrested John Bowne in 1662 and deported him. Bowne's subsequent adventures brought him to Holland, where he successfully argued his case in front of the Dutch West India Company, who then ordered Stuyvesant to desist from punishing Quakers as long as they were not fomenting social disruption. The Flushing Remonstrance is sometimes described as a forerunner of the First Amendment.

John Bowne's 1661 house is still standing and was occupied by nine generations of Bowne's family. The site is a National Historic Landmark and is open for tours; call for information.

Crowds line the temple's grounds for Ganesha Chaturthi, a nine-day celebration honoring the deity Ganesha. Photo: Martha Cooper.

At the Ganesha Hindu Temple. Photo © Hazel Hankin Photography.

say—by adding new deities to the prayer area, for example, to appeal to differing traditions.

Yet the temple is more than a place for prayer. It is also an important cultural and community center and a magnet for Hindus from throughout the tri-state area. It's a beehive of activity, with committees of volunteers directing and managing, mediating problems, coordinating youth programs, raising funds, decorating, and so on. All week long, group activities, performances, and classes take place to entertain participants, enhance devotion, and transmit cultural traditions and knowledge. Instrumental music; vocal traditions; language instruction in Hindi and Sanskrit; religious instruction in Hinduism, Vedas, and meditation; and classical and folk dance styles—all are offered, as are the mundane yet critical trappings of the workaday world, such as college-admission prep courses. Many classes and performances take place in the basement rooms and stage area, where the gift shop also is located. Behind the temple is the *yagna kunda,* a space for ritual that is reserved for priests. In the 1990s, the temple's growing prestige encouraged its leadership to add new spaces. Next door, its posh, three-floor Hindu Community Center, designed in a nondescript style more indigenous to Queens (though with granite imported from India), includes a large auditorium and stage, a canteen serving vegetarian meals whose long hours match the temple's, a dining hall and conference room, and a spacious wedding hall, the *kalyana mantapam,* for marriages and large events. (The temple maintains a marriage registry to help parents matchmake for their children.) And up and down the block, single-family homes have been transformed into temple offices and accommodations for priests.

A NEIGHBORHOOD TEMPLE

It often happens that enormous achievements begin with the passion of one individual. Ganesha Temple's dreamer was one Alagappa Alagappan, a United Nations civil servant from India who believed himself guided by divine instruction to build temples in the new land of Indian immigration. He also slowly built a community of fellow dreamers into the Hindu Temple Society of North America. Of all the neighborhoods in all the cities in America, the society chose to locate its first temple in Queens, because by 1970 the tri-state area was already attracting growing numbers of Indian immigrants, many of them Hindus and most of them locating in Queens. The Hart-Celler Act of 1965 recently had done away with immigration discrimination based on national origin, bringing to the United States not only Indians but immigrants from all over the world, and profoundly changing local and national demographics.

Pursuing their self-appointed task, Alagappan and his colleagues discovered what seemed to be a perfect site in Flushing when a Russian Orthodox congregation put up their Bowne Street building for sale in 1971. The site long had been associated with houses of faith. Not all the temple's supporters approved of the Bowne Street purchase. Many believed the new temple should be built where square footage was less expensive—somewhere in Long Island, say. But Alagappan's group had envisioned a neighborhood temple, where worshippers could come frequently,

SISTER SITE: IRT 7 TRAIN, A K A INTERNATIONAL EXPRESS

Running from Forty-second Street/Times Square in Manhattan through Main Street/Flushing in Queens is the number 7 line—dubbed "the International Express" by the Department of City Planning for the number of ethnic and immigrant communities it serves. This is the subway to take to Ganesha Temple, as well as many of Queens's Indian, Pakistani, and Bangladeshi neighborhoods. When Ilana Harlow, then folk arts program director at the Queens Council on the Arts, documented the places, the people, and the cultural traditions she found along this train line, she was so impressed that she nominated the route to a contest for heritage trails being run by the White House. First Lady Hillary Clinton concurred, and in the year 2000 the IRT 7 train route was designated a National Millennium Trail, recognizing the International Express as representative of the American immigrant experience. It was one of sixteen trails designated nationwide.

"The train's route is a festival of culture every day," says Harlow, and she encourages New Yorkers to explore their city. "Communities exist in shared social space, not necessarily shared physical space. We become members of New York City's multicultural community by choosing to participate in it; by interacting with our neighbors, learning about their lives and traditions and sharing our lives and traditions with them."

hindered by neither lack of time nor double transit fares (in the dark days before Metrocards allowed free transfers between subways and buses).

Things really surged ahead when Tirupati Devasthanam—the largest temple in India, located in the southern state of Andhra Pradesh—decided to support the project. A work camp of about 150 artisans was established near Hyderabad to produce the key architectural elements such as the stone sanctum and the carved *rājagopuram* (royal tower) that rises above the temple. Pieces of the structure were then shipped to New York and assembled here. Khandelwal writes that the "priests were selected from a pool of Brahmins who had received scriptural training in India. The temple attracted more South than North Indians, but it accommodated a range of devotees of different Indian regional subcultures, including North Indian–style *arati* (waving of lights to gods), devotional songs, and religious festivals. The Ganesha Temple also affirmed the unity of all religions; the logo on the front of its building and on its stationery bore the primordial Hindu symbol *Om* in the center and was surrounded by symbols designating Islam, Christianity, Buddhism, and Judaism." Ganesha Temple was one of the first Hindu temples built in North America, and its success helped spur the construction of a dozen or more in Queens alone.

FACTORY OF GARLANDS

For Hindus, acts of worship, or *pujas,* take place not only in temples but also at home altars, in private religious gatherings, and in public festivals. Ganesha, like many other temples, is deeply involved in festival planning, and the calendar of events is literally year-round. At festival times "the temple is a factory of garlands," Dr. Mysorekar confides. Ganesha Chaturthi (Nava Dina Mahotsavam), a nine-day celebration in honor of the deity Ganesha, is this temple's most elaborate festival. Held annually in September, the procession boasts an extravagantly decorated chariot bearing Lord Ganesha's statue that proudly parades through the main streets of Flushing, symbolizing Lord Ganesha reaching out to all who cannot attend the festival. Dr. Mysorekar estimates that approximately thirty thousand people take part, the crowds swollen not only by fellow Indians but also by non-Indian community members and well-wishers. *"Jai* Ganesh," the crowd shouts. Many chant holy mantras. *Nadaswaram* musicians play their long clarinetlike instruments, *dhol* players beat out rhythms with fast-moving hands, people stop to dance, and the crowd processes slowly over its three-mile route. During the celebrations, something like thirty thousand packets of *prasadam* (food offerings) are prepared for participants by temple staff.

Another important multiday festival is Diwali (also called Deepawali), meaning "a Row of Lamps." Diwali is a centuries-old principal festival in Hinduism whose meaning is associated with the goddess Laxmi as well as with other ancient stories and deities. During Diwali, traditionally celebrated by Hindus in the fall, rituals are observed in the homes, buildings are decorated with lights, children light fireworks, and gifts and sweets are exchanged with friends and relatives. Diwali observance at Ganesha Temple was described by a visiting *Newsday* reporter: "Parents and temple leaders were teaching about the holiday as hundreds of families came to pray. Inside the red-carpeted temple, oil lamps flickered. In the center of the room, a shrine to Laxmi, goddess of wealth and prosperity, was festooned with flowers and hundreds of boxes of orange, green, and yellow traditional sweets. Many Hindus offer the treats as a sign of thankfulness." As much else changes with immigration, so has Diwali, and the holiday is now celebrated in the United States by Hindus and non-Hindus alike. "It has become an ethnic festival for all Indians, regardless of religion or region," Khandelwal explains. So while Hindus retain the myths and meanings of Diwali for their own consumption, other Indians and non-Indians now translate Diwali into "the Indian New Year," or "the biggest Indian festival," or some other easily explained tradition that can be compared to another on the American scene.

CAPITAL OF INDIAN NEW YORK

Ganesha Temple is the Hindu community's first purpose-built house of worship in New York, located in the neighborhood where Indians first settled in any number. Flushing offered quick access to

Manhattan jobs via the 7 train and in the 1960s was an easy and inexpensive place to rent and buy property. Once a few Indian households had moved in, word of mouth and family and business links attracted others. New settlers first spread from Flushing to Corona and Elmhurst and then into many other Queens neighborhoods, of which Jackson Heights is particularly well known for its Seventy-fourth Street commercial corridor. Based on the 2000 Census, of approximately 171,000 Indians in New York, about 109,000, or 64 percent, live in Queens. (The total South Asian population is much larger.) Ganesha Temple draws worshippers from all over Hindu New York City and the tri-state area, particularly on weekends, when people can come from farther afield, drawn by the culture, the commerce, the networks of friends and families. Especially for those living in relative isolation in far-flung suburbs, an excursion to Queens is a journey to the Indian American heartland.

—*Marci Reaven*

Our Lady of Mount Carmel Grotto

Rosebank, Staten Island

Hours: Every day, 24 hours.

Public Transit: S52 or S78 bus to the intersection of Tompkins Avenue and Chestnut Avenue. Walk two blocks south (in the direction of your bus) along Tompkins to Saint Mary's Avenue. Turn right onto Saint Mary's, make the first left at White Plains Avenue, then turn right onto Amity Street and proceed to the end of the block.

Listed on the National Register of Historic Places, 2000

Our Lady of Mount Carmel Grotto is a spectacular place, a fairy-tale structure that one pilgrim likened to a "jeweled city." For Catholics it's also a sacred site, a place to light a candle and say a prayer, where one can get closer to the divine. Visitors are welcome, religious or not, to appreciate the artistry and devotion of its creators.

A STONE-STUDDED SHRINE

The Grotto faces Amity Street, a short dead-end block that people who don't live in the neighborhood often find difficult to locate. Two signs greet the visitor at this entrance: a small concrete plaque spelling out *Mount Carmel* in small stones and a large wood marker heralding the shrine's listing on the National and New York State Registers of Historic Places. The gate at the chain-link fence surrounding the property is open 24/7, unlike many houses of worship that lock their doors when there is no service. The brick-inlaid path leading from the sidewalk to the grotto is flanked by several small structures, such as a crucifix with a padded kneeler and some small shrines to the Virgin Mary and Saint Anthony. On the right of the pathway stands the meeting hall for the Society of Our Lady of Mount Carmel, a wood-frame building dating back to the early twentieth century. Its semisubmerged basement once served as a male-only social club where members gathered at night to play cards and drink homemade wine. The women's auxiliary was established after World War II and came to an end in the fall of 2004 due to a lack of active members. These days the upstairs hall is rented out to local groups like Community Board 1 and the American Legion, and for receptions celebrating rites of passage. The walkway fans out at the end into a small piazza, where a stone-studded cement fountain operates during the summer in front of the shrine.

The approximately thirty-foot-high shrine consists of a central chamber built with fieldstones, flanked by two adjoining sections stretching out in serpentine fashion. The wall surfaces are decorated with smooth round stones, as well as glass marbles, shells, translucent plastic flowers, and bicycle reflectors inlaid into cement in various shapes that include crosses, triangles, ovals, stars, and diamonds. The walls also contain built-in cement flowerpots where succulents grow. Rising from the grotto is a series of towers and crownlike protrusions, many topped by crosses. Religious statues and framed prints are found throughout the grotto's alcoves, crevices, and ledges. The society's treasurer, Michael De Cataldo, calls the shrine "the nursing home of statues" because people donate their families' old, paint-chipped, and broken religious figures instead of throwing them away. During the winter months, the statues are wrapped in plastic for safekeeping and stored in the central chamber behind a removable Plexiglas door and in the basement of the society hall.

The focus of the grotto is the central chamber with its linen-draped altar and alcove housing a statue of Our Lady of Mount Carmel cradling the Infant Jesus. Candles are available for supplicants who can pray at the padded kneeler. Written petitions, family photographs, funeral cards, and other personal and devotional items adorn the stone-studded altar walls and shelves.

The grotto is a casual site, where devout visitors just walk in without pretensions to offer their prayers. People arrive in whatever style of dress they like at whatever time of day suits best. Neighborhood residents stop by after work. Staten Islanders and Brooklynites drive over on the weekend. Catholic pilgrims from the metropolitan area and beyond will also travel to Rosebank to kneel before the Virgin Mary or

A pilgrimage site for Catholic faithful since 1938. Photo: Martha Cooper.

stand before other statues of Catholic saints in silent prayer. In the wake of the September 11, 2001, attack on New York City, people sought solace at the grotto—270 rescue workers and residents of the borough died that day—leaving photos of family members and written prayers as an expression of their sorrow. With its manicured lawn and cluster of landscaped trees, the property offers a tranquil setting for pilgrims during the course of the year, a refuge from frenetic urban life.

More organized visits take place annually during the two weekends surrounding Our Lady of Mount Carmel's July 16 feast. Devotion to Our Lady of Mount Carmel is first documented in the twelfth century with the establishment of a monastic order dedicated to the Virgin Mary at an ancient hermitage located in the cavernous sides of Mount

Carmel, Palestine. Church writings state that the Virgin Mary appeared to the Carmelite monk Simon Stock of England in the thirteenth century and offered him a scapular, a part of the order's habit. For Italian American devotees of Our Lady of Mount Carmel, the shrine is a key place in a constellation of sacred sites dedicated to this aspect of the Blessed Mother that includes the churches on 115th Street in East Harlem, in Williamsburg, Brooklyn, and in Hammonton, New Jersey. The local Rosebank Society of Our Lady of Mount Carmel sponsors the grotto's July *festa,* staging a procession through neighborhood streets and setting up food stalls and game booths on the society's grounds.

RELIGIOUS LIFE IN ITALIAN AMERICA

From pre-Christian times to the present, grottoes have been a major locus of religious activity in the West. The historical appeal of the grotto is due in part to its transitional position between the mundane world and the mysterious and often forbidding underground. The mountain's gaping hole is not only a passageway to the nether regions but also a site from which the divine springs forth. The Grotto of the Nativity in Bethlehem marks the site of Jesus' birthplace, and Easter celebrates his resurrection from a cavernous tomb. It is at the grotto entrance where the supernatural, often in the form of the Virgin Mary, is made manifest. Man-made grottoes are attempts to replicate and tap the sacred powers of these natural formations.

Historically, private and public sacred space was established, often without official church sanction, as part of Italian American religious life. So it was that a group of Italian immigrant men in Rosebank began constructing a grotto in honor of Our Lady of Mount Carmel in the late 1930s. As members of the Society of Our Lady of Mount Carmel, these working-class Catholics built the structure on property owned by the voluntary association. Today, the lay organization maintains the upkeep of the elaborate shrine. A granite and bronze tombstone-like memorial in honor of Vito Louis Russo rests along the pathway. The plaque proclaims that Russo was "the founder and builder of the shrine." While he was key to the creation of this remarkable structure, Russo did not act alone like some solitary Simon Rodia building his Watts Towers. The grotto was the result of a collaborative effort by society members who offered their voluntary labor to its construction.

Russo was born in 1885 in the town of Sala Consilina, in the province of Salerno. Orphaned at an early age, Vito and his younger brother Giovanni immigrated to the United States with their adoptive parents and lived for a while on the Lower East Side before settling in Rosebank around 1895.

To help themselves meet the challenge of the United States, Italian immigrants formed mutual aid societies, which offered benefits such as unemployment and burial insurance. These voluntary associations were also responsible for introducing and organizing religious processions and street feasts in honor of the Virgin Mary and patron saints of various Italian towns. Rosebank's Society of Our Lady of Mount Carmel was founded in 1903 as a self-help organization open to all Italians, irrespective of their town or regional affiliation. It was under the tenure of the Society's first president that the organization purchased land and erected the meeting hall. Russo served as the society's second president before being unanimously elected president-for-life in 1939, a position he held until his death on February 22, 1954. Russo was clearly a charismatic leader, a man seemingly groomed in the southern Italian ideal of masculine maturity: sociable, generous, and, most important, respectful of others.

It was the death of Russo's youngest son, five-year-old Vito Jr., of pneumonia in 1935 that was the impetus for the grotto's construction. The grieving Russo turned his personal loss into collective action by mustering the society's membership for this spiritual and architectural undertaking. The grotto's design was based on the elaborate domestic altar Russo had crafted out of cardboard, aluminum foil, and decorative baubles.

BUILT WITH FAITH

On May 7, 1938, the *Staten Island Advance* covered the grotto's dedication with the headline "Shrine Built in Spare Time of Members

The residential streets of Rosebank, Staten Island, enclose this extraordinary hand-made shrine. Photo: Martha Cooper.

Is Dedicated." The article reports that the grotto, which was begun in October of the previous year, was "built by the forty-six members of the Mount Carmel Society . . . during their spare time after working hours." Four men were featured in that article: The masonry work was attributed to Umberto Summa and Angelo Madrazzo; Russo was given credit for the grotto's stone decorations; and Vincent Lupoli painted religious figures (which no longer exist) on the central chamber's vault and walls. The article mentions that one hundred sacks of cement were used in the initial masonry work. The grotto was expanded over the years to its current size. The unidentified journalist failed to inform the paper's readers of the members' innovative way of decorating the shrine.

Initially, the men applied the stones directly to the grotto's cement-smeared surface. According to the late Thomas (Marsie) Tedesco, part of the society's building team, someone suggested that they could cast sections from hand-made molds that would then be attached to the shrine's walls. In this way, stones were pressed into sandbox forms into which cement was poured. The patterning was done in reverse, which was not a problem for geometric shapes like ovals and diamonds, but the workers needed to be mindful when spelling words. Russo's grandson Gianni is credited with having reversed the S's on a sign that reads "Bless All." When the cement hardened, the wooden frames were dismantled and the stone-encrusted sections were removed and secured in

GHOST SITE:
STOREFRONT CHAPEL TO THE BLACK MADONNA

447 East Thirteenth Street, East Village, Manhattan

Public Transit: L train to First Avenue.

On September 8, 1905, Sicilian immigrants from the town of Patti in the province of Messina, who had settled in the Italian community burgeoning along First Avenue south of East Fourteenth Street, came together to celebrate their first public feast in honor of their town's spiritual patroness, the black Madonna del Tindari. According to sacred narrative, a polychromed cedar statue was transported to the Sicilian town of Tindari from the Middle East sometime in the eighth or ninth century to save it from destruction during the Iconoclastic Wars. At some point in time, the Latin words *Nigra sum sed formosa* ("I am black but beautiful") from the Old Testament's Song of Songs were inscribed on the statue's base.

The following year the Sicilians established Il Comitato Pattese alla Vergine SS. del Tindari (the Pattese Committee for the Most Holy Virgin of Tindari) and commissioned a statue of the Madonna and Child. The Manhattan statue was not a duplicate of the Sicilian original, differing significantly in style. It was stored in a basement until 1913, when the group secured a storefront space at 447 East Thirteenth Street to create a chapel and social club. The chapel was a narrow room alongside a funeral parlor that accommodated approximately a dozen people. New York's Sicilian devotees of the Black Madonna festooned the statue with ex-votos in the shape of body parts in thanks for her miraculous healing. For decades, the organization sponsored an annual *festa*

place with cement, wire, and/or metal rods. The artistry of this man-made grotto is evidence of Italian Americans' pervasive and deeply felt regard for the well-crafted object.

PROTECTING THE GROTTO

Society members are increasingly concerned with the grotto's future. Membership is down to fifteen primarily older men, and rising municipal property taxes are taking their toll. The society and grotto are not exempt as either a not-for-profit organization or a religious site.

---

on East Thirteenth Street, complete with a procession through the surrounding streets for their dark-skinned Madonna.

During the 1970s, members of the lay religious association and the neighborhood's Italian American community began moving away and dying. The chapel suffered several setbacks during this time; thieves twice broke into the storefront to steal money and the jewels from the Madonna's crown. In the spring of 1987, the remaining members dissolved the organization, donated the money from the closed savings account to the sanctuary in Sicily, and gave up the lease on the space. A devotee transported the statue to her home in south New Jersey, where she created a private domestic chapel.

On September 8, 2004, a new generation of Italian Americans met at 447 East Thirteenth Street, now a gay bar called the Phoenix. They decorated the exposed brick walls with images of the Madonna as they chatted and drank beer. Attuned to a multicultural perspective and progressive politics, these artists, scholars, and community activists have reclaimed the Black Madonna as a potent symbol of an inclusive spirituality that reveals the historic connections between Italian Americans and people of color. Meeting in this place, they are adopting and transforming the religious and cultural legacy of those early twentieth-century immigrants in the service of the ongoing journey in search of self, community, and the divine. For information about future Black Madonna events, log on to the Malìa Collective's Web site, www.maliacollective.org.

—Joseph Sciorra

With these concerns in mind and with a deep appreciation for the history and artistry of this unique structure, the folklorist Joseph Sciorra suggested to the membership that they attempt to landmark the grotto. Sciorra relied on fifteen years of research and interviews to write a detailed report and nominated the grotto to be listed on the National and State Registers of Historic Places. In 2000 the grotto was listed and designated a "traditional cultural property," the first in New York State, which the National Park Service defines by a site's "association with cultural practices or beliefs of a living community that are rooted in that community's history and are important in maintaining the continuing cultural identity of the community." While the grotto's new official status is more honorific than substantive, it is has been welcomed by the society membership and Rosebank residents.

At the June 2001 ceremony marking the shrine's listing, current present Vito Russo, grandson of the grotto's muse, recalled: "My father used to tell me, 'Someday, something big is going to happen back here. You gonna get a miracle or something. You watch.' And I used to say, 'Yeah, yeah, yeah.' Maybe this it. Maybe he got his wish." The miracle of the Rosebank grotto was not its official recognition but its construction by a small group of working-class immigrant men who joined forces in religious conviction and artistic vision to make manifest the mystery of the divine and the magic of their creative brotherhood.

—Joseph Sciorra

Urban Remembrance

A block party in the Bronx commemorates the completion of a memorial mural by Per, honoring Cheíto, a sixteen-year-old boy killed in a bus accident. Photo: Martha Cooper.

As human beings, we are made of perishable stuff; not rock or wood or precious metal, but flesh and blood. Yet our ability to create and manipulate symbols enables us to associate ourselves with the durable. Many of us leave a succinct record of our lives carved into stone, in headstones and gravestones; and we encase our bodies in wood and padding to lay them in the earth. We use commemorative art to provide a measure of immortality in an object that can outlast our mortal bodies by years, sometimes centuries. At the neoclassical tomb of Ulysses S. Grant, adorned with Greek columns and overlooking the Hudson River, or the headstones crammed into cemeteries in Queens, more cramped than a Manhattan studio apartment, the remains of many New Yorkers are marked with stone. Tours are even available of Brooklyn's Green-Wood Cemetery, a 478-acre park founded in 1838. Among the famous headstones: Leonard Bernstein, Al Capone (Albert Anastasia), Joey Gallo, Horace Greeley, George Tilyou (proprietor of Coney's Steeplechase Park), and Boss Tweed.

PLACE MOMENT: CARA DE SILVA, SHEARITH ISRAEL GRAVEYARD, WEST TWENTY-FIRST STREET BETWEEN SIXTH AVENUE AND SEVENTH AVENUE

"The third graveyard (1829–1851) of the Spanish and Portuguese synagogue, Shearith Israel, New York's first and oldest Jewish congregation, an apparition-like remnant of the city's past, whose grass, trees, weeds, and headstones make time travelers of those who come on it unexpectedly, a country cemetery in the heart of the metropolis."

But in this city, we also memorialize with flowers and candles, symbols of life's evanescence. After September 11, 2001, in the great public gathering places of Washington Square and Union Square, New Yorkers

The Manhattan skyline as seen from First Calvary Cemetery in Queens. Photo: Audrey Gottlieb.

re-created the towers in miniature using tin, papier-mâché, and oil-based paint. At shrines, red, white, and blue candles flickered alongside Christian votive candles, Jewish *yahrzeit* memorial candles, and offertory candles petitioning a range of intercessors from Saint Anthony to the Virgin of Guadalupe to the "Siete Potencias de Africa" of the Afro-Cuban religion of Santeria. The wax from the candles dripped into and onto each other, as our differences seemed to melt away.

The permanence of stone and the impermanence of candles and flowers merge at places where the departed are honored throughout the city, brought together by ritual activity. Atop gravestones Jewish mourners often place tiny pebbles rather than the flowers and candles of the Christian faiths. On the Chinese holiday of Qing Ming, Chinese families pay respects to their ancestors at local cemeteries, where they often will burn incense, make ritual offerings of food and symbolic money, share holiday eats, and set off firecrackers.

FIRST PERSON: AMY CHIN

"It's a Chinese folk tradition to go to the cemetery every year and present offerings to your ancestors. In the folk religion that we followed when we were kids, when you die there's no heaven or hell—it's all hell. And in the afterworld, you are dependent on your descendants to feed you, to give you clothing, to provide for you. So in some Chinatown stores you'll find these things—I guess they're called joss papers, and sometimes they say 'hell bank notes' on them. So once a year you go to the cemetery, you go to the grave of an ancestor, and you burn the paper money and you give offerings of food.

"When my father died, we buried him in a cemetery in Canarsie. And we would go there every year and burn stuff for him, and also for my uncles who are also buried there. I have one uncle who was a heavy smoker, and he died in the 1950s. And every year when we would go to the cemetery we would—in addition to the food and the wine and the money—we would burn packs of cigarettes for him. One year we went to the cemetery, and we brought all the offerings, and I'm watching my mother go through the ritual, and I realized she forgot the cigarettes, she didn't bring cigarettes for my uncle. So I said, 'You forgot the cigarettes.'

"And she said, 'Smoking's not good for you. He has to cut back.'"

Not as permanent as the Egyptian pyramid or the large bronze sculpture of the goddess Minerva at historic Green-Wood Cemetery, but more lasting than the flowers and pebbles, stand New York City memorial murals, painted by graffiti artists on city walls, a familiar part of today's urban landscape. In the 1980s, particularly in the Bronx, in Harlem, and on the Lower East Side, young graffiti artists began creating murals on public spaces such as handball courts and empty brick walls on the sides of stores. Often memorializing those who died young, sometimes violently, on the city's streets, these vibrant splashes of color amidst the gray of the city celebrate the lives of those who used to liven the streets with their presence. Unlike the mausoleums in the cemeteries of Brooklyn and Queens, these memorials keep the dead in the community, in the places where they lived.

In this section, we explore the memorials of Battery Park as well as John Lennon's Strawberry Fields in Central Park, a work of memorial art that, like many others, serves as a locus for rituals and celebrations on the anniversary of a death. Increasingly, city residents establish places where, they believe, the spirits of the dead reside, even if their physical remains lie elsewhere. When the folklorist Barbara Kirshenblatt-Gimblett's sister died, her nephew sensed the presence of his mother, who had been a piano teacher, in the house. "Where is she?" asked the grown-ups. "On middle C," he said.

For many families and communities, that middle C can be found in the memorial walls, private memorials and altars, and cemetery plots—places of remembrance throughout the five boroughs.

The Memorials of the Battery

Eight huge granite monoliths make up the East Coast War Memorial in Battery Park at the southernmost tip of Manhattan. Up and down the front and back of each massive block are listed the names of 4,601 servicemen and women who died in the American coastal waters of the Atlantic Ocean during World War II. Invisible, of course, are the identities of all the loved ones left behind. One bereaved family member, Robert Downey of Illinois, wrote to the New York City Parks Department to find out whether his brother John, former ship's cook third class, was among the listed. Jonathan Kuhn wrote back to assure him that he was.

Southern tip of Manhattan, bounded by State Street and Battery Place

Public Transit: R, W trains to Whitehall Street. Walk one block west along Water Street to Battery Park.

1, 9 trains to South Ferry. Walk north on State Street. Battery Park is on your left.

4, 5, trains to Bowling Green. Walk south on State Street and find Battery Park on your right. Or walk west on Battery Place and find Battery Park on your left.

"Your letter arrived today," Downey responded to Kuhn. "After forty-seven years it is as though I have located my brother's grave. Recently, as a product of my search, I received a picture of his ship. At that time and now, the tears of sorrow and loss became released, perhaps not until now because of having been conditioned to a feeling that started when he was first listed as missing. . . . It was September 12, 1942, when the U.S.S. *Muskeget* was lost with no survivors. She was a converted freighter being assigned to weather services but loaded with depth charges. . . . My brother remarked that if hit, the ship would go quickly. It was only nine years ago from the Coast Guard that I learned that the boilers blew up and then the depth charges a minute later. I will be forever grateful for your response to my inquiry."

MEMORIALIZING MEMORY

Seagulls call and circle overhead, crowds line up for ferries to Ellis Island and the Statue of Liberty, bike messengers on break sun themselves on newly renovated benches, and tourists pore over maps, all intermingling with vendors of food, trinkets, and ten-dollar Rolex watches, all washed by steady breezes off the water. Standing on the Admiral Dewey Promenade, looking out over the harbor and surrounded on three sides by water, one understands why the Battery is the place for memorials and monuments. If there's a place at the heart of New York City where a spirit might soar, it's here. Odd, then, that its name recalls gun batteries once lodged at this junction of harbor and river to fortify the city against invasion by sea.

Almost two dozen memorials reside in the park's twenty-three acres. Five are wholly dedicated to those lost in war, and one—the Wireless Operators Memorial—includes both war dead and other radio and wireless operators who went down with their ships. The largest monument to military sacrifice is the East Coast War Memorial, so forbidding and non-park-like—its granite blocks framing a fierce thirty-five-foot bronze eagle—that coming upon it unexpectedly is disorienting, then humbling. (The Bedi Makky foundry in Greenpoint, Brooklyn, which cast the giant eagle, is still in operation.) President John F. Kennedy, a World War II veteran, dedicated the monument in May 1963. A similar honor roll on the West Coast recognizes those who died in the Pacific.

The smallest war memorial at the Battery is Norway's. Made from timeworn Norwegian stone, the piece fits comfortably in its waterfront-park setting. It is dedicated to four thousand World War II sailors and naval gunners who went down on 570 Norwegian ships lost while hauling supplies from U.S. ports to war theaters around the world. "In memory of help and hospitality shown during our mutual struggle," the Norwegians wrote on the plaque. Parks Department text explains that three hundred thousand men manned these ships. "Many of them looked to New York, the principal port of call, as their home port during the war." Norwegian American seamen, many of whom live on Staten Island, have set up a small endowment for the care of the memorial.

The most surprising piece is the American Merchant Mariners

Memorial, dedicated in 1991 to American merchant seamen of all wars but inspired by a tragic scene from World War II. Poised on a little pier just off land's end, lifelike figures of three men stand on a portion of up-ended boat and bend over a fourth who is literally in the water. When the tide is out it looks as though the man might be saved. When the tide is in, the prospect is grim. The sculptor Marisol Escobar created the scene from a real photograph taken by a Nazi submarine crew after attacking a supply ship. There were no survivors.

The Coast Guard Memorial was designed in the immediate wake of

When the tide ebbs, the man in the water appears to have a chance of survival in Marisol's powerful sculpture of a merchant marine ship under attack during World War II. Photo courtesy of The Battery Conservancy.

World War II but not installed until after the Korean War. The sculpture shows three soldiers in heroic scale, two of them supporting a wounded comrade. What makes the sculpture unique is that the wounded man is African American—representing the first time the armed forces commissioned a sculpture that depicted the shared sacrifice of both white and black soldiers. It wasn't until the Korean War that the American armed forces desegregated. Two years before, in 1948, President Truman began the process with Executive Order 9981, but not until midwar did practice catch up with law. Fittingly, the Battery's Korean War Memorial was dedicated in 1991 by the first African American mayor of New York City, David Dinkins, who served in World War II in a segregated Marine Corps. Six thousand people attended the unveiling for one of the nation's first major memorials to the Korea combatants.

Aside from memorials to military sacrifice, the Battery also hosts many monuments to early settlers, great inventors, successful explorers, and other notable Americans.

A MUSEUM OF OUTDOOR ART

Jonathan Kuhn is the director of art and antiquities for New York City's Department of Parks and Recreation. Not all monuments are located on parkland, but many are. Under Jonathan's care are the monuments and memorials in Battery Park and approximately twelve hundred other monument sites throughout New York City. One site might contain a single monument or many. All together they present a colossal variety of conservation issues. In Jonathan's database are monuments whose size and complexity range from the mammoth Washington Square Arch commemorating the centennial of George Washington's inauguration as the first U.S. president down to the tiny plaque commemorating colonial Fort George, named after the English king. Laid at the Battery in 1818, it is the oldest historic marker in the city. To Jonathan, the city's monuments and memorials comprise a "museum of outdoor art"—a collection distinguished by being open to the public seven days a week. But unlike other museum directors, Jonathan is also curator, educator, preservationist, and press officer. The one role he unfortunately cannot fill is security guard. "It's not easy to maintain this collection because there are so many fewer restrictions on the public in an outdoor setting. For example, there's a lot of damage done by Rollerbladers and skateboarders. Here in Battery Park, they're jumping off the Emma Lazarus monument every day, as soon as the park workers are out of sight." He points to the squarish two-foot-high block bearing a plaque. "See, now it's behind a barricade—a little imprisoned monument—until the paving around it can be modified to discourage jumpers. But you can still see a residue of wax on it, and the places where it's been broken."

With a tiny staff of trained conservators and maintenance workers—some of whose salaries must be raised by Jonathan from private funders—taking care of all this stuff is a significant concern. Annual maintenance for every piece in his custody is Jonathan's goal, and he's often not far off the mark. What makes the job both challenging and rewarding is that the public cares. "You have no idea how upset people get when a monument is stolen—or when they go to lay a wreath and the monument's been defaced." His expression changes; his discomfort is palpable.

In New York's older, landmark parks, such as Central Park, Battery Park, Union Square, and Madison Square, the Parks Department has for decades discouraged the erection of new permanent memorials. Too many monuments inhibit other uses. "We've inherited these memorials and monuments," Jonathan explains. "We need to preserve them as distinct moments when someone had the wherewithal, enthusiasm, and drive to erect a monument. It's kind of a pact we have between the present and the past. It's not necessarily a precedent for the future."

What explains this quandary is that the city does not commission monuments; the public does. Various city agencies, including the design review body called the Art Commission, approve the placement of monuments and are often involved in their design. But with the rare exception of a government commission—as in the East Coast War Memorial in Battery Park—virtually all these statues, tablets, obelisks, steles, and flagpoles reflect private, citizen initiative. "There's no master plan," says Jonathan. "The monuments collection has grown by accretion. All these works of art were done through popular subscription, often to commemorate those who had honored their community."

He continues: "Veterans' memorials, especially from World War I, represent the largest category throughout the city—people thought it was the war to end all wars. There was barely room for monuments for all the wars that came after. Another significant category is immigration. Groups that have sustained a certain clout, or are ascending in the political firmament of New York, wish to honor their heroes from the old country. For example, in recent times we've had monuments to Benito Juarez, the Mexican independence leader; to the Czech composer Antonín Dvorák; and to Juan Pablo Duarte, the first president of the Dominican Republic."

So what does this all add up to? The positive spin is that New York's assortment of memorials and monuments is probably the most democratically created and curated collection of artworks anywhere on earth. The downside is that many New Yorkers know little about the lives honored in the monuments. The Parks Department is trying to balance this tension for newly commissioned monuments: on one hand, respecting the desire of various interest groups to honor their departed heroes with physical landmarks, and on the other, trying to ensure that the artworks, with all their long-term requirements, are appreciated by the general public. Installing informative signage near some existing monuments has helped. The information also appears on the Parks Department Web site, www.nycgovparks.org (click "Your Park," then "Historical Signs"). A strategy for new memorials is to aim for thematic matches between subject and setting—Duke Ellington at Fifth Avenue and 110th Street, for instance. Yet another solution is to aim for universal appeal. A case in point Jonathan offers is "someone like Mahatma Gandhi, who speaks to many people, not just those of Indian descent. And by setting the Gandhi statue in Union Square, there's a real connection to the place because of the way that the square is used for public protests and gatherings."

ANNUAL CALENDAR OF THE CITY'S PASSIONS

The challenge of overseeing this massive outdoor art collection has caused Jonathan to think long and hard about the pluses and mi-

In one of the first major memorials to Korean War veterans, a universal solider is present in his absence. Photo courtesy of The Battery Conservancy.

nuses of permanent memorials. He points out that physical objects outlast the living links between memories and monuments. "It's an occupational hazard of monuments and memorials that they long outlast the people who commission them, and as time marches on, the memory of the events and the people they commemorate fades from general knowledge. Of course, even when that happens—when a disassociation develops between spectator and memorial—the memorial is still doing its job by perpetuating memory. But how good a job is it doing?" He poses an interesting question. When a city becomes cluttered with old memorials to individuals whose achievements are no longer remembered, does it unnecessarily burden the present? Does it inadvertently cause people to lose interest in new memorial objects because their vision is clouded by tedium-inducing old ones? To address these concerns the Parks Department now requires that for each new monument it approves, citizen sponsors must provide a private endowment to fund on-

SISTER SITES:
THE COMMEMORATIVE LANDSCAPE OF LOWER MANHATTAN

The Battery contains the densest concentration of public memorials in New York City. It also anchors a more extensive commemorative landscape that reaches beyond the park itself to embrace nearby sections of lower Manhattan, as well as Liberty, Ellis, and Governors islands. This befits the Battery's role as New York's oldest civic space, in continuous and evolving use since the construction of the first Dutch fort in 1626.

Its first two hundred years saw the Battery's gradual transformation from an administrative center and military installation into a public promenade. Although by the early 1800s no longer the seat of official authority, it would continue to serve for generations as the port city's principal gateway to the harbor and the wider world. Broadway processions for arriving dignitaries began at the Battery and were the origin of today's ticker-tape parades along the same route. (This ongoing tradition links the Revolutionary War hero the Marquis de Lafayette with the aviator Amelia Earhart, the astronaut John Glenn, and scores of others.)

With far less ceremony, the Battery also welcomed the nearly eight million European immigrants who landed at Castle Clinton between 1855 and 1890, and the millions more who arrived there after their transit through Ellis Island in the years that followed.

The waters just offshore have been a place of commemoration as well, with grand marine parades to mark such events as the completion of the transatlantic telegraph cable (1858) and the dedication of the Statue of Liberty (1886). The 1825 opening of the Erie Canal was solemnized with a floating "wedding of the waters," as a cask filled in the Great Lakes was emptied into Upper New York Bay. Even the air above the harbor has played its part, for balloon ascents, fireworks displays, and the watery arcs of fireboat salutes.

Around the turn of the twentieth century, the Battery's first major public memorials were built, each dedicated to a single public figure. As memorials in the park congoing maintenance. And in addition to finding the right match between object, theme, and setting—as in the memorial to writer Ralph Ellison at 150th Street and Riverside Drive, adjacent to his onetime home—the Parks Department offers alternatives to statuary and flagpoles. Naming opportunities are one. Another is the creation of living memorials made from plantings, such as the recent memorial to victims of the

---

tinued to accumulate, the Battery's symbolic scope broadened: When the Wireless Operators Memorial was dedicated in 1915, the focus had clearly shifted from individual memorials to collective ones, and from local interests to world events. All but two subsequent monuments honored groups rather than individuals. Even contemporary public events, such as the annual Veterans Day observances, have the same broader focus.

Since the 1980s, this constellation of commemorative projects has expanded beyond Battery Park itself to include a number of sites elsewhere along the shoreline of lower Manhattan: the Vietnam Veterans Memorial, near the East River at the former Jeanette Park (1985), and the New York City Police Memorial (1997), the Museum of Jewish Heritage Living Memorial to the Holocaust (1997), and the Irish Hunger Memorial (2002), all on the Hudson in Battery Park City. Three of the four look beyond the city itself for their significance.

The Battery's most recent memorial weaves together both local and world events with special immediacy, commemorating the victims of the September 11, 2001, attack on the World Trade Center. In 2002, Fritz Koenig's 1971 sculpture *Sphere* was reerected in Battery Park, after its recovery from the rubble at Ground Zero only a few blocks away.

With its four-hundred-year cargo of memory and memorials, the Battery marks New York City's historical epicenter. Poised between the changing skyline and the distant horizon, it preserves a link between today's metropolis and the natural harbor that nurtured its beginnings. It is a place to bear witness to those who have come, those who have gone, and those who remain in the city's thoughts. While no single site can ever represent New York in its entirety, the Battery comes closer than any other—it is one part of this city that can stand for the whole.

—*Chris Neville*

Holocaust created in Riverside Park. And at the Battery, private funds and a commission from the Battery Conservancy produced the Gardens of Remembrance, a special planted place for memory and healing created after the terror attacks of September 11, 2001.

Such musings aside, the Parks Department actively supports the public in its use and enjoyment of existing memorial art. Monuments offer places for gathering where people can share in a sentiment or idea embodied by the object. All year round, wreaths are being laid and gatherings held at commemorative sites around the city. Jonathan stays a step ahead of events, getting his crews out to spruce things up before the ceremonies. It's not that he's receiving press releases or even monitoring permit requests because not everybody files the paperwork. He anticipates this complicated calendar of events and tries to schedule annual maintenance just before the ceremonies. "Whether you're washing down pigeon excrement or doing more sophisticated work like recoating bronze to keep it from corroding in acid rain, why not schedule it so that those showing up can benefit? This week we'll be at the Straus memorial before the anniversary of the Titanic's sinking. Two weeks ago we were at the Happy Land memorial [commemorating the 1990 fire that killed eighty-seven people at the Happy Land social club in the Bronx] in time for the fifteenth anniversary of the event. There were hundreds of people there. We were at Athens Square in Astoria before Greek Independence Day to make sure the sculptures of Socrates and Athena were looking their best. We'll be in Battery Park with John Ericsson in July before his birth date on the thirty-first. There are events related to the Battle of Long Island in 1776 that whole contingents of historians and preservationists care about, so every year before August 27 we give extra attention to the five or six monuments in Brooklyn that relate to that battle. And then there's the Gay Liberation Monument in Christopher Park to clean before Gay Pride Week in the third week of June . . ."

A HEROES' WALK

Just as there is no preexisting master plan guiding the creation of public monuments, neither do most of them have a permanent lease on a single spot of parkland. Over the decades at the Battery, many of the monuments have been disturbed more than once to accommodate expanding landfill, redesigns in the park's layout, and huge construction projects like the Brooklyn Battery Tunnel. And it's happening again, under the watchful eye of numerous public agencies and the Battery Conservancy—a private, not-for-profit "friends" organization of the kind that is proliferating throughout the city as public funds for parks and other social amenities diminish.

Battery Park is being totally redone. The plans for the new park are grand, geared toward a physical landscape of grasses, trees, and flowers at the sacrifice of concrete; where park users can relax, play, and view assorted spectacles from morning to night. Not surprisingly, many of the memorial objects scattered around the park are moving to the perimeter and forming a heroes' walk of sorts. The highly thought-out new design doesn't accommodate the helter-skelter existing placement of the monuments—something that gave the park a lot of charm, since one was always stumbling over something surprising, but presented an impediment to creating the new spaces.

Even while the monuments shuttle around the park, they prove to be potent memory devices. Reporting from the construction front, Jonathan shares the discovery of historical treasure during the temporary move of Giovanni da Verrazzano from one site to another. (Under an earlier Parks Department regime, poor Verrazzano unceremoniously lost his bottom half when receiving a new and hardier granite pedestal.) Buried underneath the statue was a time capsule filled with American, British, French, and Italian currency, including coins from as far back as 1861 and two commemorative medallions of Verrazzano and Columbus. They corresponded to the inventory of a time capsule discovered in 1947 when the monument was last moved, so the contents must have been carefully replaced.

More dispiritingly, the war memorials in Battery Park evoke not just memory but current events. In a postscript to our interview, Jonathan writes that he has "learned on the job a better understanding of the genuine sacrifices that those on the front lines have made in various military engagements whose merits we may debate. I have made it an essential component of the job to honor those sacrifices, and preserve the monuments and memorials to them."

—*Marci Reaven*

Strawberry Fields

Overshadowed by trees and buttressed by a grassy, planted knoll is a round black-and-white mosaic, the word *Imagine* at the center of an inlaid starburst. Over this little area of Central Park looms the Dakota, the apartment

Seventy-second Street and Central Park West, Central Park, Manhattan

Public Transit: B, C trains to Seventy-second Street. Enter Central Park at West Seventy-second Street. It's a short walk straight ahead to Strawberry Fields.

building where John Lennon spent the last few years of his life, and outside of which he was shot to death on December 8, 1980. Each year people gather here on the anniversary of the tragedy to honor the memory of the former Beatle.

A GARDEN OASIS

Strawberry Fields continues to be a pilgrimage site for fans and visitors from around the world, who come here year-round to reflect and sing in memory of Lennon. Each year on December 8, at 10:50 p.m., the time when Lennon was shot by Mark David Chapman, and at 11:15 p.m., the official time of his death, admirers observe moments of silence in his honor.

At the intersection of two park paths, the mosaic memorial, created by Neapolitan artisans, acts as a focal point for the people who have come to remember. Although just off Central Park West, the shape of the landscape and surrounding foliage block traffic and street noise. Musicians jamming on guitars play Beatles songs all day, one musician replacing another, just as the well-wishers come and go in a steady stream. Those in attendance sing along to the songs, creating a feeling of shared purpose and respect that links the crowd of strangers. One man flies here from Japan every year just to take part.

For Naomi Haruta and Eric Paulin, musicians and Beatles fans who play at happenings at the memorial throughout the year, the enclosed space of Strawberry Fields is particularly significant. Eric remarks: "One of the beauties of Strawberry Fields is that it's an oasis, one hundred feet away from the corner of the park, and when you're there you don't hear much noise from the street. People can sit there and have some peace and quiet. After all, Yoko [Yoko Ono, John Lennon's widow] wanted it to be known as a place of reflection, and it definitely is. It's serene and tranquil and a beautiful place to sit. There is something about the way that the mosaic is placed, the way the benches are shaped, and that you can see the Dakota." Naomi adds, "When you see the word *Imagine* sculpted in the ground, you automatically hear the song itself. Just thinking about the song is a kind of message. Just one word, but it contains a lot of meaning."

Imagine no possessions,

I wonder if you can,

No need for greed or hunger,

A brotherhood of man,

Imagine all the people

Sharing all the world . . .

You may say I'm a dreamer,

But I'm not the only one,

I hope some day you'll join us,

And the world will live as one.

HOW THE CITY CAME TO HONOR JOHN LENNON

Just nine days after John Lennon died, City Council member Henry Stern (later commissioner of parks and recreation) introduced this resolution to the council:

> **Whereas,** The Council has learned with deep sorrow of the death on December 8 of John Lennon, musician and lyricist, and
>
> **Whereas,** Born to a working-class family in Liverpool, England, on October 9, 1940, he grew up in modest circumstances and without formal musical training, and
>
> **Whereas,** In co-operation with Paul McCartney, George Harrison

and Ringo Starr, he founded the Beatles, a group that earned a world-wide reputation through the strength of its compositions, the significance of its lyrics, the style and force of its performance, and

Whereas, Since 1969, he has lived in the city of New York, waging an important struggle with the aid of Congressman Edward I. Koch and others to be admitted to the United States as a permanent resident, and

Whereas, He and the Beatles, through such songs as "Give Peace a Chance" lent strength to the international effort to bring an end to the war in Vietnam, and

Whereas, The music of the Beatles has provided enjoyment to a gen-

"When you see the word *Imagine* sculpted in the ground, you hear the song." Photo: Martha Cooper.

eration of people around the world, combining high art with popular culture, and

Whereas, Last Monday, he was tragically murdered as he entered his home at One West 72nd Street in the borough of Manhattan in the City of New York, and

Whereas, Millions of people, of all nations, of all walks of life, have joined in respect for his memory and in protest at his senseless death, now therefore, be it

Resolved, That the Council of the City of New York does hereby tender this expression of its sorrow and joins with all others in mourning his passing, and be it further

Resolved, That copies of this Resolution be sent to his widow, Yoko Ono Lennon, and his sons, Julian and Sean.

Council member Angelo Arculeo, representing districts in Brooklyn and Staten Island, objected to the resolution on the grounds that Lennon was not the kind of person the city should honor. The resolution was sent for further study to the Committee on General Welfare.

Once that happened, Henry Stern says, he and his fellow council members decided to take things a step further. "I was a fan," Stern says,

FIRST PERSON: JOHN LENNON

"[Strawberry Fields] is a Salvation Army home that was near the house I lived in with my auntie in the suburbs. There were two famous houses there. One was owned by Gladstone, which was a reformatory for boys, which I could see out my window. And Strawberry Fields was just around the corner from that. It was an old Victorian house converted for Salvation Army orphans, and as a kid I used to go to their garden parties with my friends Ivan, Nigel, and Pete. We'd all go up there and hand out and sell lemonade bottles for a penny and we always had fun at Strawberry Fields. Apparently it used to be a farm that made strawberries, or whatever. I don't know. But I just took the name, it had nothing to do with the Salvation Army. As an image—Strawberry Fields forever."

—Quoted in All We are Saying:
The Last Major Interview with John Lennon and Yoko Ono

"of Lennon's lyricism, of the beauty of his words and his thoughts. I figured this was a man who should be honored by making his name a permanent part of the city's geography. And since we had to go through the whole committee process, we might as well name something for him." A teardrop-shaped piece of park land in front of the Dakota emerged as a strong candidate. Some say it's because John and Yoko used to walk there. Stern brainstormed with friends to find a name for the proposed memorial site, and the late journalist Jack Newfield suggested Strawberry Fields. It seemed to fit, Stern remembered, because it evoked one of Lennon's best-known songs and it described a physical place.

Local Law 957 designated the place called Strawberry Fields. It's a little bit of Central Park, but its meaning is big.

IMAGINING STRAWBERRY FIELDS

Now that the city had honored Lennon, Yoko Ono helped turn Strawberry Fields into a garden oasis by donating one million dollars to the Central Park Conservancy to design and build the memorial and maintain it in the years to come. To the east of a paved area that surrounds the Imagine mosaic is the Garden of Peace, designed by the landscape architect Bruce Kelly. After Ono ran an ad in the *New York Times* requesting rocks and plants from around the world for the memorial, 150 nations contributed the trees and plants that fill the garden today. An earlier attempt to literally transform the area into fields of strawberries failed when hungry birds devoured the twenty-five thousand plants. On October 9, 1985, the day when John Lennon would have turned forty-five, Strawberry Fields was officially dedicated.

Strawberry Fields continues to be a site of contemplation and tribute, not only to Lennon and the Beatles but to the ideal of world peace it has come to symbolize. For Yakov (Jack) Tsibushnik, who emigrated from the Ukraine in 1993, the memorial is a very special place. John Lennon and the Beatles changed his life, he claims. "I remember I was nine years old, 1967, when I first heard a Beatles song. I did not understand the words, but the music touched my heart so deeply. The Beatles songs broke the Iron Curtain. Through the BBC Radio, Voice of

The night John Lennon was murdered in front of the Dakota apartment house on Central Park. Photo © Harvey Wang

America radio, we started to listen and to realize that somewhere else there was a life different from the Soviet way of life. That's how me and my friends got the idea of freedom." Jack stops by Strawberry Fields just to sit. "If I feel tired or have problems, I come here for advice. I sit here, I realize what happened, and somehow the answer is here for me. This magic circle with the sign, Imagine, it brings you the answer." Strawberry Fields regular Eric Paulin says, "When you dedicate a place like this to somebody like John Lennon, it's not just for them, it's for anybody like them. It's for anybody who has that kind of respect for humanity and for world peace and unity."

Gatherings materialize in this place at other times of sorrow, such as after the deaths of musicians like Jerry Garcia and fellow Beatle George Harrison, and following the attacks of September 11, 2001, when mourners found their way here to light candles and seek communal solace. So the memory of John Lennon and the meaning of the site evolve. Those of us who grew up listening to the Beatles, as well as younger folks who have grown to love their music, still grieve for Lennon's loss. Those of us who love New York still mourn the death of a beloved world figure who chose to make this city his home.

—Marci Reaven

Notes

INTRODUCTION

The comments about the mosaics at Grant's Tomb were made by Tom Goodridge as part of his nomination of the site to our Census of Places That Matter. The quote from a resident of the Street of Little Doors is from Mimi O'Connor, *Time Out,* "Essential New York," October 24–31, 1996. For Edward Casey's notions of place memory, see *Getting Back into Place: Toward a Renewed Understanding of the Place-World* (Bloomington: Indiana University Press, 1993). See also the excellent work by Dolores Hayden, *The Power of Place: Urban Landscapes as Public History,* 2d ed. (Cambridge, Mass.: MIT Press, 1997). Somini Sengupta's "My City: Plotting Your Winter Days to Gather the Light" appeared in the *New York Times,* January 14, 2000, p. E43. Stephanie Nilva's unpublished poem is called "City Lights." Thanks to Cara De Silva for the image of the historic plants at the Cloisters. The quote from Fred Ferretti comes from his "City Games," in *1976 Festival of American Folklife,* ed. Bess Hawes (Washington: Smithsonian Institution, 1976), p. 31. Robert Hershon's poem "The Driver Said" first appeared in *How to Ride on the Woodlawn Express* (New York: Sun Press, 1985). The quote from Alan Lomax comes from a personal conversation between Steve Zeitlin and Bess Lomax Hawes, 1989.

URBAN GATHERINGS

Bohemian Hall and Beer Garden

The Great Good Place: Cafés, Coffee Shops, Bookstores, Bars, Hair Salons, and Other Hangouts at the Heart of a Community is by Ray Oldenburg (3d ed., New York: Marlowe, 1999).

The General Society of Mechanics and Tradesmen

The Sean Wilentz quote is from his *Chants Democratic: New York City and the Rise of the American Working Class, 1788–1850* (New York: Oxford University Press, 1984), p. 38.

Webster Hall

The quote from Kathy Peiss on the importance of meeting halls is from her *Cheap Amusements: Working Women and Leisure in Turn-of-the-Century New York.* (Philadelphia: Temple University Press, 1986), p. 93. The "competition" quote is from the *New York Times,* April 8, 2003. Irwin Silber's observations about hootenannies are from the LP *Sing Out! Hootenanny with Pete Seeger and the Hooteneers,* Folkways Records FN2513, 1963. The 1920s flyer both cited and pictured appears in Andrea Weiss and Greta Schiller, *Before Stonewall: The Making of a Gay and Lesbian Community*, an illustrated historical guide to the film (Tallahassee: Naiad Press, 1988), p. 21.

George Chauncey's comment about Webster Hall as a site for gay balls is drawn from his *Gay New York: Gender, Urban Culture, and the Making of the Gay Male World, 1890–1940* (New York: Basic Books, 1994), p. 293. The report of the Committee of Fourteen is quoted in Chauncey, p. 236.

Terry Miller's comments on nudity are drawn from his *Greenwich Village and How It Got That Way* (New York: Crown, 1990), p. 267. Our observations on the hall's legal troubles are from the *New York Times,* December 30, 1886. Information on Webster Hall's first owner, Charles Goldstein, is from his obituary in the *New York Times,* November 29, 1898. Stanley Nadel's observations are from his *Little Germany: Ethnicity, Religion, and Class in New York City, 1845–1880* (Urbana: University of Illinois Press, 1990), p. 1.

The Sister Sites description of the library and clinic is from Andrew Dolkart and Matthew Postal, *Guide to New York City Landmarks,* 3d ed. (Hoboken, N.J.: John Wiley and Sons, 2004), p. 60.

CITY PLAY

Introduction
Erving Goffman's "Fun in Games" appears in *Encounters* (Indianapolis: Bobbs-Merrill, 1961).

Stickball Boulevard and the Stadiums of the Street
Gaston Bachelard's ideas about the durable nature of childhood are from his *Poetics of Reverie: Childhood, Language, and the Cosmos,* trans. Daniel Russell (Boston: Beacon Press, 1971), p. 20.

Thomas Jefferson Park Pool
The description of the pool from the era when East Harlem was largely Italian is from *The WPA Guide to New York City* (New York: Pantheon Books, [1939], 1982), p. 269. The quotes from Robert Caro's *Power Broker: Robert Moses and the Fall of New York* (New York: Vintage Books, 1974), are from pages 513, 457, and 514 respectively. The passage by Edwin Torres is from his *Carlito's Way* (London: Prion Books, [1975], 1999), pp. 2, 4.

Empire Roller Skating Center
Barry Brown's description of the World War II–era Empire is from Barry Brown, "The Life of a Roller Skater," *Roller Skaters' Gazette: The Artistic Roller Skater's Monthly Newsletter,* July 2001, p. 1.

Coney Island
The Charles Denson quote is from his *Coney Island Lost and Found* (Berkeley, Calif.: Ten Speed Press, 2002), p. 113. Our comments about Coney Island's walkways derive from Melissa Baldock's Columbia University master's thesis, "Preserving the Honky-tonk: Coney Island's Future in Its Amusement Past," 2003. The Richard Snow quote is from his *Coney Island: A Postcard Journey to the City of Fire* (New York: Brightwaters, 1984), p. 115. The quote from the historian Elliot Willensky is from Ric Burns's documentary *Coney Island,* PBS, 1985.

URBAN PALATE

Coney Island Bialys and Bagels

The First Person quote is from Mimi Sheraton, *The Bialy Eaters* (New York: Broadway Books, 2002), p. 42.

Sahadi's Specialty and Middle Eastern Foods

The First Person quote is from Abdeen Jabara, "Being Arab American in New York," in *A Community of Many Worlds: Arab Americans in New York City,* ed. Kathleen Benson and Philip M. Kayal (New York: Museum of the City of New York; Syracuse: Syracuse University Press, 2002), p. 227.

Arthur Avenue Market

The story about Annie Lanzillotto's mother and the heart-cooking advice both appear in the privately printed booklet "Annie and Mario: How to Cook a Heart: Verbatim," 1997. For more on the New York City municipal markets, see Suzanne Wasserman's doctoral dissertation, "The Good Old Days of Poverty: The Battle over the Fate of New York City's Lower East Side during the Depression," New York University, 1990.

ART AND MUSIC, CITY STYLE

The Village Vanguard

The first quote by Lorraine Gordon is taken from Ashley Kahn, "After 70 Years, the Village Vanguard is Still in the Jazz Swing," *Wall Street Journal,* February 8, 2005. All other Lorraine Gordon quotes are from an interview conducted by Roberta Singer and Elena Martínez, December 14, 2004, at the Village Vanguard. The Max Gordon quotes are from his *Live at the Village Vanguard* (New York: Da Capo Press, 1982), pp. 4, 16. The First Person quote is from Pete Hamill, *A Drinking Life* (Boston: Back Bay Books, 1994), p. 210.

Richmond Barthé's Frieze at Kingsborough Houses

The quote from Romare Bearden and Harry Henderson is from their

History of African-American Artists: From 1792 to the Present (New York: Pantheon Books, 1993), p. 140, as is the Barthé quote in the next paragraph. Our interview with Joan Maynard draws upon an oral history done by Hilary-Anne Hallett for the Center for the Study of Women and Society Activist Women's Voices Oral History Project, based at the Graduate Center, CUNY, on March 18, 1997, and a 2004 telephone interview with Steve Zeitlin.

METROPOLITAN MEANDERINGS

Introduction

Barbara Rothman's essay about her childhood appears in *Voices: The Journal of New York Folklore* 27 (Fall–Winter 2001): 36–37. The comment about loving everyone at varying distances is from Aimar Arizmendi. The quotation from Kamillah is from the documentary film *Ferry Tales,* directed by Katja Eson and distributed by Women Make Movies, 2003.

Quirky Features of the Landscape

The reference to the "gaunt stump" is from *The WPA Guide to New York City* (New York: Pantheon Books, [1939], 1982), p. 305. The Place Moment about the dioramas at the American Museum of Natural History is from Gillian Fassell, *Time Out,* "Essential New York," October 24–31, 1996. Christopher Gray's essay "Streetscapes: On Waterfronts of the Present, Rail Bridge Relics of the Past," appeared in the *New York Times* on November 7, 2004. Barbara Kirshenblatt-Gimblett's comments are from her article "The Future of Folklore Studies in America: The Urban Frontier," *Folklore Forum* 16 (1983): 222. Eric Miller's Place Moment about Jim Power is taken from his paper "Festive Art in a Festive Neighborhood: Street Mosaics in New York City's East Village," available at http://ccat.sas.upenn.edu/~emiller/mosaics _paper.html. Brandon Holley's quote about the Tic Tac Toe Chicken appeared in a brief write-up in *Time Out,* "Essential New York," October 24–31, 1996.

Art in the Subways

Thanks to Laura Silver, who wrote an early draft of this essay. For the "alligators in the sewers" legend, see Jan Harold Brunvand, *The Vanishing Hitchhiker: American Urban Legends and Their Meanings* (New York: Norton, 1981), pp. 90–98. Pynchon's *V* was published by Lippincott (Philadelphia and New York, 1963); pp. 42–43 quoted.

URBAN NATURE

Community Greening

The Michael Gold quote is from *Jews Without Money* (New York: Carroll & Graf, 1930), p. 41. The quote from Joseph Sciorra is from his "'We're not here just to plant. We have culture.' An Ethnography of the South Bronx: Casita Rincón Criollo," *New York Folklore* 20, nos. 3–4 (1994). The quotes from Hattie Carthan about the Magnolia Tree Earth Center are from Fred Ferretti, "Urban Conservation: A One-Woman Effort," *New York Times,* July 8, 1982, p. C6. The First Person poem by Edgardo Vega Yunqué is from his *Mendoza's Dreams* (Houston: Arte Publico Press, 1987).

CITY SPIRITS

Introduction

For two excellent essays on the Stations of the Cross celebrations in New York, see Joseph Sciorra, " 'We Go Where the Italians Live': Religious Processions as Ethnic and Territorial Markers in a Multiethnic Brooklyn Neighborhood," and Wayne Ashley, "The Stations of the Cross: Christ, Politics, and Processions on New York City's Lower East Side," both in *Gods of the City: Religion and the American Urban Landscape,* ed. Robert A. Orsi (Bloomington: Indiana University Press, 1999).

Ganesha Hindu Temple

The quotes from Madhulika Khandelwal and the First Person quote are from Khandelwal's *Becoming American, Being Indian: An Immigrant Community in New York City* (Ithaca: Cornell University Press, 2002), pp. 78, 84, 60, 1. The description of the Diwali observance at the Ganesha Temple is from Emily Wax, "Chasing Evil with Joy," *Newsday,* October 21, 1998, p. A29.

URBAN REMEMBRANCE

Strawberry Fields

The First Person quote by John Lennon is from David Sheff, *All We Are Saying: The Last Major Interview with John Lennon and Yoko Ono* (New York: St. Martin's Griffin, 2000), pp. 154–157. Song lyrics from "Imagine" used with permission.

About the Authors

Marci Reaven is a public historian and media producer, transplanted from the Bay Area of California to the Lower East Side of New York City, where she has lived for many years. With an abiding interest in cities and in people, her films, exhibits, and writing showcase people struggling to make a difference. She is the managing director of City Lore, where she directs the Place Matters project to promote and protect places that connect New Yorkers to the past, sustain community life, and keep the city vital.

Steve Zeitlin is a folklorist, writer, filmmaker, and cultural activist. He is the founding director of City Lore, a commentator heard on public radio, the coauthor of *City Play* and *Giving a Voice to Sorrow: Personal Responses to Death and Mourning,* and the author of a volume of poetry, *I Hear America Singing in the Rain.* He has documented, recorded, and fallen in love with carnival pitches, children's rhymes, family stories, subway stories, ancient cosmologies, and oral poetry traditions from around the world.

From our offices on the corner of First and First (First Street and First Avenue, a corner Kramer on *Seinfeld* once termed "the nexus of the universe"), City Lore is engaged in the crucial work of documenting, preserving, and presenting New York City's—and America's—living cultural heritage. For twenty years, we have been working to celebrate the city's grassroots cultures and to ensure its living legacy in stories and histories, places and traditions. We encountered many of the places in *Hidden New York* through our Place Matters project—a joint effort with the Municipal Art Society to promote and protect places that connect us to the past and keep our communities vital. For suggestions about how to protect places that matter in your own community, log on to www.placematters.net.

About the Contributors

Natalie Westbrook DeYoung received a bachelor of fine arts degree from the Cooper Union School of Art in 2003 and a master of arts in critical and curatorial studies from the University of Louisville in 2004. She currently resides in Detroit, Michigan.

David Hochman writes for the *New York Times, Esquire, National Geographic,* and many other publications.

Robert Maass is a writer and photographer of news and features as well as children's books. He recently added filmmaking to his repertoire with the documentary *Gotham Fish Tales,* which ran on the Sundance Channel and appeared in many festivals.

Elena Martínez is a folklorist and City Lore's primary fieldworker and researcher for the Place Matters project. Specializing in documenting Latin music in New York City, she is coproducing the upcoming film *Mambo to Hip-Hop: Music and Survival in the South Bronx.*

Joseph Sciorra is a folklorist and the assistant director of academic and cultural programs at Queens College's John D. Calandra Italian American Institute. He is the author of *R.I.P.: Memorial Wall Art,* a collection of photographs by Martha Cooper documenting memorial graffiti.

Roberta Singer, Ph.D., is the director of music programs at City Lore. She has researched, written, and produced films about Latino music in New York and Puerto Rico for more than three decades and produces festivals and tours of Puerto Rican and Cuban music.

Caitlin Van Dusen recently moved from New York City to San Francisco, where she works at the *San Francisco Bay Guardian* and at 826 Valencia, a pirate supply store and writing and tutoring center for children.

Planning an Outing

Index